# Transformative Change

# Peace and Conflict Studies
## Series Editors: Thomas G. Matyók, Sean Byrne, Jessica Senehi, Maureen Flaherty, and Hamdesa Tuso

Within a global context, this interdisciplinary series advances the work of recognized scholars in the field of Peace and Conflict Studies (PACS) as well as emerging and marginalized voices. Peacebuilding and conflict transformation are activities that address the world's wicked problems—a task that requires a broad range of global actors. The series seeks a balance of western and non-western approaches to peacebuilding and conflict resolution practice, and a wide range of theoretical and methodological approaches to peace and conflict studies is encouraged. Particular interest is placed on scholarship and practice developing in the Two-Thirds World. As an integrated field of study and practice it incorporates a substantial number of sub-disciplines: alternative dispute resolution, conflict analysis and resolution, peacebuilding, human rights, social justice, reconciliation and forgiveness, narrative and peacemaking, indigenous peacemaking, gender, and religion, among others.

### Titles in the Series

*Transformative Change: An Introduction to Peace and Conflict Studies* by Laura E. Reimer, Cathryne L. Schmitz, Emily M. Janke, Ali Askerov, barbara T. Strahl, and Thomas G. Matyók

# Transformative Change

## *An Introduction to Peace and Conflict Studies*

Laura E. Reimer, Cathryne L. Schmitz,
Emily M. Janke, Ali Askerov,
barbara T. Strahl, and Thomas G. Matyók

Foreword by Sean Byrne

LEXINGTON BOOKS
Lanham • Boulder • New York • London

Published by Lexington Books
An imprint of The Rowman & Littlefield Publishing Group, Inc.
4501 Forbes Boulevard, Suite 200, Lanham, Maryland 20706
www.rowman.com

Unit A, Whitacre Mews, 26-34 Stannary Street, London SE11 4AB

British Library Cataloguing in Publication Information Available

**Library of Congress Cataloging-in-Publication Data Available**

ISBN 978-0-7391-9812-4 (cloth : alk. paper)
ISBN 978-0-7391-9814-8 (pbk. : alk. paper)

♾™ The paper used in this publication meets the minimum requirements of American National Standard for Information Sciences Permanence of Paper for Printed Library Materials, ANSI/NISO Z39.48-1992.

Printed in the United States of America

We dedicate this book to:

our children, our grandchildren, and the generations that will follow; and to the students

who we hope will be guided by this book to begin a journey toward the creative use of conflict as a platform for peace.

# Contents

# Foreword

## *Peace and Conflict Studies: The Cutting Edge*

## Sean Byrne

Ours is a field of great importance, with the potential to transform much that is a challenge in our world. One of the critical steps in this process is the introduction of new student scholars to the field of peace and conflict studies, through providing a foundation that scans the history, current trends, and expanding areas of the field with relevance and application. In this co-authored volume, Laura Reimer, Cathryne Schmitz, Emily Janke, Ali Askerov, barbara Strahl, and Tom Matyók, provide a sophisticated and insightful exploration of the current, broad-reaching state of the Peace and Conflict Studies (PACS) field. Throughout the interesting and creative chapters are foundational principles, contemporary practices, and applications that take readers from the pages of the text to the applicability of peace and conflict studies and practices to the world around us. While reflecting the growth and expansions of how the PACS field has evolved over the past fifty years, the authors have carefully crafted a unique and important contribution to the PACS literature.

Building upon the early stages of the field as Appropriate or Alternative Dispute Resolution (ADR), Conflict Management and Peace Studies wave of the 1960s and 1970s, to the Conflict Analysis and Resolution wave of the 1980s, to the Conflict Transformation wave of the 1990s, and to the PACS wave that includes peacebuilding, human rights, and social justice era of the twenty first century, the book[1] also contains some of the Conflict Analysis and Resolution processes. These are facilitation, mediation, and negotiation as well the more contemporary cutting edge processes of the PACS field like community engagement, storytelling, restorative justice, the arts and the humanities, and transformational change. A sustainable and just peace is a holistic endeavor that includes multiple actors, activities, and institutions at multiple levels working toward peaceful nonviolent transformation,[2] and this is made clear throughout the pages.

These pages highlight the importance and significance of creative and innovative peacemaking and peacebuilding approaches to nurture peaceful coexistence and conflict transformation. This volume provides a comprehensive understanding of existing and new approaches to conflict transformation and peacebuilding among communities at the local, national, and international levels.

The evolution of the PACS field is best captured by Oliver Richmond who makes the point that PACS has gone through four phases in its development:

1. Conflict management tied to ADR and the realist paradigm of power over, operating in a negative peace or the absence of war milieu; the best that can be hoped for is managing relationships between groups or states.
2. Conflict resolution and interactive problem solving advocated by Jay Rothman and Ron Fisher, and tied to John Burton and Edward Azar's basic human needs approach, and the liberal paradigm of regional and international institutions working in the role of conflict resolution safety valves at the global level.
3. The idea of integrating elite and grassroots peacebuilding as well as multi-track diplomacy plus humanitarian aid, addressing genocide and human rights violations that are tied to the neoliberal paradigm after the Cold War, an approach often championed by John McDonald and Louis Diamond among others.
4. Hybridization, creativity, and innovation whereby emancipatory peacemaking and peacebuilding is critically tied to the arts and humanities, and storytelling as well as new and emerging issues (LGBTTQ, the environment, youth, women, and Indigenous) in the PACS field.[3]

The cutting edge approach in PACS is best represented by John Paul Lederach's Strategic Peacebuilding Paths that includes the following key components and subcomponents of strategic peacebuilding that work at all levels of society simultaneously. They are law-advocacy and solidarity, restorative justice, transitional justice, trauma healing, humanitarian action, government and multi-lateral efforts. There are also nonviolent social change, dialogue/conflict resolution strategies, education, development and dealing with transnational and global issues to achieve structural and institutional change, justice and healing, violence prevention, conflict response, and transformation.[4]

In addition, Roger MacGinty and Oliver Richmond contend that the liberal peacebuilding model needs to be deconstructed, and localized peacebuilding efforts and hybrid models of peacemaking taken into consideration.[5] A sustainable and just peace is a holistic endeavor that includes multiple actors, activities, and institutions at multiple levels working toward peaceful nonviolent transformation.[6]

Students and scholars alike will appreciate how the authors integrate theory, research, and practice with current pedagogy to facilitate expanded understandings of the knowledge building that has occurred across the phases of PACS, while acquiring some of the skills and techniques that make PACS scholars practitioners. This book is a must read for anyone new to the field, or to anyone who wants to explore meaningful ways to move forward, based on the newer frameworks, practices, and cutting edges of Peace and Conflict Studies.

Sean Byrne
Professor of Peace
and Conflict Studies
Director, Arthur V. Mauro
Centre for Peace and Justice
University of Manitoba
Winnipeg, Manitoba
July 22, 2015

## NOTES

1. Byrne, Sean and Jessica Senehi, Conflict Analysis and Resolution as a Multidiscipline: A Work in Process. In *Handbook in Conflict Analysis and Resolution*, Dennis Sandole, Sean Byrne, Ingrid Sandole and Jessica Senehi 17–29, (New York, NY: Routledge, 2009); and Senehi, eds., Jessica and Sean Byrne, Conclusions: Where Do We Go From Here? In *Critical Issues in Peace and Conflict Studies: Implications for Theory, Practice, and Pedagogy*, Tom Matyok, Jessica Senehi and Sean Byrne eds., 397-405, (Lanham, MD: Lexington Books, 2011).

2. Barash, David and Charles Webel, *Peace and Conflict Studies*, (Thousand Oaks, CA: Sage, 2013); Philpott, Daniel and Gerard Powers, eds. *Strategies of Peace: Transforming Conflict in a Violent World*, (Oxford: Oxford University Press, 2010); and Richmond, Oliver and Audra Mitchell, eds. *Hybrid Forms of Peace: From Everyday Agency to Post-Liberalism*, (New York, NY: Palgrave Macmillan, 2011).

3. Oliver Richmond, ed. *Advances in Peacebuilding: Critical Developments and Approaches* (New York, NY: Palgrave Macmillan, 2010).

4. John Paul Lederach, 2015 Strategic Peacebuilding Paths. http://kroc.nd.edu/strategic-peacebuilding-pathways Retrieved April 21, 2015.

5. Roger MacGinty, *International Peacebuilding and Local Resistance: Hybrid Forms of Peace*. New York, NY: Palgrave Macmillan, 2011); Roger Mac Ginty, *No War, No Peace: The Rejuvenation of Stalled Peace Processes and Peace Accords* (New York, NY: Palgrave Macmillan, 2008); and Oliver Richmond, Ed. *Palgrave Advances in Peacebuilding: Critical Developments and Approaches* (New York, NY: Palgrav Macmillan, 2010).

6. Barash, David and Charles Webel, *Peace and Conflict Studies*, (Thousand Oaks, CA: Sage, 2013); Philpott, Daniel and Gerard Powers, eds. *Strategies of Peace: Transforming Conflict in a Violent World*, (Oxford: Oxford University Press, 2010); and Richmond, Oliver and Audra Mitchell, eds. *Hybrid Forms of Peace: From Everyday Agency to Post-Liberalism*, (New York, NY: Palgrave Macmillan, 2011).

# Preface

The pursuit of peace is ancient, but its entrance into academia as Peace and Conflict Studies (PACS) has brought a new dimension to understanding conflict. *Transformative Change* is a comprehensive introduction to the theory, research, and practices of this field, which have the power to positively transform the interpersonal relationships of daily life, build and restore communities, and influence state relations around the world. The multidisciplinary scholarship of the field helps make sense of conflict in a way that shifts the paradigm from merely ending war to building comprehensive and sustainable peace. This pursuit is exclusive to the human capacity for empowered relationships.

The study of conflict transformation now stands as a respected field of study and practice within academia. It is taught in over three hundred undergraduate and graduate programs around the globe. The number of colleges and universities establishing and expanding programs in and related to peace and conflict studies increases annually.

## AN OVERVIEW OF THE BOOK

*Transformative Change* reflects the dynamic and fluid nature of peace and conflict studies, offering a practice-based education in an introductory format. PACS practice stands on a foundation of theory and research, which is guided by the purposeful significance of peacebuilding. The energy inherent in the field is reflected through the breadth of models and concepts presented. Current theories, frameworks, and models are included. The transformative and empowering inquiry methods include engaged, Indigenous, and participatory academic research. The large practice section focuses on the responsive and empowering trends in transformative conflict and peacebuilding practice for change among the many types and levels of conflict. The practice section concludes with an exploration of artistic expressions that are reshaping the study of conflict.

## AUDIENCES

This book is written for students of peace and conflict. The primary audience is members of the post-secondary community. For students in other disciplines, the book provides opportunities to integrate PACS into the frameworks of their chosen fields in order to explain, predict, and influence the world around them. The frameworks and practice models are also written to inform students who are drawn to the field of peace and conflict studies from other areas of education and expertise, including international relations, education, business and organization studies, public and education administration, the military, and social work. The authors were drawn to peace and conflict studies from these areas. This book provides all readers with the knowledge and paradigms needed for a solid foundation upon which to launch their work.

## THE AUTHORS

The authors came together at The University of North Carolina Greensboro in the United States, as faculty members in the graduate and undergraduate programs in the Department of Peace and Conflict Studies. Working as professors we realized that between us we have the education, experiences, and expertise to offer the field a unique textbook built on the values that guide the field and our teaching. The book facilitates meaningful educational experiences in order to make a difference in real life. In the spirit of democratic engagement and collaboration, it seemed fitting to extend the writing of the book to include the work of our students. Their work is strategically placed in this text. It is our students and alumni who keep us growing and expanding. They are leading us in embedding the use of the arts and sports across our models of practice.

Although we have different backgrounds, nations, faiths, and expertise, the similarities between us have been the strength of this work. The project has tested us in ways we did not anticipate, challenging us to grow. In the process we again learned that the principles and practices of peacebuilding and transformative change contained within these pages truly work in all contexts.

## HOW TO USE THIS BOOK

Because there is no single path to peace, this book is designed with conflict transformation at its core. This work is designed to be more than a textbook. It is meant to impact the way readers address conflict, interpret peace, and foster transformation. This may include making notes, highlighting, and doing whatever helps to make this book useful.

The chapters of the book are organized according to knowing (theory, models, and praxis) and practice. Each chapter represents a critical area of the field and presents tools of practice to engage peacebuilding and conflict transformation. The number of chapters is deliberate so that instructors may use the textbook as a comprehensive and engaging resource. The chapters are constructed with learning outcomes in alignment with the latest pedagogical practices and within reasonable course expectations. These will orient both the reader and the instructor to what we believe is significant in each chapter. Of course, our desire is for students to engage with material as constructivist learners, creating new knowledge that is meaningful to each individual in a unique way. Questions guide this engagement at the end of each chapter.

Our intent has been to equip instructors and students with a book that embodies an introductory survey course in peace and conflict studies. The following chapters contain the mechanisms for recognizing the patterns of conflict and for responding appropriately. The lessons learned here can be applied at all levels of conflict for transformative change.

# Acknowledgements

This book is a collaborative effort, enriched by the contributions of many people. The authors wish to thank and extend our public appreciation and respect to Dr. Sean Byrne for setting aside the time to write the Foreword for *Transformative Change*. Many of us were his students. We especially wish to acknowledge his inspiration to all of us. He is a true scholar.

We could not have written this book without the ongoing contributions of our students—the people who sit in our classrooms, explore new frontiers in PACS, share their insights with us, and generally animate our work day at university. We encourage our students to be pracademics and to apply their passions and knowledge to expand the field, and they do! The people below provided importantly to the development of this book, and many are at the edges of our field, pushing out. We are proud of them as representatives of the new generation of PACS scholars and invited them to share their passions for the book.

**Jeff Aguiar** holds a Bachelor of Fine Arts in Theatre Education, a Post-Baccalaureate Certificate in Nonprofit Management and is currently pursuing his Master of Arts in Peace and Conflict Studies at the University of North Carolina Greensboro. With over twenty years of experience in the arts, nonprofits, and community building, the praxis of community building in the arts as both a product and a process has been his primary professional focus, spanning multiple industries and levels of community. Jeff has developed a hybrid model that merges narrative with formal theory for conflict analysis, and is the author of the theatre section of chapter 12.

**Philip Allinger**, BA Political and Administrative Science, holds a double MA from the Universities of North Carolina Greensboro and Konstanz, Germany, and met the authors of this book as an exchange student at UNCG, where he animated the classes with his vibrant imagination and brilliant analyses. Philip wrote the story of the Knight Errant and the Big Big Dragon, which originates from participation in the class "Skills and Techniques of Conflict Transformation" taught by Laura Reimer in 2014. Philip's main academic interests are the contribution of religion to peacebuilding and the study of genocide.

**Michael Barkman** studied political science and urban and inner city studies at the University of Winnipeg, Canada. He has had a deep passion for improv theatre from a young age. He has performed with many groups across Canada and has facilitated youth improv and theatre in Winnipeg, working especially with newcomer and refugee students in peacebuilding activities with energy and laughter. He met Dr. Reimer in a community democracy course at U of Winnipeg in 2015. Michael is keenly interested in applications of peacebuilding processes for community engagement, and is the co-author of the improv section in chapter 12.

**Jacob Bridges** is a graduate of the University of North Carolina Greensboro with a Bachelor of Arts degree in political science. He is keenly interested and educated in music's impact on social change as conflict transformation. In addition, he has worked on multiple political campaigns as a community organizer. Jacob wrote the section about American folk music and protest songs in chapter 12, which originated in coursework completed for peace and conflict studies at the University of North Carolina Greensboro with Dr. Reimer.

**Jessica Cruz** completed her MA degree in peace and conflict studies at the University of North Carolina Greensboro where she has focused specifically on workplace conflict. Her research and professional focus is on conflict management, interpersonal relations, organizational structuring, and professional development within organizations. As the graduate assistant for the peace and conflict studies department at UNCG, Jess maintained her standard for excellence and provided outstanding editing, review, and copyediting support throughout the book project.

**Chuck Egerton** has been an instructor and Department Head of Photography at Randolph Community College in North Carolina for twenty-five years. He holds a BFA in drawing and painting, an AAS in commercial photography and an MA in peace and conflict studies. He begins work on a PhD in Peace and Conflict Studies at the University of Manitoba in fall 2015, focusing on photography as a means to transform conflict. Chuck is an educator, photographer, and passionate peace and conflict studies practitioner, responsible for the photography section of chapter 12.

**Jenna. E. Reimer** is a conflict resolution student at Menno Simons College at the University of Winnipeg. Jenna received mediation training from Dr. Strahl in Las Vegas, Nevada in 2014. Her interests are in identity conflict and peacebuilding practices, particularly focused on transforming conflict for people living in post-Troubles Northern Ireland. Jenna conceived the title of this textbook and provided invaluable insight and suggestions throughout the final weeks of the project. Many of the questions at the end of the chapters have been shaped by Jenna's student experiences and her interests, passions, and applications of peace and conflict studies. She intends to pursue an MA and possibly a PhD in PACS.

**Frannie Varker**, MS is completing an MA in Peace and Conflict Studies at the University of North Carolina Greensboro. Her focus of study is the nexus of experiential education as peace education. Employed as the

Director of Team QUEST, UNCG's experiential education program, she believes understanding team and group dynamics is essential to community and peacebuilding. Frannie contributed to the experiential education portion of the Group Processes chapter.

**Margo Wilson Kehler** is an award-winning educator, having taught high school drama in the public school system in central Canada for over twenty-six years. Margo recognizes the powerful influence of improv to assist students as they work through and represent conflict, on the stage and off. Her passion for improv has led her to workshop with some of the great names in the various forms of this art: Keith Johnstone, Del Close, Charna Halpern, David Shepherd, and Paul Sills to name a few. Over the years, Margo has led her teams to multiple regional and national victories. Margo co-authored the improv section of chapter 12.

We want to acknowledge the professionalism and support of the Lexington Books publishing team, and our editors, Justin Race, Kathryn Tafelski, and Ashli MacKenzie in particular, who caught our vision immediately and were steadfast encouragers and our champions throughout the process.

Finally, but not least, we acknowledge our families. In many ways, it is at home on the anvil of family relationships that we all learn to navigate conflict, build peace, and experience firsthand the power of transformative change. No work like this can ever be completed without the ongoing love and support of the people closest to us. To each of our family members, friends, colleagues, and students that walked the journey of this project with us, thank you.

Laura Reimer
Cathryne Schmitz
Emily Janke
Ali Askerov
barbara Strahl∗
Tom Matyók

∗ correctly spelled with lower case 'b'

# ONE

# Introduction to the Field of Peace and Conflict Studies

LEARNING OUTCOMES

- To understand the basic concepts of PACS scholarship and practice
- To remember the four phases of development in the field
- To evaluate the differences among conflict resolution, management, and transformation
- To analyze the differences between war and terrorism

OVERVIEW

Rising from a broad foundation of interdisciplinary theory, research, and practice, Peace and Conflict Studies (or PACS) is one of the fastest growing academic fields of study. PACS integrates theory from multiple disciplines in the humanities and social sciences, and is now shifting and expanding to explore the role of the Indigenous ways of knowing, and integrating with the arts and design fields, and peace scholarship. The growing literature within the field engages conflict analysis toward peaceful, positive, and sustainable conflict transformation.

INTRODUCTION

There is a common assumption that conflict is a simple collision between two parties. In fact, the origins, processes, outcomes, and consequences of conflict are deeper and longer lasting than a simple collision. Another assumption for many people is that in every conflict there is a winner and a loser. This assumption, whether at the local or global level, keeps groups and communities stuck in cycles of violence. There are many interpretations of the term conflict, and many theories and models offering explanations of its causes, triggers, paths, resolutions, and ultimate sustainability or transformation. Despite the many erroneous or simple understandings of conflict, the field of peace and conflict studies emerged into the world of academia and practice in recognition of the complexity of conflict. The contributions of theory, frameworks, and models provide a foundational knowledge for practice in which conflict is recognized, acknowledged, addressed, and ultimately transformed.

Conflict analysis begins with the repercussions of action and seeks patterns to predict the path of conflict. The traditional images of peace and of conflict are static doves or guns. In fact, both peace and conflict are intimately integrated and more accurately depicted as a swirling hologram, alive and fluid, full of potential. It is this potential that compels the field forward to study conflict, to transform conflict, and to build peace. Through the careful study of the patterns and habits of conflict, scholars are discovering important trends at multiple levels and in multiple contexts. PACS research has determined that conflicts waged between nation states contain the same elements as disputes between neighbors or family members. Models and frameworks represent the inquiries and curiosities of some of the greatest minds in the field; people with substantial theoretical grounding but who are also impassioned to transform the daily experiences of people in conflict for good.

In the dynamic relationship between theory and practice, research has produced significant alternatives to the age-old pattern of resolving conflict through violence. Conflict is transforming around the globe as theory guides practice, and practice prompts further inquiry. Simultaneously, peacebuilding is a methodology and in some ways, a guiding ideology. The practices of building peace are numerous and creative, and the potential for sustained peace through conflict transformation is only limited by our understandings of conflict.

## CONFLICT

At its simplest, a conflict is recognized as a disagreement through which one or more parties involved in a specified situation perceive threats to their needs, interests, or concerns. It can come from a variety of sources, like perceived goals, personality differences, competition over resources, relationship styles, values and perceived values, and communication styles. The sources of conflict are not generally simple; they can be complicated by history, context, culture and identity, positionality, and technology. Conflict can also take place at multiple levels of human engagement—local, regional, national, and/or global. It can be interpersonal, community-based, or both.

While conflicts often appear to be different at the positional level, there are often common interests that can provide bridges to transformation. Interests are those matters of importance underlying the stance or position of parties in a conflict. While positions might appear to be obvious, interests must be discerned, generally by listening to the message behind positional statements. Conflicts are frequently either values conflicts or interest conflicts. Values tend to be more stable and fundamental. They can be non-negotiable because they are deep within. On the other hand, interest conflicts can be more accessible for change. Discerning the difference is an important early step in peacebuilding.

Typically there are four general types of conflict that lay the foundation for the earliest phases of conflict analysis—interpersonal, intrapersonal, interstate, and intrastate. Although it is preliminary conflict analysis, all conflicts can be codified into one of these categories. Each type of conflict is recognizable by its patterns.

Intrapersonal conflicts take place within an individual. They are typically developed based on the perceptions people have about their own thoughts and feelings, and about the thoughts and feelings of others. Intrapersonal conflicts can exist for a while without expression through anger, disappointment, fear, or even hurt. Once they are expressed or communicated to someone else, however, they are recognized as interpersonal conflicts. Interpersonal conflict is conflict between individuals, and is often simply avoidance. The principle of conflict threshold, however, states that in order for conflict to exist, parties must recognize that they have opposing interests.[1]

Interstate conflict occurs between governments and employs armed forces. An armed conflict is an organized collective and violent conflict, usually between two groups. The World Wars were interstate wars. Interstate conflicts usually commence with an official or formal declaration, and can take place anywhere, at any time. Intrastate conflicts take place inside state borders and are usually predicated by ethnic, religious, or ideological incompatibilities, and armed forces are involved in some way. Sometimes there is involvement or support from a foreign government, but not always. Civil wars are considered intrastate wars.

## Categories of Conflict

The categories of conflict have identifiable general characteristics that offer important distinctions for approaching conflict and are important factors in the design of appropriate interventions. These are introduced below as social, structural, ethnic, identity-based, environmental, and organizational conflicts. As the research grows and as the field expands into new areas, these general categories continue to provide useful ways to organize conflict and serve as a second level toward informing intervention design and peacebuilding. These are general categories only, and it is important for the reader to know that within these categories, and within the types outlined above, there are divisions among micro and macro levels from personal to global, divisions among academics and practitioners, and divisions among specialists and generalists.[2]

Social conflict is one of the broader categories or varieties of conflict. According to James Schellenberg,[3] social conflict refers to the opposition between individuals and groups on the basis of competing interests, different identities, and differing attitudes. The conflict takes place in the context of society. Kriesberg and Dayton[4] have also researched and written extensively about social conflict, and have identified the characteristics of social conflicts.[5] Social conflicts are natural, inevitable, and universal. They can be beneficial. Social conflicts are waged with varying destructiveness, so that not all social battles are battles for survival. Social conflicts entail contested social constructions, meaning that participants in a conflict usually have differing views of what they are fighting about, and sometimes about who they are fighting against. All social conflicts can be transformed in a positive direction, especially with different stakeholders engaged in different approaches at different times. Social conflicts are dynamic and tend to move through stages of emergence, escalation, de-escalation, and a settlement, termination, or outcome that indicates conflict resolution.

Structural conflicts[6] occur as a result of the way an organization (often governmental) is organized, or structured. They may be defined as the conflict that results from the allocation of scarce resources or a shift in the structure of a system or environment that changes the status quo of a situation. Structural conflicts do not include individuals or groups in their analysis, except as they are affected by the conflict. Theories of structural conflict find their origins in the work of Karl Marx, who did not attribute any of the interactions of economics or society to be the result of individuals or their personalities.

Ethnic conflicts are group conflicts, but they are difficult to define. Ethnic conflicts are complex and multi-causal, steeped in history. One distinguishing factor is that the goals of at least one party are defined in ethnic terms.[7] Ethnic conflicts are identified when the primary conflict is taking place over ethnic distinctions.[8] That is, ethnic conflict occurs when some aspect of how a group defines itself or how it is defined by another group becomes politicized. This means that there are times when one party to the conflict will claim that its ethnic identity is the reason why their members cannot achieve their interests, their claims are not satisfied, or they do not have the same rights as the members of the other group(s). In this way, ethnic conflicts form group conflicts in which at least one party interprets the conflict, the cause of the conflict, and any potential resolution as an existing or perceived ethnic divide. Not every ethnic conflict is characterized by violence, but inter-ethnic violence is always a sign of underlying conflict.[9]

Identity conflicts are also group conflicts, similar but importantly distinct from ethnic conflicts. Essentially, identity is defined as an abiding sense of the self and of the relationship of the self to the world.[10] This is why these conflicts are sometimes called identity-based conflicts. Northrup[11] explains identity as a system of beliefs or a way of constructing the world that makes life predictable rather than random, and provides people with a reasonable level of ability to predict how their behavior affects what happens to them as they function in society. Identity conflicts and identity-based conflicts are not identity crises, which are intrapersonal conflicts.

According to Kriesberg,[12] people have many characteristics that may be the basis for identity and for opposition to people whose characteristics are different from theirs.[13] John Paul Lederach explains that identity is lodged in how people talk about themselves, who they are, where they have come from, and what they fear.[14] Identity is the meaning that individuals give to their membership in a given community and it is those attributes or qualities that bind them to that community and distinguish it from others. Jessica Senehi has stated that identities shape the way we interact with other people and also the way we intervene or respond to conflict.[15] According to many scholars, it is in the context of many relationships that identity conflict can best be understood.

Environmental conflicts can be defined as the destabilizing interferences in the ecosystem's equilibrium.[16] They are comprehensive and integrate with other conflicts. As a result, they may manifest as political, social, economic, ethnic, religious or territorial conflicts, or in relation to resources or national interests. Environmental conflicts are numerous and complex, including migration, natural resources, loss of biodiversity, human security, and even business. Environmental conflicts have potentially far-reaching consequences, including violence in several forms. The cause and principal characteristic of the conflict are the importance of environmental degradation resulting from the overuse of renewable resources, the increase in pollution, the general impoverishment of living spaces, and the misuse of plants and other non-human life.

Organizational conflict refers to how people respond to and within over-arching societal systems and structures.[17] They can take place inter-organizationally (for example, a business takeover), or intra-organizationally (for example, among departmental employees). Workplace conflict is one form of organizational conflict that is often addressed through policy changes, labor disputes, and the filing of a grievance. Typically, the response is to avoid addressing conflict and instead to reassign an employee, or to increase rules and regulations in an effort to transform relationships and the workplace back to a stable environment.

*Conflict Actors*

Conflict actors are the individuals, groups, organizations, or institutions involved in a conflict. They are both readily identifiable but sometimes require careful consideration before they are identified. Analysts carefully determine the conflict actors before they begin to consider intervention. The conflict actors may include governments, international organizations and financial institutions, identity groups, factions within groups, single-issue groups, potential peacemakers, and potential spoilers. Within groups, analysts engage another layer of conflict analysis in order to distinguish between top leadership, middle-range leadership, and grassroots leadership. Gaining a clear understanding of all the actors involved in a conflict is critical.

Typically, the primary actors are thought of as those directly involved in the conflict, and so they are less difficult to identify than the other actors. Secondary actors are not actual parties to the conflict but they have a high degree of interest in and influence over the conflict, frequently due to their proximity. For example, sometimes these are the governments of countries that border on a country in conflict.

In addition to the primary and secondary actors, analysts determine that there are other parties with interests in and influence over events. These external actors often include regional and global players, like governments, government organizations, non-governmental organizations, and institutions. For example, the external actors may be large global organizations like the United Nations and the European Union.

## WAR

War is a brutal form of politics and has many definitions, yet most people feel a sense of dread, fear, and foreboding that suggests there is a common conceptualization of war. All theories of international relations recognize that war is a central problem for everyone in the world.[18] In his book, *On War*, Karl von Clausewitz defines war as an act of violence used with the intention to force opponents to comply with the wishes of the first.[19] He identified war as a continuation of politics by means other than formal political ones. Others recognize that war is a sustained, coordinated violence between political organizations.[20] War is dynamic. In the west, there are essentially three main positions surrounding war. These are the convictions that war is never legitimate (which is pacifism); that anything is acceptable in times of war; and that there must be restraints on the conduct of war.[21] This latter position contains the roots of Just War theory, which is an important and foundational concept in peace and conflict studies.

## JUST WAR THEORY

Just War is one of the traditional paradigms for approaching the relationship between war and politics. Just War theorists explore the moral and legal justifications for engagement in war, but Just War theory is more an ethical paradigm than it is a practice. Just War theory led to rules of war, the Geneva Convention, and the International Criminal Court. Usually wars are justified by states on historical or theoretical grounds. Although not all states provide justification for their decision to engage in war, scholars try to make sense of what happens by applying common principles recognized in the literature as Just War theory. Just War theorists are concerned that warfare should be suspended in general, and settled in ways that help provide justice after war, while preventing more of the same.

There are two groups of consideration for a war to be judged "just." These are *jus ad bellum* and *jus in bello*, two Latin terms that describe conditions and justifications.[22] *Jus ad bellum* refers to the right to go to war, and includes authority, cause, and intention. When there can be no other way to resolve conflict, as the "just cause," *jus ad bellum* also includes a "last resort" consideration. *Jus in bello* refers to the conditions for the conduct of war for nations, armies, and individual soldiers. All armies maintain standards of lawful and criminal behavior and have police, prisons, and courts to enforce the standards. Although the treatment of the enemy is often merciless, armies that act in contravention of the just war criteria are also in violation the international rule of law, which does hold them accountable. Although Just War theory is not a direct form of conflict transformation, it does place parameters and expectations around the engagement and practices of war and in this way, attempts to manage the most violent form of conflict.

## TERRORISM

Terrorism is a political term and has its roots in state terror.[23] Terrorism is not war, although it uses force and violence. The concept of terrorism is complex and combines different aspects of human experience, such as politics, psychology, culture, military strategy, and justice, among others. Terrorists have strong feelings concerning the rightness of the use of violence. In order to fight terrorism effectively, it is important to understand the rationale behind terrorism.

Terrorism has a global character. Terrorism can be defined as "the threat or use of violence by a group or individual against noncombatants in a struggle to achieve political goals,"[24] and deliberately targets innocent people as victims.[25] Terrorism is a form of violence designed to attain political achievements. Moreover, terrorists aim to demoralize a civilian population in order to diminish its support for the national governments that are fighting terrorism. Terrorism is an asymmetric form of warfare; a concept with political, legal, and military tentacles, but without the rules of engagement or restrictions of war between states.

In late modern times, states, as legitimate actors of the international system, still use war as a means to reach their objectives. Non-state actors such as terrorist organizations have to rely on violence to reach their targets. The main elements generally differentiating between them are the notion of legitimacy and the methods of action, though states do also enlist violence against their citizens. Unlike terrorist organizations, states are legitimate actors and usually do not use the immoral methods, such as suicide bombings and beheadings, that terrorist groups employ. The field of peace and conflict Studies exists to transform any form of violence, and especially war and terrorism.

## CONFLICT STUDIES

### The Four Waves of the Field

Waves on the ocean flow into one another and overlap one another in a steady pattern that manifests the water differently with each wave. This is an appropriate description of the trends and developments that frame the history and practice of conflict resolution studies.[26] These are called the four waves; they are not timelines.

Before the 1960s, the world of conflict resolution was very different from today. Power-based bargaining resulted in zero-sum agreements, mostly among management and labour. This meant there were significant losers and winners, and rarely satisfactory compromise. In the international system, the foreign policy of nuclear Détente held conflict in balance between the military superpowers, but there were prolific outbreaks of conflict among other, smaller nation states. There were many problems and few ways to resolve them. Problem solving workshops by early scholars in the field like John Paul Lederach, John Burton, and Ronald Fisher emerged as a direct response to both the arms race and the proliferation of ethnopolitical conflicts.[27] These were the early days of Alternative Dispute Resolution (ADR), and served to build trust by promoting group understandings of basic human needs and of other's views. This in turn forged a willingness to focus on consensual decision-making, and the emergence of the first of the four waves.[28]

The first wave is directly associated with people's growing distrust in government and the changing political values of the 1960s. In North America especially, cars, music, and clothing reflected new values. This was the age of "power to the people," Dr. Martin Luther King Jr. and the Civil Rights movement in the United States, man on the moon, and the women's movement. The peace movement was born in direct protest against US military involvement in Vietnam. There were many conflicts and many ways that people were striving to make sense of widespread change but they began to take power back through community engaged processes, and socially, people sought to solve their problems locally.[29]

The conflict resolution movement emerged as a distinct field of study in the late 1960s and early 1970s. In universities, Professor Ken Boulding founded the *Journal of Conflict Resolution*, and Professor Johan Galtung created the *Journal of Peace Research*. The International Peace Research Association (IPRA) was founded in 1965, and in 1973 the University of Bradford created the first School of Peace Studies.[30] During this period, conflict management was tied to ADR and the realist paradigm of power. Most research and practices in the field focused on the absence of war, so that this was a period of conflict management.

The second wave established the professionalization of the field. This was a time when mediation became a formal dispute mechanism, and formal organizations dedicated to conflict resolution were founded. These included The Society for Professionals in Dispute Resolution (SPIDR), which eventually merged with Conflict Resolution Network (CRenet) and the Association of Family Mediators (AFM) in 2001 to become today's Association of Conflict Resolution (ACR).[31]

The third wave is characterized by a focus on the structural roots of conflict, on basic human needs, and by an exploration of the connection between micro and macro levels of conflict intervention.[32] Formal programs of conflict resolution were founded during the third wave, including the Center for Conflict Resolution (CCR) at George Mason University, which established a comprehensive multidisciplinary Master of Science. The Department of Dispute Resolution of Nova Southeastern University offered a Master degree in Dispute Resolution, then renamed it the Department of Conflict Analysis and Resolution in 1994.

In 1984 the United States Institute of Peace was founded, and the next year, the Canadian Institute for International Peace and Security and Conflict Resolution Network Canada were established. The formalization and professionalization of the field were well established during the third wave.[33] In 1987, the first doctoral program was created in Conflict Analysis and Resolution in the United States. In 2005 in central Canada, the Arthur V. Mauro Centre for Peace and Justice established the first doctoral program in peace and conflict studies at St. Paul's College at the University of Manitoba, inspired by the belief that while religion has often been a cause of violence, coalitions of individuals inspired by different religious faiths can be significant peacebuilders. In many ways, conflict resolution took the form of interactive problem solving, tied to the basic human needs theories of John Burton and Edward Azar.

The fourth wave introduced the umbrella of peace and conflict studies and a focus on conflict transformation, led by scholars Johan Galtung and

John Paul Lederach. The fourth wave represents a growing attention to multi-track diplomacy, humanitarian aid, dealing with genocide, and the defence of human rights. Transformation of relationships and structures through grassroots efforts characterizes the literature and curriculum of the fourth wave.

Some conclude that the field is now in a fifth wave as a theory-based discipline with a "defensible place in the academy."[34] However, the field is not simple to define and is loosely structured within itself.[35] Trends from recent research indicate a steady movement toward peacebuilding, which combines the technical skills of conflict resolution with the academic discipline of research and applied theory. Yet there are also many indications that the discipline is expanding rapidly to include Indigenous research methods and peacebuilding practices, and into newer expressions of conflict transformation that include sports, music, environmental studies, and new, less violent forms of military engagement.

One of the most exciting characteristics of peace and conflict studies is the recognition that relationships are not static. This means that as the field continues to expand and explore relationships at all levels, knowledge will increase, and a continuously more peaceful and sustainable world will emerge.

## Three Forms of Conflict Engagement

Conflict engagement has taken three primary forms with three different goals. Conflict resolution, conflict management, and conflict transformation contribute in different ways to peace and conflict studies. Although they are separate, both conflict resolution and conflict management are platforms that inform practice for conflict transformation.

## Conflict Resolution

One of the originally recognized mechanisms for peacebuilding is conflict resolution. Conflict resolution refers to the methods and processes involved in facilitating the peaceful ending of conflict and retribution and seeks to move conflicting parties away from the positions of one winner and one loser toward positive outcomes. Conflict resolution practices are heavily reliant on the identification of the conflict styles of individuals and often involve external actors for resolution. The critical distinction for conflict resolution is the implied reduction, elimination, or termination of conflict. According to the principles of conflict resolution, conflict is over when the immediate issue, or conflict, is resolved to the satisfaction of the parties involved. Resolved conflict means that a balance has been achieved between the parties.

## Conflict Management

Typically, conflict management principles are associated with the workplace and with minimizing or managing conflict so that organizational outcomes may be achieved with minimal discomfort or conflict. Conflict management refers to behaviors and strategies, usually undertaken by organizational managers to minimize the effects of conflict in a group, but does not assume or require conflict resolution.[36] Conflict management strategies include a variety of behaviors that can be engaged in order to deal with conflict, but the goal is neither conflict resolution nor conflict transformation.

## Conflict Transformation

The term conflict transformation was first used in the field of peace and conflict studies by professor and practitioner John Paul Lederach of Notre Dame University. It is both a framework for understanding and a description of responses to conflict, or processes. Most importantly, conflict transformation is about relationships, how they converge, and that the desired change can be encouraged.

As a framework for conflict analysis, conflict transformation practices identify root causes of conflict in the context of other potential causes by explicitly recognizing and exploring the relationships and connections surrounding difficult or negative responses to conflict. This provides a base for exploring how such responses may turn into positive, or more peaceful, responses to conflict.[37] History can be considered and individual narratives can be included in a conflict transformation analysis in order to help shape a change process. The structural conflicts built into institutions and organizations like governments, corporations, and even civil society are relevant to study.[38]

Each conflict encountered by an individual or by a group results in a choice or response. That response can set the stage for movement toward positive or negative change. This is a process, not one event in time, and is recognized as conflict transformation. Lederach[39] identifies four ways that conflict transformation may be considered prescriptive for positive change.

1. As a way to understand how individuals are affected by conflict in both positive and negative ways, conflict transformation can acknowledge effects at the physical, emotional, and spiritual levels.
2. As an intentional intervention to minimize misunderstanding and to maximize mutual understanding, conflict transformation can bring the relational fears, hopes, and goals of individuals to the surface.

3. Conflict transformation also represents intervention in order to gain insight into underlying social structural conditions and causes of conflict.

4. Finally, as a framework for understanding, conflict transformation can help people in conflict understand cultural patterns that contribute to their setting, and to build upon resources that can help them constructively respond to conflict.

In this way, the changing nature of conflict, or the transformation of conflict, can influence positive change in personal, relational, structural, and cultural ways. The recognition of the many relationships inherent in conflict is at the core of conflict transformation principles.

## PEACE STUDIES

Peace studies is often confused with the peace movement, but they are very different. Peace studies is an academic discipline, and it is a complex and practical process with the goal of changing lives and transforming societies. Peace studies is closely tied to increasing our understanding of violence and to the eradication of war. This is important to the sustainability of the world. Overcoming conflict involves overcoming psychological and structural obstacles that are the result of prolonged and violent conflict. Actual peace-building involves a wide range of functions and rules, affected by human interactions and perceptions, and by the post-conflict social environment.

By the 1990s, peace research was established in academia. Over three hundred research institutes, professional associations, and academic journals supported the ongoing, integrated, and expanding work of the field. Formal peace research has resulted in an ongoing expansion of the knowledge base and the development of peace practices. The number of scholars and the level of scholarship, has increased resulting in the emergence of peace studies onto the world stage to inform peace workers.

Paul Rogers and Oliver Rathsbotham, well-known scholars from the University of Bradford in the United Kingdom, argue that the distinction of peace research from other overlapping disciplines is "its central concern with issues of peace and conflict, its multi-disciplinarity, its holistic approach combined with quantitative and empirical methodologies, and its normative commitment to the analysis of conditions for non-violent social and political change."[40] This unique contribution means that although peace research is centrally focused on alternatives to conflict, the search for conflict transformation does not hesitate to cross disciplinary boundaries or to explore the applicability of frameworks for understanding from other scholarly research and practice. In this way, feminist research, environmental research, and critical theory have contributed significantly to advances in the field.

Peace research is recognized by the International Peace Research Association[41] to be inclusive of many integrated fields: peace culture and communications, peace journalism, conflict resolution and peacebuilding, peace and ecology, global political economy, human rights, internal conflicts, non-violence, peace education, peace history, peace movements, youth, tourism, peace theories, refugees, religion and peace, security and disarmament, gender and peace, reconciliation, art and peace, and Indigenous peoples rights.

There are numerous approaches to conflict as a result of distinguished and expanding scholarship. The international recognition of peace studies is underscored by the nomination for the Nobel Peace Prize to two of the early scholars in the field. First Johan Galtung, who established the first Peace Research Institute and is often recognized as one of the founders of the field, was recognized. Next was Adam Curle, who established the concept of Conflict Progression. John Paul Lederach explains Curle's foundational framework this way: "Conflicts progress from situations of unbalanced power and low awareness, or latent conflict to situations of unbalanced power and increasing awareness, or overt conflict. Negotiations attempt to bring overt conflicts to a situation of balanced power and high awareness. When this situation is stable, Curle calls it peace."[42] Until these scholars emerged through peace study work, the world considered peace to be only the absence of armed conflict.

Canadian scholar Anatol Rapoport, credited with the development of Game Theory, describes peace research as an "infrastructure of peace, which . . . ought to be the source of an antidote to the ideational poisons generated by exacerbating destructive conflicts. . . . They ought to be 'armed' for the inevitable struggle against the infrastructure of war."[43] Although this is a very brief introduction it is apparent that peace studies, as a purpose, an academic stream, and a goal, provides scientific analysis as one of the important frameworks influencing the progress and development of peace and conflict theory, research, and practice.

Peace and conflict scholarship has points of tension between the desire for scholarly excellence and contribution, and the desire to leave the objective detachment of the academy to share university knowledge through practice toward the building of peace. It resides in the desire to make a positive difference in the lives of people in our communities, cities, nations, and world. Effective study requires a strong knowledge base, and the field continues to attract people drawn by the ongoing and combined tension between the high standards and objective scientific demands of scholarship, and the subjective values commitment to help people and make the world better.[44]

## PEACEBUILDING

Peacebuilding is the practice arm of academic research and the focus of teaching and scholarship. Building sustainable peace is central to peace research and to conflict studies. Peacebuilding has been defined as "the creation and nurturing of constructive relationships across ethnic, religious, class, and racial boundaries."[45] It is practice-based and aimed at transforming individuals, societies, and even government policy, from a state of violence or deep injustice to one of greater peace. One scholar has claimed that despite the media agenda to report conflict, global politics are in fact "in an age of peace-building."[46] The practices of peacebuilding stand on the foundations of just peace, scholarly research, community engagement, and local strengths and assets.

Peacebuilding is not restricted to post-war settings and in this is its strength and appeal. While the public news media seems to be constantly negative, there is overwhelming evidence that the early years of the twenty-first century are characterized as an era of peacebuilding. Since 1988, for example, the United Nations has been aggressively involved in peacebuilding operations as global public policy, based primarily on the scholarship of peace and conflict studies. As a result, since the end of the Cold War an unprecedented number of civil wars have ended with negotiated settlements. Over eighty countries have moved toward democracy, the protection of human rights, and the rule of law. The World Bank reports that since the turn of the new century, economies in the developing world are growing faster than they are in developed countries.

In the United States, the United States Institute of Peace (USIP) is an example of peace-time peacebuilding. The United States Institute of Peace is an independent, nonpartisan institution established in 1984 and funded by the American Congress to increase the nation's capacity to manage international conflict without violence. In 2005, USIP established a professional training center for practitioners in conflict prevention, management, and resolution.

According to one of the world's leading non-profit agencies changing the face of poverty, the World Bank and the United Nations[47] report that since 1990, extreme poverty rates have been cut in half, 17,000 fewer children die every day than they did in 1990, 2.3 billion people got access to clean water, and the number of pregnant women and new mothers who die dropped 45 percent in these same twenty-five years! During the same period, adult illiteracy has been slashed in half, and the world has reached equality in primary schooling between boys and girls.

The number of families that have improved their relationships, the number of workplace relationships that have transformed, and the number of marriages that have survived and thrived, and the peaceful resolution of conflict on the streets and in the prisons are not measured here, but all share their successes in the study and practices of peacebuilding.

Peace, like conflict, takes place in global systems, regional politics, national governments, local municipalities, community matters, and among and within individuals. The scope is vast, but the principles of peacebuilding and of understanding and transforming conflict are durable and sustainable.[48]

## Challenges to Peacebuilding

There are three major considerations and challenges confronting the peacebuilding agenda around the globe. These challenges provide an important context for the frameworks and evaluation approaches developed in peace and conflict studies. First, the international culture is committed philosophically and economically to arms production and has an unsophisticated understanding of non-violent approaches to conflict transformation. Second, war is a comprehensive system that will only be transformed or prevented from escalating through concepts, approaches, and actions that deal with the specific nature of armed conflict, the people that operate it, and the settings in which war is rooted. History has shown that non-systemic approaches do not work. Finally, time is the third challenge to building sustainable peace throughout the world. Peacebuilding is complex and requires a comprehensive, long-term and multi-faceted strategy to transform conflict, end violence, and achieve sustained resolution; finite timelines, though politically popular, cannot guarantee sustained peace. Although these are serious challenges, they can be overcome. The recognition and ongoing research into these three challenges represent some of the important ways peace and conflict paradigms influence the international order.

## SUMMARY

The foundational concepts of Peace and Conflict Studies (PACS) provide a broad platform from which models, frameworks, strategic interventions, and a vast collection of skills equip scholars and practitioners to approach conflict for transformative change. With its origins in multiple disciplines, PACS has expanded in four waves that each provided important contributions to transformative change. Wave One corresponded with the countercultural revolution of the 1960s, Wave Two established the field professionally, and Wave Three explored the structural roots of conflicts, basic human needs, and began to examine interconnections between micro and macro level conflict intervention. The fourth wave culminated in conflict transformation and peace and conflict studies, which has seemingly become a fifth wave. The distinctive contributions of conflict resolution, conflict management, and conflict transformation weave through the four waves. While conflict styles assist people to understand how they and others respond to conflict and why, these same interventions are useful at the organizational level and on a global scale. There are a number of foundational concepts, but the differences between war and terrorism are particularly relevant today. Peace studies and peacebuilding are the goal and the constant methodology of PACS. The growing literature within the field engages conflict analysis toward peaceful, positive, and sustainable conflict transformation. The foundational concepts are launch pads for the research and practice that will ultimately transform the way the world responds to conflict.

## QUESTIONS

1. Write a working definition of conflict.
2. What are the four waves and how was each significant to the PACS field?
3. Define, compare, and contrast conflict resolution, conflict management, and conflict transformation. Look for examples of each of these in movies or television shows.
4. What are the important differences between war and terrorism? Consider this in the context of current events.

## NOTES

1. Rachel N. Remen, "Helping, Fixing or Serving?" *Shambhala Sun* (September, 1999): 207.
2. James Schellenberg, *Conflict Theory: Theory, Research and Practice.* (Albany, NY: State University of Albany Press, 1996).
3. Ibid.
4. Louis Kriesberg and Bruce W. Dayton, *Constructive Conflicts: From Escalation to Resolution.* 4th Edition (Lanham: Rowman and Littlefield, 2012).
5. Ibid., 2.
6. See the work of Ho-Won Jeong, *Understanding Conflict and Conflict Analysis.* Los Angeles: Sage, 2008.
7. Judy Carter, George E. Irani, and Vamik Volkan, "Ethnopolitical Conflict in Perspective." In Judy Carter, George E. Irani, and Vamik Volkan, eds., *Regional and Ethnic Conflicts: Perspectives from the Front Lines.* (Upper Saddle River, NJ: Pearson Prentice Hall, 2009): 1.
8. Ibid., Kriesberg and Dayton, Wolff.
9. Wolff., 3.
10. Kriesberg and Dayton; Lederach, 2003; Senehi.
11. Terrell Northrup. "The Dynamic of Identity in Personal and Social Conflict." In Louis Kriesberg and Terrell Northrup, eds. *Intractable Conflicts and Their Transformation.* (Syracuse, NY: Syracuse University Press, 1989): 55–82.
12. Kriesberg and Dayton.
13. Kriesberg and Dayton.
14. John Paul Lederach, *The Little Book of Conflict Transformation: Clear Articulations of the Guiding Principles by a Pioneer in the Field.* (Intercourse, PA: Good Books, 2003).
15. Jessica. Senehi, "Building Peace: Storytelling to Transform Conflicts Constructively." In Dennis Sandole, Sean Byrne, Ingrid Sandole-Staroste and Jessica Senehi,

eds., *Handbook of Conflict Analysis and Resolution.* (New York, NY: Routledge, 2008):199–212.

16. Stephen Libiszewski, "What is an Environmental Conflict?" (1992). http://www.css.ethz.ch/publications/pdfs/What_is_Environment_Conflict_1992.pdf

17. Maire Dugan, "A Nested Theory of Conflict." *A Leadership Journal: Women in Leadership-Sharing the Vision* 1, July 1996: 9–21.

18. Dougherty and Pfaltzgraff (2001): 188.

19. Von Clausewitz, 1989. Full details to come from Ali

20. Levy and Thompson (2010): 5.

21. Nicholas Rengger, "On the Just War Tradition in the Twenty-First Century." *International Affairs (Royal Institute of International Affairs 1944–)* 78, No. 2, Apr., 2002: 354.

22. Jon Dorbolo, Oregon State University, "Just War Theory," 2002. Available at http://oregonstate.edu

23. Cindy C. Combs, *Terrorism in the Twenty-First Century* (Fourth Edition). (Upper Saddle River: Pearson Prentice Hall, 2006).

24. William Nester, *Globalization, War, and Peace in the Twenty-first Century.* (New York: Palgrave Macmillan, 2010): 78.

25. Rosemary O'Kane, *Terrorism.* (Harlow: Pearson Longman, 2007).

26. Thomas Matyók, "Peace and Conflict Studies; Reclaiming our Roots and Designing Our Way Forward." In Thomas Matyók, Jessica Senehi, and Sean Byrne, eds., *Critical Issues in Peace and Conflict Studies: Theory, Practice, and Pedagogy.* (Lanham: Rowman & Littlefield, 2011): 295.

27. Sean Byrne and Jessica Senehi, "Conflict analysis and resolution as a multidiscipline:A work in progress." In Dennis Sandole, Sean Byrne, Ingrid Sandole-Staroste, Jessica Senehi, eds., *Handbook of Conflict Analysis and Resolution.*(New York: Routledge, 2009):3.

28. Ibid., 4.

29. Matyók, 295.

30. Ibid.

31. Ibid.

32. Ibid; and Byrne and Senehi, 2009: 4.

33. Byrne and Senehi: 4.

34. Matyók, 296.

35. Ibid, 297.

36. M. Aflazur Rahim, "Toward a Theory of Managing Organizational Conflict." *The International Journal of Conflict Management* 13, (2002): 207.

37. Lederach., 30.

38. Lederach, 69.

39. Lederach, 24–35.

40. Paul Rogers and Oliver Ramsbotham, "Then and Now: Peace Research-Past and Future." *Political Studies*, 47, no. 4 (1999): 740–754.

41. International Peace Research Association. Accessed February 2, 2015. http://www.iprapeace.org/.

42. John Paul Lederach, "Process: The Dynamics and Progression of Conflict." In *Building Peace.* (Washington, D.C.: United States Institute of Peace, 1997): 63–72.

43. Anatol Rapoport, *The Origins of Violence.* (New York, NY: Paragon, 1989).

44. Stephen Ryan, "Peace and Conflict Studies Today." *The Global Review of Ethnopolitics* 2, no 2 (January, 2003): 78.

45. Kroc Institute for International Peace Studies, "Strategic Peacebuilding," *University of Notre Dame,* 2012, accessed January 31, 2015.http://kroc.nd.edu/research/strategic-peacebuilding.

46. Daniel Philpott, "Introduction: Searching for Strategy in an Age of Peacebuilding." In *Strategies of Peace: Transforming Conflict in a Violent World,* Daniel Philpott and Gerard F. Powers, eds. (Oxford, UK: Oxford University Press, 2010): 3.

47. Compassion Canada, *Annual Report: The Changing Face of Poverty*. (London, ON: Compassion Canada, 2013–2014): 8.

48. Johan Galtung, "After Violence: 3R, Reconstruction, Reconciliation, Resolution: Coping with Visible and Invisible Effects of War and Violence." Accessed February 4, 2015 at https://www.academia.edu.

# TWO
## Models and Frameworks

### LEARNING OUTCOMES

- To recognize the discernible patterns of conflict represented in common models
- To acquire working definitions and understandings for conflict, transformative change, and peacebuilding
- To examine the inherent potential for change in conflict maps
- To recognize the influence of major frameworks and models for conflict analysis and peace practice

### OVERVIEW

Successful interventions into conflict situations are dependent on thoughtful and accurate analyses of conflict, a process that is initiated with a grounding in theoretical underpinnings. The historical and theoretical influences provide a framework for analyzing conflict and developing models of transformation. Disciplinary models and frameworks guide the analysis of conflict and the building of transformative practices in the field of Peace and Conflict Studies.

### INTRODUCTION

Although people tend to think of conflict as a simple collision between two parties, in fact, the origins of conflict are deeper. It is in this deeper analysis that the smallest seeds of conflict transformation are found. Because it is unfamiliar, understanding conflict and the transformation of conflict requires a paradigm shift for all newcomers to the field of Peace and Conflict Studies (PACS).

The field builds upon theory drawn from multiple disciplines. This theory created the base for the development of the models and frameworks that guide peace practice and scholarship. In this way, frameworks and models guide the conflict analyst and are critical for meaningful conflict transformation and peacebuilding.

## HISTORICAL INFLUENCES

Issues of war and peace have always captured an interest among philosophers and scholars. Cultures have historically glorified the warrior while remaining conflicted over the nature of war itself. They have simultaneously struggled with a desire for just and lasting peace. The collision of cultures through armed warfare has had benefits and costs. Too often, international politics were defined only as power politics. Conflicts were resolved by waging war, and a single power paradigm dominated academic discourse and government policy for centuries. This struggle led to the formal study of peace and conflict post-World War II, with an increasing focus by academics, government leaders, and the public at large on sustainable peace. The pursuit of conflict transformation through negotiation, mediation, and peace talks is increasingly opening opportunities to rethink relationships at multiple levels. There is hope, especially as peace and conflict scholarship advances, that one day people "will not learn war anymore."[1]

One of the additional contributing factors to today's peace dialogue is the Cold War of 1947–1965, a period of increased tension between west and east. This was intensified by the threat of nuclear war, framing in part, the response by the western military allies including the United States and other partners of the North Atlantic Treaty Organization, and the eastern bloc countries, including the Soviet Union and members of the Warsaw Pact. There was no direct fighting between the two superpowers so it was called the 'cold' war. There were, however, armed conflicts in three countries that represented vested interests for the west and the east: Korea, Afghanistan, and Vietnam. The Cold War divided the globe along East and West lines. Dialogue has shifted and currently tends to be framed in terms of the Global North and the Global South.

Following the horror of two World Wars, and in a global context of increasing tensions, the Cold War set the international stage for the development of research into the dialectical relationship between conflict and peace.[2] The multi-disciplinary nature of PACS allowed scholars to shift from the state-centric studies of international relations to respond more effectively to the complex contemporary world in which conflict was recognized to implicate all levels of society.[3] This shift in recognition that conflict was not just the business of governments and armies, has meant an expansion from studying conflict as war to thoughtful practice of peace, peacebuilding, and post-conflict transformation.

The convergence of post-Cold War circumstances, including a growing sense of danger and threat, and the fear of more war in the mid twentieth century, coincided with the tenacity of a handful of scholars. A scholarship base for the discipline has developed with contributions from both sides of the Atlantic. This has led to an increased understanding of conflict, conflict transformation, peace, and peacebuilding. As a result, frameworks and theories informing the developing field provide the underpinnings for analysis and practice.

## THEORETICAL UNDERPINNINGS FOR TRANSFORMATIVE CHANGE

Theory is a conceptual model that defines a set of actors and conditions, and proposes affiliations and causal connections among them.[4] The set of conditions may include intervention strategies, outcome conditions, and other factors that affect the result. As such, theory plays an essential role in guiding the development of models for peace and conflict practice. Theory provides an inter-relational framework through which analysts can better understand what has happened in the past, what is happening now, and how past and current dynamics along with patterns of interaction might inform a prediction of what will likely happen in the future. Among its many contributions, the field of PACS discerns patterns of conflict so that effective and meaningful interventions can be developed and implemented.

Theories and frameworks produce dependable generic knowledge that help practitioners identify the best intervention for a specific circumstance. There are three common ways to engage theory for meaningful conflict transformation: theory for analysis, theory for practice, and theory for research. In PACS, theory, practice, and research share a vital and intrinsic link that strengthens the processes of transformation across all types and levels of conflict. The applied success of each one of these components is dependent on engagement with each of the others, so that peace and conflict theory, practice, and research are fundamentally integrative in nature.

## THEORIES OF INDIVIDUAL AND SOCIAL IDENTITY

Understanding the ways that people define themselves and the groups that they belong to is a critical component of conflict analysis for transformative change. Theories of individual and social identity seek to explain shared group conflicts based on the core ways that people define themselves as belonging to a group. This might be best explained in the way that people relate to their identity as an American or a Canadian. When citizens feel threatened or attacked in some way that discredits or minimizes their identity as citizens, people experience a form of group conflict called identity conflict.

Identities are dynamic, variable, and unique. Identities may emerge, develop, change, disappear, and shift in salience. Some types of identities are related to the factors of gender/sex, ethnicity, religion, sexual orientation, class, and nationality. This is particularly relevant to PACS because conflict most typically begins to germinate in threats to identity. Terrell A. Northrup[5] has examined the role of identity in the development, maintenance, and transformation of intractable conflicts. She argues that identity is a psychological sense of self as it relates to the world. Self may occur on interpersonal, community, organizational, cultural, or international levels. Whenever conflict involves a threat to identity, it becomes intractable. Identities may vary from individuals to groups; they may be long and enduring or relatively short-lived.

Identities and identity theories are closely tied to social identities, especially in matters of identity conflict. Understanding the subtle differences between theories of individual and social identities is an important tool for conflict analysis and critical information for conflict transformation practice. It is widely accepted that conflicts and identities have strong relationships with one another. Identities can cause conflicts, but they can contribute to conflict transformation as well. Mutual trust and acceptance, cooperation, and consideration of mutual needs help the formation of peaceful relations that, in turn, contribute to the shift in social identities, and then are consolidated by social identities.

*Social Identities*

Social identity theories are also significant to PACS because social identities have been a driving force behind most of the world's intractable social conflicts. Avruch and Black[6] define identity as a concept that refers to the social use of cultural markers to claim, achieve, or ascribe group membership. This means that social identities have shared markers like language, faith, historical celebrations, and even eating habits that unite them and distinguish them from other groups. At the same time, some groups share markers with other groups, which provide opportunities to transform conflict.

There are controversies over the formation and persistence of social identity. How identities are formed and reformed is integral to understanding how conflicts erupt, escalate, de-escalate, and become transformed or resolved.[7] The protection of one's identity is one of the most important basic needs. Non-satisfaction of identity needs is seen as one of the major sources of conflict. This notion of identity plays an important role in the development of a sense of belonging that is a central concept to the dynamics of groups. Social identity theory is important to understanding conflicts that may be based in conditions of inequality, which often include conflicts framed in terms of gender, ethnoracial positioning, sexual orientation, and/or religion. Social identity theory is especially powerful when employed in interaction with other theories, like basic human needs, to better understand the origins of conflict.

*Basic Human Needs*

Basic human needs theory is among the fundamental PACS theories. It has attracted the interest of PACS theorists due to its potential to explain the causes of conflict. Human needs theory identifies that people have basic needs that must be met in order for them to maintain a particular level of harmony. This does not refer to material gain, and in some ways provides a foundation for the human rights discourse. Theories in the human needs category identify needs somewhat differently, but what unites them is the conclusion that unless these needs are satisfied, conflict can not be resolved or transformed.

PACS scholars, in particular Johan Galtung and John Burton,[8] discuss a more horizontal and integrated table of needs. John Burton[9] argues that there are universal basic needs such as identity, recognition, and security that must be met for people to not be in conflict. He says that people of all races and beliefs have common values and similar aims. When these needs are satisfied, people function well. When they are not satisfied, people struggle within the norms of society, even though they find the norms to be wrong and inoperative. In these situations, the person formulates their own rules to justify action that is incompatible with social norms, and consequently labeled deviant. The underlying struggle is related to their feeling that their basic human needs have not been satisfied. Differentiating action from behavior, Burton argues that action is observable, whereas behavior is the motivation, thus it is the reason for action. He distinguishes needs from interests and values, since needs are universal, whereas values are cultural. Burton argues that values are not generic and though there is a level of stability, they may change over periods of time. He also makes a link between needs satisfaction and social harmony, arguing that human beings do anything to satisfy their basic needs. In this way, basic human needs theories postulate that needs act as a motivational force.

Galtung further develops basic human needs theory to include security, welfare, identity, and freedom needs. Galtung identifies the needs which, when violated, exacerbate ethnic conflict. He recognizes that the more common theories of human needs have "a Western bias and may be of some use as a checklist to discuss problems of Western societies"[10] Galtung's expansion is more inclusive. Scholars who offer theoretical frameworks placing conflict within a human needs framework contribute to the foundational understandings of PACs. Although the perspectives vary to include psychological, social, and biological needs, the common thread is that the lack of satisfaction of basic human needs is a major cause of conflict.

## MODELS FOR UNDERSTANDING THE PROCESSES OF TRANSFORMING CONFLICT

*Peace Triangle and Violence Triangle*

Peace and violence are interrelated and even interdependent in terms of explaining one another. Johan Galtung[11] has defined three basic forms of violence, all of which are rooted in ideology—structural, cultural, and direct. Violence can begin with any of these forms and then easily transmit to the others. The violence triangle contrasts the three types of violence. Structural violence expands our knowledge of violence as more than physical; cultural violence involves an aspect of the culture that can be used to legitimize direct or structural violence. Structural violence arises from social, political, and economic systems that give rise to the unequal distribution of resources and power. Cultural violence incorporates religion, ideology, language, art, stars, crosses, crescents, flags, anthems, and like aspects of culture. Direct violence is the physical manifestation of violence such as war, murder, rape, assault, and verbal attacks. Direct violence is the result of conditions created by structural and cultural violence, and cannot be eliminated without eliminating them. Direct violence is cyclical. It has its roots in cultural and structural violence; then strengthens them. Bonds between structural, direct, and cultural violence are a triad.

Many existing protracted ethnic conflicts around the world have all three aspects of violence. Galtung[12] expanded the framework to include peace. He put forth six divisions which can be divided into two triangles, one of violence and one of peace: direct violence, structural violence, cultural violence, direct peace, structural peace, and cultural peace. Here, the triangle of violence engenders conditions for developing strategies to reach peaceful outcomes in a particular situation. The violence triangle can be contrasted with the peace triangle. This frames the necessity to understand and examine violence as a base for peace development. The conflict triangle used concurrently with the peace triangle helps produce a process supporting the development of the peaceful conditions crucial for conflict transformation. A researcher may employ this theory to explain social or ethnic conflict. Practitioners, on the other hand, may formulate a more effective approach by understanding the situation or event.

*PACS Conceptual Frameworks*

Several prominent models for understanding the processes of transforming conflict represent another important framework for students of peace and conflict. Each of these are maps or conceptual diagrams that have had a significant influence on the field and expanded conflict analysis to encompass the multiple and complex relationships inherent in conflict. The ones included are the Inquiry Model developed by John Paul Lederach, the Social Cube Model developed by Sean Byrne, the ARIA Model developed by Jay Rothman, and the Nested Foci Model developed by Maire Dugan. These scholars are currently researching, writing, and practicing in ways that continue to contribute significantly to the field. The models explained here provide foundations for current, ongoing, and expanding peacebuilding practice.

*The Inquiry Model: Development of the Change Process*[13]

The Inquiry Model is about relationships. John Paul Lederach is recognized as one of the major contributors to the establishment and development of conflict transformation as a core concept in PACS. Lederach maintains that relationships are at the heart of conflict transformation, and his Inquiry Model, also called The Big Picture of Conflict Transformation, provides a framework for inquiry into how human relationships are and can be transformed by conflict, positively and negatively, constructively and destructively. It is a comprehensive model for making sense of complex conflicts. The model focuses specifically on the interconnectedness of patterns and relationships, in part because relationships change conflict, and they are changed by conflict. Important to this model for understanding conflict transformation is the recognition that all of these subcomponents work in relationship to and with each other to facilitate better understanding of the conflict being explored. Lederach's Big Picture of Conflict Transformation is used increasingly in PACS to understand complex conflicts. The model is particularly useful for ethnic or identity conflicts.

The Inquiry Model explores the nature of conflict as the base for the development of change across three components. The relationships between these three subcomponents, called Inquiries, help conflict analysts explore meaningful action.

The Presenting Situation (Inquiry 1) contains three subcomponents, issue, patterns, and history. Issue is the situation, or perhaps the conflict, that prompts the inquiry. Patterns are those recurring events relevant to the issue. History includes factors, relationships, and events that provide context; and an issue is rooted in situation and history. Immediate issues are rooted in relationships and structures that are embedded in an historical context. Within it "lies our ability to recognize, understand, and redress what has happened."[14] An historical understanding of the conflictual situation is established. According to this conflict transformation model, the perspectives of the participants within an historical record assist in generating recognition of how conflict develops. In this way, an avenue exists for exploring the structural, cultural, and relational conflicts and relationships that may have influenced the contemporary trend.

The Horizon of the Future (Inquiry 2) has three subcomponents called Solutions, Relationships, and Systems. Solutions encompass responses to conflict that are considered to provide one or more answers to the problem. Relationships between people, institutions, and/or organizations constitute part of the desired future. Systems are the social groupings or networks of organizations and institutions that form part of the desired future. This inquiry helps one to recognize that social systems like education, health, and social welfare are in relationship with people, both collectively and individually. It is important to acknowledge that their desires for the future provide an important orientation for people as they respond to conflict and that knowledge and information illuminate the full context of what influences change.

The Development of Change Processes (Inquiry 3) helps with the defining of what people hope to build that is new and not destructive. Change processes are defined as "the transformational component and the foundation of how conflict can move from being destructive toward being constructive."[15] This means that " . . . movement can only be done by cultivating the capacity to see, understand, and respond to the presenting issues in the context of relationships."[16] This component is more complicated than the first or second Inquiry. It has six subcomponents instead of three—personal, relational, cultural, structural, episode, and epicenter. Lederach refers to these as aspects, perspectives, and dimensions of change.[17] These six subcomponents represent the complexities of conflict transformation and how change is both developed and supported. Personal involves the cognitive, affective, behavioral, and spiritual aspects of change. Specifically, it is through the individual's voice that concern is expressed and conflict understood. This is one of the important links between identity and conflict.

The next three subcomponents are closely intertwined. Relational, the second subcomponent, is a dimension that helps researchers and practitioners explore the interactional patterns underlying conflict transformation. Conflicts and changes in conflicts must be considered through the lenses of relationships between people and other conflicts. Structural, the third subcomponent, focuses attention on the influences of institutions or organizations on the transformation of conflict from one state to another by meeting basic human needs, providing access to resources, and the making of decisions that affect groups, communities, and societies. Cultural, the fourth subcomponent, focuses on changes produced by conflict among the broadest patterns of group life, and is about understanding how people construct meaning.

At the center of the process within the third inquiry are the episode and epicenter. The episode of conflict engages exploration of the visible conflicts that have taken place within a distinct time frame; while the epicenter of conflict situates issues and crises within a framework of social context and relationships. Specifically, the epicenter reflects the relevance and accountability of all relationships surrounding conflict and what might be useful to shape the future. Together, the epicenter and the episode create a figurative platform for responses to conflict.

The depiction of conflict transformation as circular underscores the continuous nature of conflict. This model highlights the contexts of relationship patterns at all levels. The model allows for analysis and potential understanding of complex and complicated conflicts by facilitating mapping the components of conflict, creating opportunities to consider how responses to conflict are developed, and then designing an appropriate intervention.

## Social Cubism

Social Cubism is about interaction among conflict mechanisms. The Social Cube Model[18] was developed in response to the limitations of older theories and models for explaining the causes and escalations of ethnoterritorial conflicts. These models seemed either too simple or too complex, and explored the material and psychological mechanisms of ethnoterritorial conflict as competing interests. Sean Byrne proposed that studies of ethnoterritorial conflict explore the *interaction* of material and psychological mechanisms.

The model depicts a cube as a graphic representation of interaction and interrelationships (see Figure 2.1), and is specifically designed to assist in the analysis of ethnoterritorial or identity conflicts. This model identifies six interrelated facets or forces that are inclusive of the history, religion, demographics, political institutions, and non-institutional behavior, economics, and psychocultural factors of conflict. These six facets or social forces combine to produce patterns of intergroup behavior that give conflict transformation practitioners and policymakers better knowledge in order to constructively reduce conflict and tension. When trying to better understand conflict, analysts can use the model to examine the interrelationships between the conflict mechanisms and, in this way, begin to make sense of and design intervention for protracted ethnic and identity conflicts.

With reference to the diagram, one notes that the six dimensions are interconnected and intertwined, like the faces of a cube. This interconnection is the primary contribution of Social Cubism. Conflict mechanisms, history, religion, demographics, political institutions, non-institutional

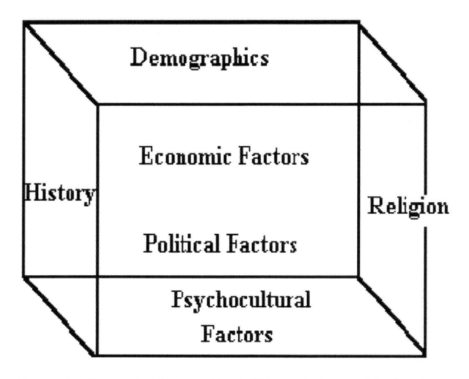

Figure 2.1.   Byrne's Social Cubism Model. With permission as originally published by Sean Byrne and Neal Carter. "Social Cubism: Six Social Forces of Ethnoterritorial Politics in Northern Ireland and Quebec." *Peace and Conflict Studies* 3, no. 2 (1993): 52–72

behavior, economics, and psychocultural factors are intertwined in relation to the others. Understanding the dimensions within this holistic framework for conflict analysis supports informed analysis and practice. The history of groups in conflict is of great influence on the conflict, and very important in a social cube analysis. The force of history comes from each group's golden past and historical experiences, including folklore and stories, from which they take comfort and identity, and which in turn devalue the histories and identities of other groups. Closely related are the demographic and economic dimensions. Encompassed in the demographic dimension are multiple forces including ethnicity, socioeconomic factors, and gender factors. Economic factors are connected to resources and power. Ethnic and economic issues manifest through the social and also the structural.

The other three dimensions cross religion, politics, and psychocultural factors. These personal, social, and political factors interact and are sometimes used by elites to manipulate power and conflict. Religion can be manipulated as a political instrument by elites to escalate tensions and divide communities. For example, the "other" can be demonized by claiming that they follow a false god. The political force is situated in power and its unequal distribution across the "ingroups" and "outgroups." Over time, the history of each group becomes politically entrenched in the collective memory, usually of select events from the past in which groups have been victimized. Psychocultural issues are critical to any analysis. Essentially these are psychological and cultural issues that are meaningful to the group. Emotions connected to these issues shape perceptions and future interaction between and among groups.

Others have expanded the social cube to include additional dimensions of analysis. Social Cube 2.0[19] introduces time and space as elements of analysis. Within this model time is further broken into the secular and the sacred, and space includes the physical, emotional, and spiritual.

A great strength and distinction of the Social Cube Model is that it illustrates dimensions and the relationships that comprise the underlying driving forces of conflict in a way that had not been considered before. The model encourages analysts to pause and reflect on the roles and implications of each of the interacting issues, and the consequences of that interaction, in order to facilitate meaningful and more successful conflict transformation and peacebuilding.

## ARIA CONFLICT ENGAGEMENT MODEL[20]

The ARIA framework, developed by Jay Rothman, is a model for conflict analysis and creative engagement that captures the fluid nature of conflict by presenting it in musical terms as both a metaphor and an acronym (see Figure 2.2). An aria, which means song in Italian, is a structured form of music that is the result of simple melodies. Musical arias are usually self-contained. Similarly, the ARIA Conflict Engagement Model is a diverse and intuitive model that can be readily applied to all kinds of conflict. The model provides structure to guide analysts and intervenors in a systematic way. In the same way, the aria is a musical system with a definite structure of simple melodies. The ARIA model flows through four stages that form the acronym: Antagonism, Resonance, Invention, and Action.

According to Rothman, conflict can be destructive or creative depending on how and whether or not it is well-guided. The ARIA model is most often applied to identity-based conflicts at all levels, including nations, organizations, and communities. People embracing the ARIA method identify and focus on the needs and motivations of all parties to a conflict; they are equipped to create joint agendas for groups engaged in passionate, adversarial conflict. Each stage encourages the exploration of who, what, where, when, and why. In the process, people in conflict are encouraged to unpack the conflict and recognize the crucial differences between identity, goal, and resource based conflicts and respond accordingly. The ARIA website (http://www.ariagroup.com/) is an excellent resource and provides worksheets and other useful tools for applying the ARIA Conflict Engagement Model for conflict transformation for individuals, pairs, and groups.

This diagram, which is a transitional model developed by Rothman and modified with Laura Reimer, reflects the musical nature of the ARIA model. The tail of the note represents the conflict, and the place where the process begins. The first stage is Antagonism. This is the actual conflict; those things that antagonize one side against the other. This has been described by the blaming, attributing, and anger that fuels the conflict. Antagonism is characterized by binary thinking and an "us versus them" or "me versus you" mindset. The conflict is framed "adversarially." One of the transformative qualities of the ARIA method is the shift to an engaged "our" mindset. This is a product of "Reflective Framing." By acknowledging and voicing the matters that have hurt and angered them, the identity needs of both sides are brought forward. At some point, conflict parties may determine that they want to escape from the destructive conflict cycle they are locked within. The parties are then ready to reframe their situation interactively, as a new harmony may arise out of the expression of each side's needs and narratives.

After the realization that they do not wish to be caught in the destructive conflict dynamic of "Us" versus "Them," parties move into the Resonance phase, where they recognize that they are in the conflict together: "We." This in turn encourages the parties to work together cooperatively. They brainstorm and invent acceptable options that are mutually agreeable and meet the stated needs of all parties as articulated during the Resonance stage. After mutually acceptable solutions to the conflict are "Invented," the "who" and "why" of the conflict are addressed by the parties. They enter into the Action phase of ARIA in order to determine the tangible "what" of the solution. Thus, a consolidated plan is developed that details who does what, why, and how. By their actions, the formerly conflicting parties have transformed themselves from adversaries to allies. They may proudly proclaim, "This is our shared and concrete plan" and just as the plan was invented and developed together, they carry it out together. The model indicates that like the simple but structured musical aria, each important piece leads to harmony. Resonance, Invention, and Action are effective ways to resolve potential conflicts, guided by the phases of ARIA.

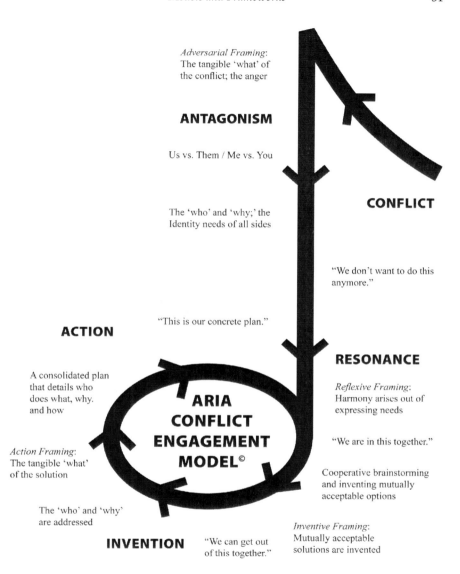

**Figure 2.2.   Aria Conflict Engagement Model. With permisson. Source: Jay Rothman with Laura Reimer.**

THE NESTED FOCI MODEL

The Nested Foci provides a paradigm for relating conflicts to the larger, systemic aspects of a particular conflict. It is applicable to most issue-based conflicts. The Nested Foci Model was developed at a time when conflict was recognized as organic and dynamic, but conflict models were mechanistic and static, offering little connection between theory, analysis, and appropriate conflict intervention. Maire Dugan developed this integrated model to reflect how conflicts sit, or nest, within the context or environment of other nests. The concept for the model emerged within the context of two conflicts: the integrated but ignored contributions of women to the field of conflict resolution by the late 1990s and the ongoing problem of systemic socialized racism in the southern region of the United States.[21] This is a systems model that locates the source of conflict within four related categories or levels of conflict[22] depicted as four elongated pods sized from smallest to largest and nestled within each other. Each pod represents one of the four levels at which Dugan suggests conflict emerges.

The smallest center pod rests within the other three and is labeled Issues-Specific conflicts, which are analytically the simplest and most frequent types of conflict and can occur between or among individuals or groups of any size. The source of the conflict involves any number of issues. The next larger pod focuses on the interpersonal level. This reflects the observation that sometimes an issue is not the actual source of conflict. A relationship conflict is described by Dugan as the product of the interaction patterns and feelings between parties.

The Structural Sub-system level conflicts mirror system-level conflicts and are evident in the inequities that accompany them. These are racism, ageism, sexism, classism, and heterosexism for example. It is important to recognize that just as conflict is relational, so each pod is in some way related to all the other pods. Other times, the source of conflict is beyond the relationships of the parties and is located in the institutions or structures of the social system. The largest pod is called the System-level conflict and refers specifically to the "inequities that occur as the result of human constructs."[23] In this way, conflicts between people may be rooted in the system level, which recognizes an additional and broader conflict in which parties struggle to transform their conflict.

Notably, although an Issues-specific conflict may exist on its own, each of the other levels will have manifestations of the issues within them. This means that a Relational conflict also has Issues-specific conflicts; a Structural Sub-system conflict contains both Relational and Issues-specific conflict; and a system-wide, System-level conflict has all of the conflict manifestations of the other levels.

Dugan's model has been modified and the levels renamed to attenuate the relational nature of the Nested Foci so that analysis and intervention would focus on the relationships among the levels rather than on the levels themselves. John Paul Lederach adapted the model, renaming the components as Issue, Relationship, Subsystem, and System. According to his adaptation, conflicts can be best understood in the context of the relationship of issues to larger contexts. This is a common sense approach to conflict and one that provides opportunity for conflict analysts to consider structures and relationships together and among each other in the quest for greater understanding.

The four models outlined above, the Inquiry Model, Social Cubism, ARIA, and Nested Foci, share the similarity of being relational and systemic approaches to conflict. As explained earlier, until the advent of these models, conflict analysis tended to be linear and static. These models not only added the dynamic nature of conflict to the analytical process, the models also borrowed liberally across disciplinary and relational boundaries. Additionally, the Inquiry Model, Social Cubism, ARIA, and the Nested Foci Model represent the major models and frameworks that guide conflict transformation practice today from the interpersonal to the interstate levels and from local to global levels.

## INDIGENOUS WORLDVIEWS

The Indigenous worldview shares the circular, dynamic, integrated, and non-linear qualities of the models outlined in this chapter, but provides an additional framework for ongoing peace work. Around the world, the voices of Indigenous peoples are being heard and consulted after centuries of silencing. Understanding Indigenous perspectives occupies one of the central spaces of national and international dialogues. In Canada, for example, the relationship between the Canadian state and Indigenous peoples is the primary social, fiscal, and policy issue of the times. In Africa, renewal is taking place in countries that have been ravaged by imperialism, colonialism, and decades of military dictatorship. Although they differ around the world, there are central principles to Indigenous cultures, which are presented here as an important framework for peacebuilding and conflict transformation. Although the core characteristics of Indigenous worldviews are seemingly universal from modern Africa to Israel to China to South and Central America, the following characteristics rely primarily upon the North American Indigenous worldview.

One of the first guiding tenets of the Indigenous worldview is the focus on principles, of which relational accountability and reciprocity are constant values in social interactions. This is an immediate conflict with traditional academic worldviews and with traditional conflict analysis, which is objective and linear. The Indigenous scholarship available for theoretical foundations occupies the contested space between Indigenous scholarship and western, or whiteness scholarship. It is a difficult space to navigate. This literature traverses the western paradigm, carefully includes what the authors respectfully interpret as cultural relevance, and then applies that perspective to Indigenous peoples and the complex conflicts that typify contemporary life. Stated harshly, this is assimilation literature with unique twists or applications for local relevance but it is ultimately about applying mainstream public policy paradigms onto Indigenous people. Until recently, much of the literature about Indigenous conflict was not written from an Indigenous perspective nor built upon Indigenous research methodologies. This is a fundamental conflict and a guiding framework that is in the infant stages of remedy. The western model of historical methods of analysis still characterizes much of academia and public policy and has perhaps confounded peaceful coexistence since the early days of contact.

Indigenous leadership literature comes from oral testimony and Indigenous cultural understandings and so is not literature in the western understanding of the term. The insistence on the credibility of the written text within the university setting is described by Indigenous scholars as foreign and dangerous to Indigenous people.[24] The oral traditions of Indigenous people contain many leadership stories and principles that provide a framework for understanding peace and conflict. Writing from the Indigenous paradigm, Linda Tuhawai Smith stresses that "history is power and is mostly about power."[25] Historical references place Indigenous experiences into the western paradigm, and this results in the loss of the essence of Indigeneity. In North America, many Indigenous activities and rituals were simply outlawed by the federal governments. Some Indigenous scholars now use the vehicle of general knowledge and education to press the validity of traditional ways of knowing. Peace and Conflict Studies is expanding the academic literature by including Indigenous perspectives, and those provided through research include and elevate the voices of Indigenous people directly.

The Indigenous worldview is powerfully portrayed through the leadership selection processes of Canadian Aboriginal tribes. Although Chiefs were primarily male, that has changed in modern times. The following describes the development and selection of leadership among the Pacific West Coast Salish and demonstrates the circular worldview:

> Leaders were looked upon for leadership, role modeling, and know-how. The Chief had to be knowledgeable about a wide variety of things to ensure the survival of the people. Such leaders looked to their family elders and other specialists . . . and they especially called upon their spiritual helpers. They were expected to be dignified, tolerant, generous, and modest and be expert in inter-village affairs. In short . . . deeds spoke for him. . . . He was the individual who possessed the power of wealth. . . . He was also the well-spoken individual who others looked to for advice.[26]

Similarly, accounts of Treaty-making and leadership instances recorded in western history demonstrate this message of interconnectedness and respect. Many of the Chiefs recognized that education would assist their people to adapt to the agricultural economy and new structures of the settlers into North America. Chiefs like Poundmaker, Big Bear, Powhatan, Geronimo, and Shingwauk worked hard to assure the means for their future generations to learn to live with the settler communities in prosperity and strength. In these oral accounts, Chiefs exhibited tremendous personal sacrifice, which was expected of great leaders.

There was a highly visible accountability for leaders in Indigenous communities, and so their leadership status was an important symbol for the community. Prior to the establishment of Canada's *Indian Act* to administer the relationship between government and Indigenous communities, the communities could quite literally support their leaders by voting with their feet. That is, when they were dissatisfied with their leadership, tribal families could pack up and leave their chief and live with another tribe. Leaders had to commit to acting for the betterment of their nation, to work toward unity and to do the best for their people or risk losing the support of their followers. Leadership was measured in numbers of followers. The Rotinohshonni (Mohawk) culture identifies peace, power, and righteousness as the cultural imperative for leaders. Indigenous leadership is principle-based and principle-driven, whereas western leadership is prescribed and described.

Leadership, character, track record, and community values are inextricably combined in the Indigenous worldview. All forms of living things are to be respected as being related and interconnected. In the *Great Law of Peace* the Iroquois rendition of this principle is phrased as thoughtful attention to continuing generations of families, thinking of grandchildren and those yet unborn. Among the Indigenous tribes of the Pacific region, ceremonies like the Potlatch, outlawed in the early 1900s because of the strength of their governance practices, were national decision-making events. Decisions were either agreed to by everyone or they were not taken. Like other Indigenous cultures, the concern of leaders was for several generations into the future, and included the relationships among people, land, and the spiritual realm.

Indigenous worldviews focus on character qualities, sustainability for the entire community and for future generations, and a consensual decision-making model in which leaders represented the will of all of their followers. This forms an important framework for peacebuilding work as around the globe, efforts are being undertaken to transform the conflicts that now characterize many communities of the world's Indigenous people.

## SUMMARY

There are common and influential frameworks and models that complement theory and frame approaches to conflict, transformative change, and peacebuilding. In many ways, like the Indigenous worldview, the models and frameworks of Peace and Conflict Studies are circular. Scholars work fluidly across theory, research, practice, evaluation, and back to frameworks and theory in the pursuit of transforming conflict toward peace.

## QUESTIONS

1. Why are theories, models, and frameworks important in Peace and Conflict Studies; what do we gain from them?
2. Explain one of the models in this chapter in your own words with reference to the conflicts in a movie, television show, or book of your choice.
3. What sets the Indigenous worldview apart from historical means of analysis? How is this relevant to conflict at personal and state levels?
4. Reinterpret a model or framework from this chapter into a more circular and holistic model.

## NOTES

1. Jay Rothman, *From Confrontation to Cooperation: Resolving Ethnic and Regional Conflict.* (Aria Group Publications, www.ariagroup.com, 2012): Dedication.
2. Ibid., 75.
3. Ibid., 78.
4. Paul C. Stern and Daniel Druckman, "Evaluating Interventions in History: The Case of International Conflict Resolution." In *International Conflict Resolution After the Cold War*, Paul C. Stern and Daniel Druckman (Editors). (Washington, DC: National Academy Press, National Research Council, 2000).
5. Terrell A. Northrup, "The Dynamic of Identity in Personal and Social Conflict." In *Intractable Conflicts and Their Transformation*, Louis Kriesberg, Terrell A. Northrup, and Stuart J. Thorson (Editors). (Syracuse, New York: Syracuse University Press, 1989).
6. Kevin Avruch and Peter W. Black, "The Culture Question and Conflict Resolution." *Peace & Change, 16*, 1991.
7. Louis Kriesberg, *Constructive Conflicts* (Second Edition). Lanham: Rowman & Littlefield Publishers, Inc., 2003.
8. Johan Galtung "International Development in Human Perspective." In John Burton (Editor), *Conflict: Human Needs Theory*. (New York: St. Martin's Press, 1990b): 301–335.
9. John Burton, *Deviance, Terrorism, and War: The Process of Solving Unsolved Social and Political Problems* (Oxford: Martin Robertson, 1979); and John Burton (Editor), *Conflict: Human Needs Theory* (New York: St. Martin's Press, 1990b).
10. Galtung, 1990b: 312.
11. Johan Galtung, "A Structural Theory of Aggression." *Journal of Peace Research, 1,* No. 2. 1964: 95–119.
12. Johan Galtung, *Peace by Peaceful Means: Peace and Conflict, Development and Civilization.* (London: Sage, 1996): 32–33.
13. For a diagram of the Inquiry Model, also called the "Big Picture of Conflict Transformation," see John Paul Lederach, *The Little Book of Conflict Transformation: Clear Articulation of the Guiding Principles by a Pioneer in the Field.* (Intercourse, PA: Good Books, 2003: 35).
14. Ibid.

15. Ibid., 19.

16. Ibid., 15.

17. Ibid., 22–24.

18. See Sean Byrne and Neal Carter, "Introduction to Social Cubism." *ILSA Journal of International & Comparative Law, 8*, Summer 2002: L 741.

19. Tom Matyók, Hannah Mendoza, and Cathryne L. Schmitz, "Deep Analysis: Designing Complexity Into Our Understanding of Conflict." *InterAgency Journal. 5* No.2. Summer, 2014:

20. This model originally appeared in Jay Rothman, *Resolving Identity-based Conflict in Nations, Organizations, and Communities* (San Francisco: Jossey-Bass, 1997) in an alternate configuration. It has been expanded in Jay Rothman, Editor, *From Identity-Based Conflict to Identity-Based Cooperation* (New York: Springer, 2012). For a full discussion of the ARIA Conflict Engagement Model, see http://www.ariagroup.com.

21. Maire Dugan, "A Nested Theory of Conflict." In *A Leadership Journal: Women in Leadership-Sharing the Vision* 1 (July, 1996): 14. For a very interesting account of the influences of women scholars on Dugan and on the development of the model, see Ibid: 9–10.

22. Ibid., 15.

23. Ibid., 9–20.

24. See Smith, Linda, *Decolonizing Methodologies: Research and Indigenous Peoples.* (New York, Zed Books, 1999)

25. Ibid., 34.

26. Washington, Michelle, "Bringing Traditional Teachings to Leadership." *American Indian Quarterly, 28,* nos. 3/4, (2004): 592.

# THREE

# Empowering People through Praxis

LEARNING POINTS

- To gain awareness of research and inquiry methods that emphasize the role of community members in knowledge generation and application
- To understand the contributions of community-engaged participatory research, participatory action research, and indigenous research to various communities
- To understand the interconnectivity of scholarship with practice, and theory with experience (praxis)
- To identify strategies to advance one's own efforts for reflective practice

OVERVIEW

Research and inquiry are often perceived as within the domain of academics and professionals. From this perspective, only highly trained and specialized individuals conduct research. However, insights and knowledge that come from lived experiences, and intentional reflection on those experiences, are equally essential for authentic knowledge creation and effective practices. The value of praxis is as a process by which meaning is generated reflectively in the application and practice of theories and ideas. There are three primary approaches in which community members are critical partners and leaders in the design, implementation, and examination of conflict transformation practice and scholarship.

## INTRODUCTION

Including individuals and communities as collaborators in inquiry has a longstanding yet often marginalized history in various disciplines including community psychology, community development, public health, political science, education, and international development. However, a growing international movement of practitioners, scholars, funders, and citizens has increased the recognition, legitimacy, and support for seemingly atypical approaches that reorient the role of participants or clients to that of co-investigators and partners. Inclusive approaches question the habits and tendencies often taken by traditional research in order to consider new ways of seeing people, relationships, contexts, processes, and outcomes.

Reasons to include community members as co-investigators or co-inquirers abound. Some contend that the findings from inquiry in which key stakeholders are co-investigators are more valid and reliable.[1] By including those persons who are expected to be impacted by the ideas or interventions addressed as co-investigators, one may have greater trust in the accuracy or at least plausibility of the findings or expression of ideas. Others point to the importance of social justice and emancipatory practices. Inquiry and interventions must not repeat past cycles of hierarchy and misuses of power that perpetuate inequalities.[2] The active co-construction of knowledge leads to self-critical awareness among citizens and community members, as well as scholars and practitioners, each of which is necessary for collective social change. The emerging approaches embraced by PACS researchers seek to intentionally and proactively empower under-represented voices through reflective practices.

Reflective practice is a process of continuous learning through iterative cycles of experience and reflection about those experiences.[3] These approaches recognize community members as essential and legitimate sources and creators of knowledge who are intimately involved in all areas of scholarship. To varying degrees within these approaches, community partners work with scholars and practitioners to identify the issue or practice of focused attention. Jointly they determine their approaches to understanding the issue, whether it is through data collection and analysis, storytelling, or other creative expressions of knowing. If and when appropriate, community partners help to develop action plans and contribute to the documentation and dissemination of what has been learned. The three examples presented here were chosen to represent different types and levels of involvement among academic or practice professionals with community stakeholders.

Community-engaged methods are about entering the process with the participants. This form of scholarship is not to be confused with applied research, research anchored in inquiry, or research that is being done to, for, or on behalf of the individuals or community. Applied research extracts findings from previous studies and uses them to design and apply interventions for the purpose of further refining understanding and techniques. The activity or technique is implemented in exactly the same way. Participants are seen as the subjects of the study as they are on the receiving end of services crafted from existing research. Rather than including the community and stakeholders in the generation of knowledge and development of the intervention, applied research is commonly, though not always, conducted by researchers who are external to the community.

## COMMUNITY-ENGAGED RESEARCH

Community-Engaged Research (CER) is also referred to as community-based participatory research and community-engaged scholarship. CER is undertaken via collaborative partnerships developed among trained researchers (including faculty, staff, and students) in collaboration with community members to address topics and issues that advance both scholarly understanding, as well as community outcomes.[4] In this approach, there are two communities that are expected to benefit as a result of the research—the professional or academic communities and communities that are made up of stakeholders with vested interests in a shared topic or issue.[5] Although there are some scholars who challenge the notion that CER necessarily includes academics or scholarly professionals (i.e., CER can be done by community members alone), this approach is actually a partnership between academics/professionals and community members that allows for discussion of the challenges and opportunities of bridging the partners' sometimes very different cultures, experiences, motivations, and values.

Through community-engaged partnerships, members of academic communities (universities or colleges) partner with members outside of the academy to advance community and public interests and priorities. Furco describes the mutual benefits that are created through "a porous and interactive"[6] relationship between academics and community members. The "advantage," Furco argues, "to the community is that research draws upon community knowledge, reflects their concerns better, and ultimately yields a practical benefit."[7] The mutual benefit to the academic community is that it broadens scholarly agendas and methodologies to establish the foci of investigations and inquiry that could not be addressed without community engagement. Further, through CER and other community-engaged approaches, universities serve their public mission and promote democratic civic engagement outcomes.[8]

CER partnerships are made up of groups of individuals who approach the research from different sectors and with different assets (both academic and non-academic). There are guidelines for upholding the rigor of high quality scholarship as well as developing high quality partnerships.[9] Therefore, the quality of community-university partnerships, or community engagement more broadly, is determined by the process by which partners inform and contribute to the shared work, as well as the expressions of that work in scholarly products and artifacts.

## STANDARDS FOR HIGH QUALITY PARTNERSHIPS

High quality community-engaged partnerships are expected to be both mutually beneficial and reciprocal. Mutual benefit is the expectation that all partners will achieve meaningful outcomes. Such research begins with the premise that the process and results will have positive outcomes for both the intellectual or disciplinary community, as well as for the community of stakeholders vested in the particular topic. Therefore, the assets of academics and disciplinary professionals are brought to bear on the issue under study, as well as the assets of the key stakeholders who inform and are affected by the issue of study.

The second key ingredient of community-engaged research goes beyond requiring that the process and outcome are mutually beneficial to requiring the active involvement of academic and community stakeholders as co-investigators. Reciprocity is the respect for and inclusion of the knowledge, perspective, and resources that each partner contributes to the collaboration.[10] In reciprocal partnerships, partners are willing to think and undertake action differently as a result of coming together in collaboration. This requires mutual exchange of energy and commitments to the activity, as well as to the partners. In this way, power is shared among partners. Each partner contributes in meaningful ways throughout the activity or process. As it relates to inquiry, this includes the identification of appropriate questions, approaches, and methods, in order to interpret or make sense of the findings and to disseminate the findings and implications to the respective communities of each partner.

## SCHOLARSHIP

A community-engaged research approach emphasizes the value of high quality scholarship as a means for advancing understanding. Table 3.1 compares the criteria for evaluating traditional scholarship and community-engaged scholarship. One can readily see the differences in the two approaches in that community-engaged scholarship meets the criteria of traditional scholarship and additional community-centered aims as well (as indicated by the plus (+) sign within the Table).

**Table 3.1.   Comparison of Traditional and Community-Engaged Scholarship**

| Traditional Scholarship [1] | Community-Engaged Scholarship [2] |
| --- | --- |

| Clear Goals | Basic purposes are clearly stated; objectives are defined, realistic and achievable; questions are important to address | + Intended audience/users are clearly identified |
|---|---|---|
| Adequate Preparation | Shows understanding of existing scholarship; brings necessary skills and resources | + Builds upon prior knowledge and work in the community |
| Methodological Rigor | Methods are appropriate to the goals and effectively applied; procedures are modified in response to changing circumstances | + Authors effectively incorporate community and academic/ institutional expertise in the work and work products |
| Significant Results | Goals are achieved; work adds to the field and is open for further exploration | + Add to existing knowledge and benefits communities |
| Effective Presentation | Style of organization of presentation is suitable; uses appropriate forums for communicating work; message is presented clearly and with integrity | + Appropriateness of language and visual aids for diverse audiences |
| Reflective Critique | Critical evaluation of one's own work; brings appropriate breadth of evidence to one's critique; uses evaluation to improve the quality of future work | + Critique is informed by both academic/institutional and community feedback. |
| Ethical Behavior[3] | Appropriately cites others' work; follows guidelines for ethical behavior provided by institutional review boards | + Evidence of collaborative approach characterized by mutual respect, shared work, and shared credit |

1. Charles Glassick, Mary Huber, & Gene Maeroff, *Scholarship assessed: Evaluation of the professoriate.* (San Francisco: Jossey-Bass, 1997).
2. Adapted from Cathy Jordan, Sarena Seifer, Lorliee Sandmann, and Sherill Gelmon, "CES4Health.info: Development of a Mechanism for the Peer Review and Dissemination of Innovative Products of Community-engaged Scholarship. International." *Journal of Prevention Practice and Research*, 1 no. 1 (2009): 21-28; and adapted from Andrew Furco, "A Comparison of Traditional Scholarship and the Scholarship of Engagement. In *Promoting Civic Engagement at the University of California: Recommendations from the Strategy Group on Civic and Academic Engagement*, by Jodi Anderson, Aubrey Douglass, and Associates. (Berkeley: Center for studies in higher education, 2006): 10.
3. Ethical behavior was not included in Glassick, Huber, and Maeroff's (1997) criteria, but was added by Jordan et al. to more fully include reciprocal, as well as ethical, processes in the framework of high quality community-engaged research.

Scholarship is defined as the expressions and artifacts of scholarly generative activities. Scholarship is expected to evolve as technologies transform knowledge creation and dissemination, and ways of knowing become more inclusive and complex. Scholarship has typically included books, book chapters, articles, and manuscripts in disciplinary journals, monographs, conference proceedings, and presentation of papers at disciplinary conferences. Because of technical advances, as well as increased emphasis on and expectation to have broader impacts on communities, scholarship now also includes websites, technical reports, program evaluations, white papers, blogs, programs, curriculum, videos, and on-line tools.

Rooted in the local reality, theory and practice are dialectically linked. A foundation in practice informs theory, and theory, in turn, reflects the systemic nature of changes across conflict settings.[11] This dynamic transaction works toward social action, rather than testing theoretically-driven hypotheses.[12] Thus, the major contributions of community-engaged research to strategic peacebuilding are the processes that generate solutions to practical problems and the mechanisms that systematically monitor and reflect on the processes and outcomes of change.

In sum, community-engaged research connects disciplinary work to significant public issues. In community-engaged scholarship research is done with, rather than for, or on, a community—an important distinction. The research produces knowledge that is beneficial to the discipline, as well as to the participating community. As a result, a diverse array of products may be generated. These include scholarly papers, websites, newsletters, designs, displays, exhibits, forums, workshops, handbooks, guides, and policies.

PARTICIPATORY ACTION RESEARCH

Participatory action research (PAR) is an example of an inquiry-based approach towards social actions that can, but does not necessarily, involve academic researchers or external professionals.[13] Borrowing from Vio Grossi (1980), McIntyre defines PAR as "an approach to exploring the processes by which participants engage in collaborative, action-based projects that reflect their knowledge and mobilize their desires."[14] PAR is a form of relational practice wherein the creation of "ideas begin with practice, and are located within practice. As practice evolves, so too does the theory. . . . The kind of theory which will help us improve our social situations has to arise from learning about the practice from within the practice itself."[15]

Proponents of PAR argue that knowledge generation and the construction of meaning are contributions provided by all stakeholders in the research community. These methods include intuitive, experiential, presentational, as well as conceptual, knowing. This approach accepts that knowledge gained through those investigations and reflections are as legitimate, if not more so, than "expert" knowledge.[16]

Several models of participatory action research suggest recursive processes among adaptable steps. These include:[17]

- Questioning a particular issue
- Reflecting upon and investigating the issue

- Developing an action plan
- Implementing and refining the action plan

PAR draws upon diverse theories and methodologies. It is informed by critical theory, emancipatory theory, feminist theory, and action research among others, and it is practiced in many different ways within diverse settings by many different people. For example, PAR has been advanced, particularly in the fields of education,[18] youth development (youth participatory action research, or YPAR), and conflict transformation to empower teachers, youth, and communities to become proactive inquirers and problem solvers in their own classrooms and lives.[19] Common across these applications is the recognition that context matters and that exploration, reflection, and action must be braided together.[20]

## THEORETICAL INFLUENCES

A brief review of the theoretical influences provides some of the approaches that motivate and guide applications of PAR, and include other forms of community-engaged approaches to research, inquiry, and praxis. These are explained below.

Action research emphasizes the importance of *doing* in order to *"know."* As Kurt Lewin, a founding scholar of action research argues, "You cannot understand a system until you try to change it."[21] Further, McTaggart suggests that action research emphasizes the role of interpersonal interactions and relationships and argues that "as people examine their realities, they will organize themselves to improve their conditions."[22]

Critical theory strives to uncover and dismantle paradigms and processes that, sometimes inadvertently, end up disenfranchising and disempowering the very individuals and communities that researchers seek to serve. Critical theorists seek to uncover and illuminate how power in social, political, cultural, and economic contexts informs the ways in which people act in everyday situations and environments.[23] Applied to PAR, critical theory approaches attempt to identify, explain, and transform circumstances that oppress individuals and communities.

Emancipatory theory and pedagogies (approaches to teaching) are attributed to Paulo Freire, a Brazilian adult educator who advocated for democratic unifications of theory and practice (praxis) and conscientization—practices that develop critical awareness of one's social reality through reflection and action. Emancipatory theory is one type of critical theory that is aimed at empowering individuals and communities through knowledge gathering and enlightenment. It suggests that through thinking critically, individuals can be liberated from the dictates of tradition, habit, and bureaucracy, which limit perceived, as well as actual freedom. Progress is possible, according to emancipatory theory, through participatory democratic processes for reform. Applied to PAR, emancipatory approaches deemphasize the role of the external professional, and instead, emphasize in "the responsibility of the people themselves who [are] making their own choices about how they [live] their lives."[24]

Feminist theories inform practice to the extent that practitioners of PAR consider the ways in which women's lives, experiences, and contributions are recognized, included, valued, and empowered throughout all phases of reflection and action. In this way, special attention is paid to the often invisible but powerful structures that may limit the active participation and voice of women as significant actors in social change. Feminist PAR approaches are increasingly practiced in international efforts as a way to organize and empower not only women, but also other excluded groups regardless of sex or gender, to address injustices and strengthen collective organization and action.[25]

Describing the significance of PAR, McIntyre concludes, "conducting PAR contributes a way of thinking about people as researchers, as agents of change, as constructors of knowledge, actively involved in the dialectical process of action and reflection aimed at individual and collective change."[26] McNiff and Whitehead suggest that "(i)n conflict situations, working out ideas *is* the learning; working out how to live with one another *is* the peace process."[27] Hence, PAR is particularly well situated to identify problems and develop potential solutions to improve peace-building practices and outcomes.[28] In conflict transformation, PAR is used to address post-conflict rebuilding of communities, addressing the issues, while also building the capacity of community members to collaboratively define issues, set goals, share information, and commit to reconstruction efforts.[29]

## INDIGENOUS APPROACHES

Indigenous approaches to research, like the other approaches presented here, prioritize the relationship between and among individuals, land, social structures, and communities about which greater understanding or action is sought. Indigenous approaches, however, define and emphasize relationships somewhat differently from the other community-engaged and participatory approaches. With Indigenous approaches, one cannot understand, make meaning, or 'know' without also recognizing all relationships.

As presented by the American Indigenous Research Association,[30] in an Indigenous approach to research, "information is gained through *relationship*—with people in a specific Place, with the culture of Place as understood through [the indigenous] cultures, with the source of the research data, and with the person who knows or tells the story that provides information." Further, "the researcher acknowledges a personal relationship with the story itself and how it is interpreted by both the teller and the researcher."[31]

## Relational Accountability

Relationships are essential for community-engaged approaches. For the most part, the relationships described are of individuals serving as partners who are co-investigators collaborating together to address conflicts or other issues. However, relational accountability is distinct from these types of collaborative relationships. Shawn Wilson,[32] a Canadian Aboriginal/Indigenous scholar, established the term "relational accountability." This concept explains that "an Indigenous paradigm should aim to be authentic or credible. By that I mean that the research must accurately reflect and build upon the relationships between the ideas and the participants. The analysis must be true to the voice of the participants and reflect their understanding of the topic."[33] Relational accountability insists that research must look at entire systems of relationships as a whole. Relational accountability as a core principle of Indigenous research assures and expands the inclusion of relationships in inquiry and analysis.

Wilson uses the analogy of a fishing net to explain the Indigenous paradigm of relational accountability: "The data and analysis are like a circular fishing net. You could try to examine each of the knots in the net to see what holds it together, but it is the strings between the knots that have to work in conjunction in order for the net to function. So any analysis must examine all of the relationships or strings between particular events or knots of data as a whole before it will make any sense."[34]

## THE FOUR PRINCIPLES OF INDIGENOUS RESEARCH

Relational principles permeate all aspects of Indigenous research—the choice of topic, who is included in the study, how the research is collected and presented, and the researcher's control over the findings and conclusions. Like Indigenous worldviews in which relationships are central and integrally connected, there are four general principles for Indigenous research collectively maintained by Indigenous scholars:

- relational accountability throughout the research process,
- the recognition of the diversity and complexity of the whole being in research design and conclusions,
- the inclusion of spiritual and relational dimensions in research, and
- the creation of safe spaces in which people can express themselves.

Understanding the needs and perceptions of any Indigenous people requires a methodology that meets these four criteria while simultaneously being inductive, dynamic, and fluid.

## INDIGENOUS RESEARCH

Some non-Indigenous academics and scholars have criticized the subjective nature of Indigenous inquiry as unscholarly. Traditional quantitative research, for example, seeks to eliminate any and all relationships or subjectivity, calling these "biases" rather than recognizing them as contributing to the research as Indigenous approaches maintain. However, Wilson argues that the process of Indigenous research is a ceremony, thereby elevating Indigenous research methodology to that of a sacred concept.[35] Wilson also explains that the principles of ceremony, and the accountability that flows from such a sacred approach, are contrary to the analytic questions typifying Western research methods and epistemologies.

Others within the Indigenous community contest the placement of Indigenous research within academic institutions altogether. For example, New Zealand Maori scholar Linda Tuhiwai Smith initiated the discourse of Indigenous research with the launch of her ground-breaking book, *Decolonizing Methodologies*.[36] Like Smith, an increasing number of Indigenous scholars are hesitant to designate Indigenous research as a subcategory of qualitative research because research compliance protocols and funding agencies often use terms and methods that dehumanize the people being studied. Dehumanizing individuals was a core strategy and outcome of earlier colonization experiences; and therefore, is associated by some Indigenous people with memories of conflict and harm. Thus, to really learn about Indigenous peoples, some argue that there must be another approach to inquiry that does not cause harm. Smith's main point is that decolonizing methods, which are not personal and subjective, must be developed carefully in order for researchers to really understand the relational nature of Indigenous people and cultures as they were before they were colonized, and as many are today.

Other Indigenous scholars do not reject qualitative or quantitative research, per se, but instead have tried to help others understand better ways to conduct research with, by, and for Indigenous people. Sonya Atalay, a North American Indigenous scholar and archaeologist, says that the principles of community-based research inherent in Indigenous research makes research relevant for people involved in research.[37] The process comes alive with stories and cultural traditions that would not be discovered in any other way. Story gathering (hearing stories) and storytelling (sharing the stories) are appropriate ways of understanding and sharing ideas that recognize and value complex webs of relationships, relational knowing, and relational accountability.

The discussions surrounding the place of Indigenous research on the academic research paradigm continues. Understanding the integral role of relationships in how research is conceptualized, adopted, applied, and disseminated is critical with any population, but particularly when collaborating with Indigenous communities.

## SUMMARY

Community-engaged research, participatory action research, and Indigenous approaches to research each emphasize the necessity of including community members in the design, implementation, and analysis of research for the purpose of capacity building, empowerment, and more comprehensive and accurate understanding of lived experiences. They also highlight the role of theory and researchers in proactively promoting conflict transformation and peacebuilding. Additionally, each approach gauges success in terms of not only the quality of expected outcomes or plausibility of the findings, but also the principled way in which relationships are fostered and the contributions of diverse individuals and perspectives are honored.

Understanding different approaches for including community members as active participants in their own understanding and action-taking is an essential component in conflict transformation and long-term peacebuilding. In this way, Indigenous research mirrors the principles of conflict transformation, which recognize the larger patterns and relationships integral to understanding. Becoming a positive member of such efforts require the skills, habits, and commitments to learning not only from experience, but by reflecting on experiences and trying anew each day.

## QUESTIONS

1. What are the advantages to including community members as co-investigators? What might be some of the challenges?
2. What does "empowered practice" connote that "academic research" does not? Outline the strengths and weaknesses of each label.
3. Consider the communities that you have been or are involved with that work for conflict transformation and peacebuilding. Who are the key stakeholders?
4. Describe the three approaches explored in this chapter and identify the stakeholders. Think about one topic of interest to you and

briefly compare and contrast how the three approaches to research might effect results or outcomes.

## NOTES

1. Andrew Van de Ven, *Engaged Scholarship: A Guide for Organizational and Social Research*. (Oxford: Oxford University Press, 2007).

2. See Paulo Friere, *Pedagogy of the Oppressed*. (New York: Continuum, 1970); Saltmarsh, John, Matthew Hartley, and Patti Clayton, *Democratic Engagement White Paper*. (Boston: New England Resource Center for Higher Education, 2009).

3. Donald Schön, *The Reflective Practitioner: How Professionals Think in Action*. (New York: Basic Books, 1983).

4. Kerry Strand, Nicholas Cutforth, Randy Stoecker, and Sam Marullo, *Community-based Research and Higher Education: Principles and Practices*. (San Francisco: Jossey-Bass, 2003).

5. Barbara Israel, Amy Schulz, Edith Parker, and Adam Becker, "Review of Community-based Research: Assessing Partnership Approaches to Improve Public Health." *Annual Review of Public Health* 19, (1998): 173–202.

6. Andrew Furco, *Promoting Civic Engagement at the University of California*. (Berkeley, CA: Center for the Study of Higher Education: 2005).

7. Andrew Furco, "A Comparison of Traditional Scholarship and the Scholarship of Engagement," in *Promoting Civic Engagement at the University of California: Recommendations from the Strategy Group on Civic and Academic Engagement*, by Jodi Anderson, Aubrey Douglass, and Associates. (Berkeley: Center for Studies in Higher Education, 2005): 10.

8. Saltmarsh, *Democratic*.

9. Cathy Jordan, Sarena Seifer, Lorliee Sandmann, and Sherill Gelmon, "CES4Health.info: Development of a Mechanism for the Peer Review and Dissemination of Innovative Products of Community-engaged Scholarship. International." *Journal of Prevention Practice and Research*, 1 no. 1 (2009): 21–28.

10. Emily Janke, and Patti Clayton, *Excellence in Community Engagement and Community-Engaged Scholarship: Advancing the Discourse at UNCG*, vol. 1. (Greensboro, NC: University of North Carolina at Greensboro, 2011).

11. Robin McTaggart, "Issues for Participatory Action Researchers," in O. Zuber-Skerritt (ed.) *New Directions in Action Research*, (London: Falmer Press, 1996).

12. Agneta Johannsen, "Post-Conflict Situations: The Example of the War-Torn Societies Project." *Berghof Handbook for Conflict Transformation*. (Berlin, Germany: Berghof Research Center for Constructive Conflict Management, 2001).

13. Alice McIntyre, *Participatory Action Research*. (San Francisco: Sage, 2008).

14. Ibid., 5.

15. Jean McNiff and Jack Whitehead, *Action Research Principles and Practice*, 2nd ed. (London: Routledge/Falmer, 2002): 4.

16. Practicing Freedom: Collaboratively generating community-led change. Retrieved April 14, 2015 from http://www.practicingfreedom.org/offerings/participatory-action-research/.

17. McIntyre, *Participatory*, 6.

18. Geoffrey Mills, *Action Research: A Guide for the Teacher Researcher*. 5th ed. (London: Pearson, 2013)

19. Laura Taylor, and John Paul Lederach, "Participatory action research and strategic peacebuilding." (*Unpublished manuscript,* 2009).

20. McIntyre, *Participatory*.

21. Attributed to Kurt Lewin (1946) in *"Problems of Theoretical Psychology"* by Charles Tolman, Frances Cherry, René van Hezewijk, and Ian Lubek (eds.) (Belfast: Captus University Publications, 1991): 31.

22. Robin McTaggart, "Principles for Participatory Action Research." *Adult Education Quarterly* 41, no. 20, as cited in Alice McIntyre, *Participatory Action Research*. (San Francisco: Sage, 2008).

23. Max Horkheimer, *Critical Theory*. (New York: Seabury Press, 1982).

24. McNiff and Whitehead, J. (2002). *Action research*, (2002): 136.

25. See for example, Participatory action research: A feminist perspective and practice reader. (2013). Womin: African Women Unite Against Destructive Resource Extraction. Retrieved from http://webfactoryinternational.co.za/preview/womin/participatory-action-research.html.

26. McIntyre, Alice. (2002). "Meaning, Violence, School and Community: Participatory Action Youth Research with Urban Youth. *The Urban Review (32)* 2, 149.

27. Jean McNiff and Jack Whitehead, *Action research*, (2002): 13.

28. Julienne Meyer, "Action research" in K. Gerrish and A. Lacey (eds.), *The Research Process in Nursing*. (Oxford: Blackwell, 2006).

29. Agneta Johannsen, "Post-Conflict Situations: The Example of the War-Torn Societies Project." *Berghof Handbook for Conflict Transformation*. (Berlin: Berghof Research Center for Constructive Conflict Management, 2001).

30. American Indigenous Research Association. Accessed on April 14, 2015 from http://americanindigenousresearchassociation.org/.

31. Ibid.

32. Shawn Wilson, *Research is Ceremony: Indigenous Research Methods*. (Halifax: Fernwood Publishing, 2008).

33. Ibid., 101.

34. Ibid., 120.

35. Ibid.

36. Linda Tuhiwai Smith, *Decolonizing Methodologies: Research and Indigenous Peoples*. (New York: Zed Books, 1999).

37. Sonya Atalay, *Community-Based Archaeology: Research with, by, and for Indigenous and Local Communities*. (Oakland: University of California Press, 2012).

# FOUR

## Engaging with Communities for Change

- To understand the difference between asset-based and deficit-based approaches to change
- To understand why relationships matter in community and peace-building
- To analyze one's own approach as it relates to mutually beneficial and reciprocal engagement with others

### OVERVIEW

Community engagement enhances the field of Peace and Conflict Studies (PACS), as it describes ways that external professionals can work with communities as partners and build upon everyone's strengths and contributions. Understanding the core principles and practices of community-engaged approaches, how they work, and why they matter to all stakeholders serving communities can increase the effectiveness and durability of lasting peace.

### INTRODUCTION

While practitioners possess ideas and skills born from experience and training, transformative change requires that they must also learn about, and effectively build upon, the existing strengths and assets that community members offer. Community-engaged approaches seek to understand, from a community-driven perspective, what communities desire for their future, as a core aspect of conflict transformation.[1] Therefore, engaging communities in ways that build the capacity of all partners, but in particular, community members, to activate and sustain positive change, is foundational for conflict transformation.

## COMMUNITY ENGAGEMENT

Community engagement is a term that is used commonly and across diverse contexts. As a field of practice and academic scholarship it has defined core principles and practices.[2] A community-engaged approach describes principled, asset-based methods used by trained professionals with community members, who through reciprocal and mutually beneficial partnerships, address community-identified interests and priorities. Practitioners work with community participants as co-investigators, co-designers, co-educators, and more broadly, co-partners. The ideas, experiences, and relationships of community stakeholders are viewed as essential to the transformative process of change and the development of long-term peace. It is the community that must take ownership in transforming social, political, and economic systems that sustain or degrade potential for positive and long-term progress towards peace. If this work is to be transformative, it cannot be done by external professionals and stakeholders alone.

The following elements, both philosophy and practice, are common to community-engaged approaches:

- build relationships among key community stakeholders
- leverage existing assets
- foster reciprocal engagement to empower and build capacities of diverse stakeholders

A community-engaged approach describes how external professionals may interact with communities, broadly defined, but can also be applied to working with individuals and families as well.

### The Value of Relationships

Relationships are arguably the single most important component in community-engaged change and conflict transformation. Relationships form the base for facilitating positive personal and community outcomes. They help to humanize the "other," as well as increase a sense of affirmation and reciprocation of feelings. They also provide a sense of a safety net or social support; create new social networks; and foster caring, sympathy, and trust.[3] Relationships are necessary and promote constructive change processes that include, but go beyond, addressing immediate solutions to immediate crises.[4]

One cannot expect to engage effectively in transformative change without developing significant relationships with the parties involved. Relationships require trust and effective communication. Important processes for building relationships include active and deep listening (e.g., appreciative inquiry, reflective listening) as ways of learning about the values, preferences, and expectations of others. Trust within community-engaged partnerships is strengthened when expectations of roles and responsibilities are clearly defined and commitments are upheld. In a community-engaged approach openness among professionals and community members is necessary. Therefore, relationship building is a central activity in conflict transformation and peacebuilding, whether it is building your own relationships with others or helping others to develop theirs.

## Leverage Existing Assets

An asset-based approach[5] builds on the strengths and capabilities of individuals, associations, and institutions that exist already within a community. Assets include the knowledge, experience, skills, passions, and social relationships and networks of individuals and groups of people. Assets that exist within a community may also include physical (e.g., land, buildings, infrastructure), financial, and other resources that local schools, businesses, government and non-government agencies offer. Of these assets, social relationships, and networks are the most important for sustainable conflict transformation, yet are often under-recognized and under-valued when seeking to mitigate an immediate concern or crisis.

An asset-based approach is citizen-centered. This means that key partners include not only formally recognized leaders of neighborhoods and citizen groups, businesses, or government and non-government organizations, but also the diverse array of individuals who comprise a community and who are often left out of formal decision-making and action-taking. Partners identify issues and challenges to address and are involved in the design, implementation, and evaluation of plans, activities, and outcomes. Inclusive participation of all stakeholders helps to create buy-in and accountability among all partners as they leverage their own assets and experience ownership of ideas and activities. Success in asset-based approaches is measured primarily by the quality of social relationships and networks established.

## The Cost of Deficit-based Thinking

In our needs-based socialization, most of us focus on what is wrong or missing within individuals and communities, particularly those seeking external assistance to address concerns and conflicts. This describes one aspect of deficit-based thinking: a focus on what is not there to the exclusion of what is. Deficit-based approaches are narrowly focused. Practitioners and institutional leaders are therefore limited by not having the full scope of knowledge needed to design and implement strategies, garner resources, and offer effective services. In a deficit-based approach, success is most often defined by measures created and assessed by external or institutional stakeholders, such as the services provided, structures built, and finances contributed.

Language used by the media, well-intentioned agencies, governments, and other entities that provide humanitarian relief, social services, and funding acculturates many of us towards deficit-based mindsets. For example, news stories and photos typically depict instances of poverty with acts of aggression. Service providers and funding agencies tend to label individuals and communities by the issue for which they are seeking assistance. For example, individuals and families who have lost their homes are referred to as "homeless," rather than as individuals and families who are "currently experiencing homelessness." Hence, the labels that describe the current situation become uni-dimensional and static labels to describe, and thereby define the entire identity of a person or community. The rest of their stories, especially their strengths, are ignored.

While awareness of what needs to be addressed is critical to any change process, focusing on deficits to the exclusion of identifying assets can create real and unintended obstacles to the process of transformation. Labels describing a single condition perpetuate a deficit-based mindset. Deficit-based thinking creates, reiterates, and reinforces positions of power and dependence while ignoring the presence of rich traditions, social networks, cultures, and other characteristics that have served individuals and entire communities well.

Communities that are labeled "poor," "economically depressed," "disadvantaged," "low-income," "high needs," and "underserved" often contain very strong social networks and ties among its residents.[6] Social networks and ties are especially important and reinforced in such communities as individuals depend on one another to help with child care, cash assistance, temporary shelter, shared food, and other forms of assistance. Sharing with others is an important asset in these communities as it builds social capital[7] within and between families and establishes some degree of trust and cohesion among neighbors. Social capital is the collective value of all social networks and the resulting inclinations that arise to help each other. The social capital of these communities may be strong in the midst of, and even because of, significant economic, political, and social challenges.

While deficits should not be ignored, focusing on the things that are missing or wrong can produce a mindset that further reduces or reinforces disparities in power or feelings of dependence and helplessness. It suggests that individuals and communities do not have the ability to come up with their own workable solutions, and that they must look to others, or even so-called "experts," to solve problems for them. Tragically, deficit-based thinking can reinforce negative perspectives and stereotypes, leaving individuals exhausted, dispirited, hopeless, and looking for answers or solutions from somewhere or someone else.

### Awareness of One's Mindset

Whether one has an asset-based or deficit-based mindset makes all the difference in how one interacts with others to support conflict transformation efforts. One's mindset affects political decisions, that is, the decisions one makes about who, when, where, why, and how to engage with communities. Many come to the field of PACS with the intention to help improve the lives of others, so knowing approaches that empower and strengthen individuals, families, groups, and communities to be change agents for positive and sustainable peacebuilding is critical.

### Managing Tensions

Individuals bring to any relationship inherent differences reflecting their respective cultures, assumptions, daily practices, and formal and informal roles and positions within communities. For example, individuals may have different expectations with regards to working with others, such as how often to be in touch (frequently, infrequently), which methods of communication to use (cell phone, work phone, text, email), and what types of decisions are to be discussed jointly and which can be addressed independent of one another.[8] It can be helpful to view tensions among community members as normal and natural aspects of relationships that can be managed or transformed rather than as problems to be eliminated. Tensions may be dialectical in that they exist on a continuum as connected opposites.[9]

Three dialectical tensions[10] occur in all relationships; they are autonomy-connection, novelty-predictability, and openness-closedness. The autonomy-connection tension occurs as partners struggle with functioning together or working separately. In novelty-predictability tensions, partners struggle over creatively responding to a situation versus using well-established procedures or routines. Finally, openness-closedness tensions occur when partners choose whether to share information readily or to keep things to themselves. Rather than referring to self-disclosure of information, openness can also be defined as receptivity to different perspectives and a willingness to change one's own beliefs and attitudes.[11]

Learning effective ways to manage tensions is critical to the development of long-term and ongoing transformative change, as conflict is always present within relationships. Individuals can choose to take a learning stance to get more information and to carry out difficult conversations.[12] A learning stance describes attempts to consider more than one's own perspective and to actively work to identify and discuss the preferences of others. For example, individuals working together can openly discuss what roles each takes (autonomy/connection), whether they are open to trying new ideas and approaches (novelty/predictability), or what types of information they expect to share with one another (openness/closedness). Shared understanding and willingness to work together may be enhanced when participants take learning stances and use active-listening skills.[13]

### *Reciprocal Engagement: Empowerment and Capacity Building*

Facilitating and nurturing reciprocal engagement builds upon assets of both external practitioners and community members when they work together in true partnership. This approach is important because it affirms the power of community members, allowing them to hold ownership and stewardship of the process, efforts, and outcomes developed. At the same time, community members can benefit from the contributions that training and an outside perspective can provide. Transformative change requires individual and collective community empowerment and the building of individual and community capacity. At the individual level, such capacity and engagement include telling one's story and feeling heard, and the confidence that one can achieve one's goals. At the community level, capacity and engagement includes inclusive and participatory planning, decision-making, and evaluation of processes and progress toward shared goals.

Reciprocal engagement is not synonymous with mutual benefit or win-win situations in which each party achieves hoped for or expected outcomes. It is the seeking, understanding, and valuing of the contributions that each person has to offer.[14] Reciprocal engagement focuses on how contributions of each stakeholder are sought out and honored in the change process. Therefore, it prescribes a way of working with others in genuine collaboration to build on the assets of all involved,[15] bringing people experiencing conflict to the "same side of the table" with each other, as well as with the external practitioners supporting their efforts.[16]

### *Key Phases in Reciprocal Engagement*

Reciprocal engagement is much harder and more effortful than it may first appear. Enacting reciprocity requires that diverse stakeholders are involved in authentic ways throughout the duration of the process of transformative change and peacebuilding toward the future. Stakeholders act in partnership to define and guide the entire approach from start to finish, including the following aspects:

1. Definition of the issue and stakeholders: What is the issue, who is affected, what values and priorities need to be addressed, what are the outcomes expected and goals to accomplish?
2. Design and implementation of the interventions, activities, or events: What conversations or initiatives are needed, who else needs to be included, where and when should meetings and activities take place, what will be done or accomplished?
3. Reflection throughout and after the intervention, activity, or event to analyze or better understand what worked and why: What worked and why, how can we do better or more next time?

## *Reciprocal Engagement as a Dynamic Process*

Reciprocal engagement involves stakeholders in all phases, but the level of involvement of various partners may change with regard to level of interaction. There may be times that partners serve each other in ways that can be described as being done *on, to,* or *for* another, as well as *with* one another. Hence, reciprocity can be described as being "thin," which describes efforts in which partners provide services for one another without significant contribution from the other (i.e., on, to, for), or as "thick," representing high level of collaboration among partners (i.e., with). The cone of reciprocal engagement shows the range of approaches that professionals and community partners may use together to address community-identified priorities (see Figure 4.1 for a graphic representation).

## *From Transactional Relationships to Transformational Partnerships*

Transactional relationships are common at the start of partnership development as individuals and groups must learn about each other in order to establish collaboration norms and trust for working together. Transactional relationships describe those wherein partners are task-oriented for the purpose of exchanging goods and services. Partners who work transactionally tend to operate within established norms, structures, and power dynamics. For example, a community member may help an external professional to meet different stakeholders to learn more about the community and conflict. Similarly, an external professional may provide one-time mediation services, or provide a pre-established intervention program.

Over time and through different transactions, individuals learn to trust each other, an important precursor to and component of deepened relationships and more significant opportunities for collaborative partnerships.[17] As partners get to know one another, interactions may become more collaborative. Partners begin to work *with* each other, thinking and acting in ways not previously imagined or possible. Transformative partnerships inform and influence partners' ideas, goals, activities,

Cone of Engagement

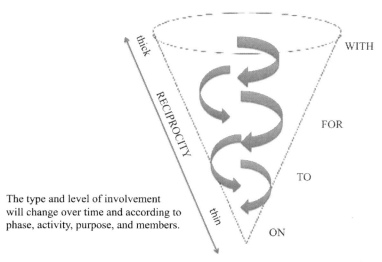

Janke, 2013; adapted from Furco, 2010

**Figure 4.1.    Cone of Engagement. Originally appeared in *Public Affairs eJournal*, Janke, 2013; adapted from Furco, 2010.**

and outcomes in ways that transcend self-interest to create larger meaning and deeper relationships with one another.[18] In transformative partnerships, external practitioners partner with those in the community to support their efforts to determine for themselves what to discuss, what their goals are, and how best to proceed.[19] External professionals offer their own assets and strengths, as well as receive and learn from the assets and strengths already present. The sum then becomes greater than the whole.

## SUMMARY

Community-engaged approaches to transformative change in which external professionals work in partnership with those experiencing conflict are defined and described. Community-engaged approaches focus on existing assets within communities, building relationships among stakeholders, empowering diverse stakeholders as they build their capacities to initiate and sustain positive change, and foster reciprocal engagement among all partners. Although social relationships and networks are critically important components of long-term conflict transformation, these assets are often not sufficiently recognized, valued, or leveraged in more traditional approaches. Relationships build trust, wisdom, and confidence within and among partners, and therefore, cannot be underestimated in efforts to transform conflicts and build lasting peace.

## QUESTIONS

1. In what ways are transactional relationships different from transformational partnerships?
2. What are some examples of policies that reinforce a deficit-based approach to working with people and communities? What are the indications that the paradigm is deficit-based? What are some recommendations you can suggest to reframe it into more of an asset-based approach?
3. Think of a time when you felt you had a good idea but others would not listen to it. What were some possible reasons why your idea was not heard? What are some approaches you might take to engage other people with your idea?
4. What would an asset-based approach to your community look like? What would be different from the way the community is defined now? What would be the same?

## NOTES

1. John Paul Lederach, *Little Book of Conflict Transformation: Clear Articulations of the Guiding Principles by a Pioneer in the Field*. (Intercourse, PA: Good Books, 2003).

2. John Saltmarsh, Matt Hartley, and Patti Clayton, *Democratic Civic Engagement White Paper* (Boston: New England Resource Center for Higher Education, 2009).

3. Michael Argyle, and Monika Henderson, *The Anatomy of Relationships: And the Rules and Skills Needed to Manage Them Successfully* (Harmondsworth: Penguin Books, 1985).

4. John Paul Lederach, 2003.

5. Jody Kretzmann and John McKnight, *Building Communities from the Inside Out: A Path Toward Finding and Mobilizing a Community's Assets* (Chicago: ACTA, 1993).

6. John G. Bruhn, *The Sociology of Community Connections* (New York: Springer, 2005).

7. Robert Putnam, *Bowling Alone: The Collapse and Revival of American Community* (New York: Simon and Schuster, 2000).

8. Rebecca Dumlao and Emily M. Janke, "Relational Dialectics: Understanding and Managing Challenging Dynamics in Campus-Community Partnerships." *Journal of Higher Education Outreach and Engagement, 16*. no. 2 (2012): 151–175. Patti Clayton, Robert Bringle, Bryanne Senor, Jenny Huq, and Mary Morrison, "Differentiating and Assessing Relationships in Service-learning and Civic Engagement: Exploitative, Transactional, or Transformational." *Michigan Journal for Community Service Learning, 16* no. 2, 2010: 5–22.

9. Teresa Sabourin, *The Contemporary American Family: A Dialectical Perspective on Communication and Relationships* (Thousand Oaks: Sage, 2003).

10. Leslie A. Baxter, "Dialectical Contradictions in Relationship Development." *Journal of Social and Personal Relationships, 7*, 1990: 69–88. Barbara Brown, Carol Werner, and Irwin Altman, "Choice points for dialecticians: A dialectical-transactional per-

spective on close relationships." In B. Montgomery & L. Baxter (Eds.), *Dialectical Approaches to Studying Personal Relationships* (Mahweh, NJ: Erlbaum, 1998): 137–154. Julia Wood, *Interpersonal Communication: Everyday Encounters* (Belmont, CA: Thompson Wadsworth, 2007).

11. Leslie Baxter, "Dialogues of Relating." In Rob Anderson, Leslie A. Baxter, and Kenneth N. Cissna (Editors), *Dialogues: Theorizing Difference in Communication Studies.* (Thousand Oaks, CA: Sage, 2004): 107: 124.

12. Douglas Stone, Bruce Patton, & Sheila Heen, *Difficult Conversations: How to Discuss What Matters Most* (New York: Penguin, 2000).

13. Dumlao and Janke, 2012: 79–103.

14. Emily M. Janke and Patti Clayton, *Excellence in Community Engagement and Community-engaged Scholarship: Advancing the Discourse at UNCG* (Greensboro, NC: University of North Carolina at Greensboro, Vol. 1, 2011).

15. Lina Dostilio, Sarah Brackmann, Kathleen Edwards, Barbara Harrison, Brandon Kliewer, and Patti Clayton, "Reciprocity: Saying What We Mean and Meaning What We Say." *Michigan Journal of Community Service Learning* 19 no. 1 (2012): 17–32.

16. William Ury, *Getting Past No: Negotiating in Difficult Situations* (New York: Bantam Books, 1991).

17. Sandra Enos and Keith Morton, "Developing a Theory and Practice of Campus Community Partnerships." In *Building Partnerships for Service-Learning* edited by Jacoby & Associates (San Francisco: Jossey-Bass, 2003): 20–41.

18. Ibid.

19. Robert Barash Bush and Joseph Folger, *The Transformative Approach to Conflict* (San Francisco: Jossey-Bass, 2005).

# FIVE

# Interpersonal Communication

LEARNING OUTCOMES

- To identify the Thomas Kilmann conflict styles
- To recognize stages depicted on the Conflict Continuum
- To know the languages of appreciation
- To learn the main interventions for interpersonal conflict transformation

OVERVIEW

There are several general principles that guide interpersonal communication and equip PACS practitioners to implement appropriate interventions for transforming interpersonal conflicts. The common techniques and strategies for improved communication and conflict transformation include active listening, the principles and power of communicating values and affirmation, and ways difficult conversations can be undertaken and navigated. These also include formal and proven steps for problem solving.

INTRODUCTION

Humpty Dumpty said, "When I use a word, it means just what I choose it to mean—neither more, nor less."[1] With these simple words, Humpty Dumpty reminds his audience about the complexities of interpersonal communication. As the story unfolds, Alice challenges Humpty Dumpty, and the early warning signs of conflict emerge in her observations: "'The question is,' said Alice, 'whether you can make words mean so many different things.'" The conflict is clearly established when Humpty Dumpty challenges Alice's views and assumptions, and then dismisses her with the statement, "'The question is,' said Humpty Dumpty, 'which is to be master—that's all.'" This excerpt from a popular children's story illustrates how easily interpersonal conflict can occur.

One of the most important characteristics of interpersonal communication is its universality. People can relate to the subtle interpersonal conflict between Humpty Dumpty and Alice. Interpersonal communication is one of the most direct tools and opportunities people have to instigate conflict (often unwittingly), but also to build relationships and transform conflict for better outcomes. When people can receive and deliver communication accurately, all kinds of conflict can be avoided or resolved. Whether this takes place between two people in a home or a workplace or between leaders of world states, conflicts can be averted through simple practices like engaging in meaningful communication, and demonstrating affirmation and respect.

## CONFLICT STYLES AND THE THOMAS KILMANN INSTRUMENT

Everyone has a conflict style. That is, all people respond to conflict in a way that is actually an effort to meet their own needs. Each style varies in the balance between emphasis on importance of issue and importance of relationship, and this variation is called the conflict style. The recognition of each conflict style and its associated behaviors and interests is important to conflict resolution, conflict management, and most definitely for conflict transformation.

How people respond to conflict involves a number of factors including their personality, experiences, training, and the type of conflict they encounter. However, the way in which people respond to conflicts is often simply based in habit, as if all conflicts warrant the same response. This means that often conflict is not responded to appropriately or productively, which produces more conflict. Unless people learn to recognize their own conflict style and the conflict style of others, there is little likelihood that people can respond to conflict with appropriate, transforming strategies.

In the early 1970s, Kenneth Thomas and Ralph Kilmann developed a conflict mode instrument (TKI) that identified five common strategies people use for dealing with and managing conflict. The five conflict styles are Competing, Accommodating, Avoiding, Compromising, and Collaborating. Each of these falls on a continuum of importance of relationship from low to high, and on importance of an issue from low to high. People tend to habitually use one dominant conflict style. This model is widely recognized, and is especially popular in organizational and workplace conflict literature and practice.

Competing is an aggressive style of communication in which people take a firm stand and are certain about what they want. When someone uses a competitive style, they tend to seek control over a discussion, in both substance and ground rules and they tend to draw on power based on expertise, authority, or their own persuasive abilities. People that have a competitive style have low regard for the outcome of the conflict on future relationships. Others are often left feeling resentful. However, this style is particularly useful in a situation where a decision must be made quickly, or if the decision to be made is unpopular.

Accommodating is the opposite of the competing style. Accommodators tend to be diplomatic and highly cooperative, but not necessarily assertive because preserving the relationship is the most important value in the conflict. They try to meet the needs of others at the expense of their own. Accommodation is appropriate when the issues matter more to the other party, or when peace is more valuable than winning. Overall, this approach is unlikely to give the best outcomes because it does not actually address the conflict.

Avoiding is a common response from people who see conflict as entirely negative. An additional dimension to conflict avoidance is called the chilling effect.[2] As a result of this style, people will evade conflict entirely, often hoping that it can resolve itself on its own. Instead, the conflict usually causes internal distress to the point that it can no longer be ignored. Since the primary goal is to avoid conflict, this style often means ending a relationship rather than dealing with conflict. Sadly, the people involved do not understand what went wrong because views and needs have not been expressed by the person with an avoidance style. This style is typified by delegating controversial decisions, accepting default decisions, and not wanting to hurt anyone's feelings. In most situations, this is a weak and ineffective approach. However, it can be appropriate when victory is impossible, when the controversy is trivial, or when someone else is in a better position to solve the problem.

Compromising is a style between Competing and Accommodating that seeks to find a solution that at least partially satisfies everyone. The central goal of a compromise style is to find the middle ground, which usually means neither party gets what they really want. Generally, it is not a satisfying resolution. Compromise is useful when the cost of conflict is higher than the cost of losing ground, when opponents are at a standstill, or when there is a deadline looming.

Collaborating is the conflict style that tries to meet the needs of all the people involved in a dispute. The goal is the best possible solution for everyone. Sometimes this is called the "win-win" solution because collaboration involves effective cooperation and an acknowledgement that everyone involved is important. It offers the chance for consensus and the integration of needs. It brings new time, energy, and ideas for resolving the dispute meaningfully. This style is useful when there are a variety of viewpoints and there have been previous conflicts in the group or when the situation is too important for a simple trade-off. Collaborating puts high importance on relationships and on issues, and involves a high level of cooperation and of assertiveness.

Typically, these conflict styles are depicted in a continuum cube.[3] The Thomas Kilmann cube in Figure 5.1 demonstrates visually that in a conflict, the importance of relationship to each party, or the importance of the issue to each party, are direct indicators of conflict styles. Notice that the horizontal axis indicates the willingness of the conflict style to cooperate with others to satisfy their needs. The further one moves to the right along the axis, the greater the level of cooperation, meaning there is a greater focus on maintaining the relationship by focusing increasingly on the needs of the other party. The avoiding style tends to be uncooperative, not focused on the relationship or the needs of the other party. In contrast, the compromising and the accommodating styles are increasingly cooperative, focused on relationship and on the other's needs.

If one observes the vertical axis, conflict styles are increasingly assertive in terms of selfish needs and desires, and on achieving their own outcomes and agenda. The avoiding style is least like this, but the compromising and then the competing style are increasingly focused on self, on their own outcomes, and on their own agenda, with decreasing concern for relationship. The collaborating style is the style most balanced between agenda or outcomes, and preservation of relationship. It is important to know that although conflict styles are habitual, they are not permanent, and people can develop a collaborative conflict style into habit.

In an effort to help people remember and recognize conflict styles, it has become a common practice for management consultants to attach the names of animals to the conflict styles. An internet search shows Thomas Kilmann's competitor style often depicted as Shark or Bull, avoider as Turtle, accommodator as Teddy Bear, compromiser as Fox, and collaborator as Owl.

Another way to remember the styles is with careful consideration of the circularity that is important to conflict transformation and peace and conflict studies.

The origins of the Timmons Strahl Conflict Style Circle (See Figure 5.2) has its roots in the Thomas Kilmann cube and a conversation between barbara Strahl and a direct descendent of Chief Geronimo in the Southwestern United States. Together, these inspired a new circular representation of conflict styles. The Apache Elder shared that a box or square is the typical shape that has been used throughout history to trap or confine people. The cube connoted that sense of restriction to the Elder in his worldview.

He shared that Indigenous people around the globe see life in a circle, which reflects creation: the seasons change in a steady and consecutive

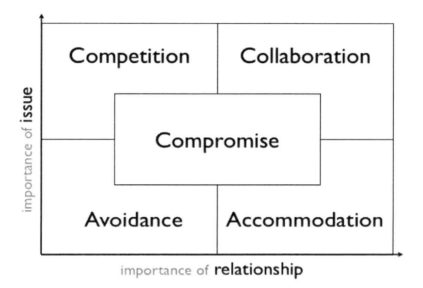

Figure 5.1.   Thomas-Kilmann Conflict Modes. Used by permission, Ralph Kilmann, April, 2015. Also located at http://www.kilmanndiagnostics.com/catalog/thomas-kilmann-conflict-mode-instrument

cycle; people are born, live, and eventually die and new people are born, live, and eventually die; morning turns to night turns to morning. Some recognize this as the circle of life; a form that permeates most Indigenous paradigms. Conflict styles are not fixed and rigid. People respond to conflict by habit, but they can choose to engage a conflict style based on the needs of the situation. In this way, conflict styles are depicted as a circle providing a visual representation of the agency people may employ when they respond to conflict.

## CONFLICT INTERVENTION

Conflict intervention is an official term for something people are involved in every day, and refers to the ways that people respond to conflict and try to change the conflicts that affect them the most. Conflict intervention is also evident in our entertainment. If one has the time to watch all of the George Lucas *Star Wars* movies, one can find an example of each of the conflict interventions at all levels of human interaction, from interpersonal to intergalactic. This is one of the critical contributions of conflict analysis; when one recognizes what kind of conflict they are confronting, the best intervention can be engaged and implemented to facilitate positive transformation.

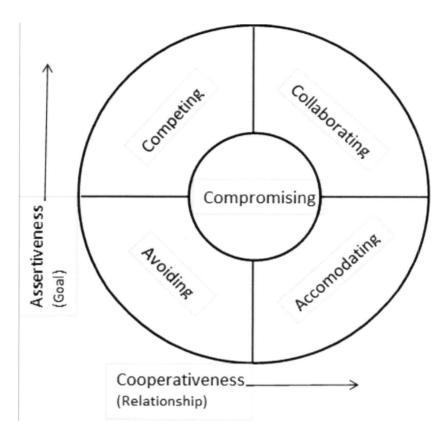

**Figure 5.2.    Timmons Strahl Conflict Style Circle. Used by permission, barbara Timmons Strahl, April, 2015**

There are several degrees, or increments among the conflict interventions. These can be readily understood as a Conflict Intervention Continuum, which was also developed by Dr. Strahl (see Figure 5.3). One end of the continuum represents those intervention practices in which the parties involved have the most control, involvement, and influence in the resolution of their shared conflict. In the *Star Wars* stories, this is often practiced by the main protagonist, Luke Skywalker. Luke talks with people, asks questions, clarifies what they are saying, and transforms conflict peacefully. At the far and opposite end of the continuum the intervention represents intervention practices in which parties have no control. With reference to *Star Wars* again, this would be the conflict intervention style of Darth Vader, the darkest villain of the series, who resolves all of his conflicts by coercion and violence.

The Conflict Intervention Continuum makes understanding conflict interventions simpler. The continuum places each well-known conflict intervention alongside the others. This way one can see the gradual shift along the agency axis, but must also remember that conflict interventions, like conflict, are fluid and dynamic and far less rigid than a continuum might suggest. The purpose of the continuum is to graphically depict how people have the most control and influence in the outcomes of their conflicts when they engage in interpersonal communication to transform conflicts; they have the least control over the outcomes of conflict in situations of coercion.

The best intervention for conflict transformation is a direct response to three key elements: the type of conflict and how it is analyzed, the actors, and the identification and implementation of the most appropriate intervention. Conflict intervention practices are most effective when they intrude into individual agency as little as possible while still achieving transformation. In so doing, the relationships between parties in conflict are preserved and hopefully improved throughout the intervention process.

## COMMUNICATION

People assume that they communicate effectively, but assumptions often lead to conflict. Ignoring how communication takes place and what is actually being communicated is a common assumption that can be more

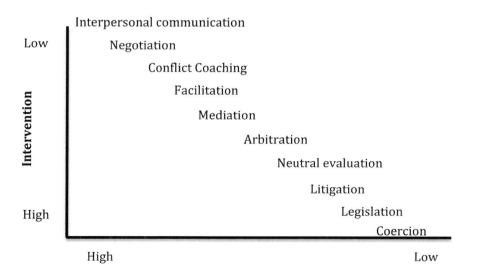

**Figure 5.3.  Conflict Resolution Continuum**

damaging to relationships than almost anything else. Interpersonal communication is about the relationships between people, which may be positive or negative, uplifting or exhausting, simple or complicated. Although verbal communication is almost universal, people involved in peace work must be diligently mindful of the complexities and potential outcomes of assuming effective interpersonal communication.

Relevant and constructive communication is essential to transforming conflict. Conflict transformation requires a number of skills and strategies, of which perhaps the most important and overarching skill is meaningful communication. Implicit in the term communication is an assumption of understanding, but this is where the conflict lies. Although the idea of information transfer seems to be common to most conceptions of communication, the mental representations, associations, and meanings attached to that information transfer are as numerous as the people sending and receiving information. Classic games like Charades and Telephone, and social media Tweets and Snapchats transfer information. Each of these is a good example of the diversity inherent in modern forms of communication and of the vast capacity of modern communication to send and receive information in ways that traditional communication devices cannot do.

Though there is a lot that is fun in communication, carelessness is fairly prevalent. Inappropriate or insensitive communication can be hurtful. Communication is affected by what is heard by a listener, regardless of what the sender intended to communicate. Factors such as identity and culture are also powerful actors in communication.

There is a true story that ends well, but demonstrates how innocent communication across identity and culture, complicated with insensitivity, can lead to miscommunication. There was a young Irish woman who moved to the Eastern United States to attend University. The young woman was placed with a family in the United States that was kind, loving, and fun. The young woman, who was homesick for her family and home in Northern Ireland was grateful to the family. She especially appreciated the décor of the home, which resembled her home among the mountains of Donegal County. One day, wanting to express her joy to her host family, the young woman spread her arms out to encompass the house symbolically, and said seriously to the family, "Your whole house is homely." The faces around her were crestfallen; they did not understand that this was a fine Irish compliment. Fortunately, one of the family members asked the young woman how the word homely was defined in Ireland (in North America, it is another word for unattractive and undesirable).

While the word homely communicated something less than complimentary to the family, the message from their Irish guest is summed in the North American understanding of homey. The home, like the family, was welcoming, attractive, and pleasing; it produced a sense of belonging in the young Irish woman. She said homely, meaning lovely; they heard homely, meaning ugly. The communication had to cross cultural lines, and was not received as it was intended! Although it was brief, the communication produced interpersonal conflict.

## REACTIVE RESPONSES

People in western societies have a tendency to listen so that they can respond. In other words, they are waiting for a speaker to stop so that they can talk, and spend the time the other is communicating with them formulating their next statements. These are called reactive responses and interfere with communication and problem solving. Most people think they are good listeners, but are usually crafting a response rather than trying to hear core concerns or emotions behind the other person's narrative.

Reactive responses describe the actions or behaviors of the listener and are obvious origins for conflict. The behaviors are readily recognized in these ways. The listener begins to offer solutions while the speaker is still struggling with the issue and has not asked for solutions, or the listener judges the speaker, either positively or negatively, and expresses the judgement verbally or non-verbally. The listener may appear disinterested or send a mixed message. This is the case when the listener hastily assures the speaker that everything is alright when there is no real indication that that is true. Reactive responses can have dreadful implications. The speaker may stop speaking, experience lowered self-esteem, and be demotivated to communicate and solve the problem at hand. Reactive responses do not transform conflict positively and peace workers must be wary of these habitual behaviors when engaged in interpersonal communication.

## ACTIVE LISTENING

Instead of reactive responses, those who strive to be peacemakers and resolve conflict need the skills of active listening. This is also called reflective listening. Active listening is possibly the single best conflict transformation technique available, and requires little more than discipline and practice. Active listening is a term that encompasses the behaviors and attitudes that communicate that one is attentive to the thoughts and feelings of another person. This conveys an understanding of what the other is saying, and meaning is conveyed according to the speaker's point of view or frame of reference.[4]

Active listening seems to be uncomplicated, but it is a challenge for many people. A strong example of active listening is clearly demonstrated in the Great Law of Peace,[5] protected within the Iroquois (or Haudenosaunee) Confederacy. The Great Law is a significant part of US and Canadian history, and provides a number of peacebuilding skills relevant to conflict transformation.

The Confederacy was and is governed by the Great Law, a peace pact established by the Peacemaker between six traditionally warring Iroquois nations at least nineteen hundred years ago. The nations were the Oneida, the Cayuga, the Mohawk, the Onondaga, the Seneca, and later, the Tuscarora. By the 1700s, these nations were identified in English history as the Six Nations. The Great Law is a living constitution that guides the world's oldest participatory democracy. It is relevant to this chapter because for hundreds of years, the Iroquois Confederacy has practiced active listening during all decision-making meetings.

According to oral history, long before North America was settled by Europeans, the nations came together in a building called the Longhouse (Iroquois means people of the Longhouse) to attend to governance matters for the Confederacy. There was one talking piece, which would be passed from speaker to speaker. The process required that before anyone could respond or express their views, they had to accurately summarize the views of all those who had spoken previously in the meeting. In this way, all listeners remained active and engaged. If a speaker was inattentive to the spoken words of the others, they were not allowed to speak. The process was monitored by a warrior in a wolf's skin with a large stick. This stick was to be used on those who did not follow the agreed and collective rules of the group. Since no decisions would be made until a decision could be made unanimously, active listening was critical to the process.

Popular versions of US history and of Iroquois oral testimony maintain that upon witnessing the democratic and effective decision-making practices of the Iroquois Confederacy in the late 1700s, Thomas Jefferson and Benjamin Franklin incorporated many of the traditions of the Iroquois Confederacy into the US Constitution for purposes of governing the new nation, including active listening. Active listening involves both attending and responding skills.

Attending skills specifically refer to the psychological and physical attention a listener provides in a communication setting. An example of attending skills that perhaps many people can relate to is the painting of the Mona Lisa by Italian artist Leonardo da Vinci, painted in the early 1500s and hanging in the Louvre Museum in Paris, France since 1797. Although the Mona Lisa is a painting, the eyes are seemingly focused intently on the person before the painting, and are alleged to "follow" as one walks around the gallery gazing at the image. For those who have been privileged to view the original painting, there is no doubt that da Vinci has reproduced an image of a woman who is intently focused and not in any way distracted with other thoughts. Physically, Mona Lisa is sitting very still and her arms are resting in the foreground. Although it is still art, the painting is a full expression of both psychological and physical attention to the one in front of the canvas; it is a painting that displays how one engages attending skills.

Attending skills are important to peaceful and effective communication and are useful in a number of peacebuilding settings, including trauma, workplace conflict, and meetings among international dignitaries. Attending skills describe the way the listener communicates verbally and non-verbally with a speaker. There are five common behaviors that describe attending skills: comfortable eye contact, relaxed posture leaning slightly toward the speaker, non-distracting gestures, and refraining from fidgeting. In contemporary times, positive attending behaviors also include concealing cell phones or other forms of electronic media so that the speaker will not be interrupted.

Another related responsibility for attentive listening includes ensuring that the setting is an environment conducive to communication and that there is enough time for listening so the speaker can take as long as is needed to speak. Attending skills keep the focus on the person who is communicating their concerns, affirming their value. Attending skills also assist the listener in refraining from thoughts or behaviors that might distract them from their goal of conflict transformation.

Responding skills are an additional and a critical part of active or reflective listening. Responding skills means that the listener's behaviors demonstrate respect and attention by reflecting the meaning and content of the speaker's experience back to the speaker. Reflection can include repeating content, feelings, meaning, or a summarization of what has been said by paraphrasing. For the speaker, these practices provide assurance that the message they are communicating is understood.

## EXPRESSIONS OF AFFIRMATION AND APPRECIATION

The sense of belonging and value is a sentiment that crosses culture, identity, and geography. No matter how diverse people may seem to outside observers, there are many shared characteristics that contain the keys for meaningful conflict transformation in interpersonal relationships. For example, a sense of value is connected to the quality of relationships shared with other people at home, at work, and in the marketplace. People are more productive and less conflictual when their value is affirmed by others.[6] When people feel unacknowledged, undervalued, and belittled in all of these contexts, conflicts are generated. Strain within relationships indicates that conflict is escalating. When people want peace in their interpersonal relationships, expressions of affirmation and appreciation constructively transform difficult relationships at home, at work, and within organizations.

The affirmation of human dignity preserves and maintains strong relationships, and there are simple skills that express an appreciation to
others in ways that are meaningful to them. Psychologists Chapman and
White[7] have identified that people communicate appreciation predomi-
nantly in one of five ways: through tangible gifts, through words of affirmation, through quality time spent with another person or persons, and
through physical touch. These have been identified as languages of appreciation, and although people tend to express one more than the others,
the expressions often change with circumstances and over time.

According to Chapman and White, people tend to express the language that affirms them in the circumstances they are in. This might
mean that a person who feels most affirmed by quality time might shift to
feeling most appreciated by acts of service if the workload at the office
becomes too intense. If they find themselves carrying the load for everyone else, when tasks are intended to be shared among colleagues, they
will begin to feel undervalued or unappreciated. To those who are astute-
ly observant, that same person alters their behavior from perhaps inviting others to take a break and share a meal, to instead appearing at the
office with a fruit tray and six cups of coffee to share with other hungry
co-workers. This would indicate that within the intense workload
circumstance, the business person would feel valued and appreciated if
others were to engage in acts of service, which can be as simple as bringing them coffee or copying a report for them.

Another example of these transformative languages in action is represented in tangible gifts. A person who feels value and affirmation when
tangible gifts are given to them may be readily recognized as the one who
buys gift cards for a co-worker at the local coffee shop, or who brings
flowers home at the end of the day for their loved one, or who may
purchase a small item like a coffee mug and give it to someone specific
who they think would appreciate it. There are no expectations attached to
these behaviors, other than a sense that the receiving party might appreciate the gesture. An observer who understands the languages of appreciation notices that the person feels valued and affirmed when they receive
tangible gifts. For this person, giving them something tangible, no matter
how small, communicates value to them far more than a hug, a slap on
the back, positive words, or an evening of dinner and entertainment
would. As peace-builders, it is important to watch for the indicators of
personal value and affirmation that are communicated by the people we
live, work, or socialize with.

Similarly, people can be hurt, discouraged, or feel undervalued when
these same five languages of appreciation are employed to intentionally
(or sometimes unintentionally) harm them. Sometimes this is done unwittingly, but for people committed to conflict transformation, it is important to look for indications of another person's language of appreciation and affirm them whenever possible. For example, the language of

words of affirmation means that writing or speaking meaningful words like "well done" can be highly motivational and encouraging. But if this same someone, who greatly appreciates words of value, is verbally criticised or called derogatory names, the result can be devastating.

As a conflict transformation technique, observing other people to understand how they express appreciation and affirmation to others is a highly effective way to repair harm, diffuse conflict, and improve interpersonal relationships at all levels. For example, media photographs of world leaders often depict the languages of appreciation: US President Barack Obama is often photographed shaking hands, touching an arm, or with his hand on the back of one of his colleagues. One might safely assume that the President's language of appreciation is physical touch, which he demonstrates in ways appropriate to the context.

Another world leader, former British Prime Minister Winston Churchill, famous for his orations, was likely a man for whom words of affirmation were his language of appreciation. Consider these few lines, delivered to the British House of Commons on June 18, 1940, as all of England braced in fear against the advancing Nazis, "Let us therefore brace ourselves to our duties, and so bear ourselves, that if the British Empire and its Commonwealth last for a thousand years, men will still say, 'This was their finest hour.'"[8]

Understanding the concept of languages of appreciation, and specifically learning to recognize each of the five expressions, assists in the transformation of interpersonal conflict so that feelings are received and interpreted as they are meant to be.[9]

## DIFFICULT CONVERSATIONS

*Intervention* is an Emmy-award winning television documentary series that anticipates and depicts difficult conversations between addicts and the people who care deeply for them.[10] People watching the show are familiar with the physiological and psychological indicators of anxiety and dread as the interventions approach. However, not all interventions or difficult conversations need to be difficult.

Recognizing the real challenges of conflicts inherent in confrontation, the Harvard Negotiation Project published a practical guide entitled *Difficult Conversations: How to Discuss What Really Matters.*[11] This seminal book asserts that there are three common forms of conversation that, when recognized, manifest a common structure to conflict and offer ready transformation.

According to the Harvard Project, each of the conversations shifts the internal stance of the listener in a difficult conversation in order to facilitate improved conversation and to overcome conflict. The three conversations help to prepare people who must engage in a difficult conversation by assisting in the clarification of what is at the root of the conflict. This is found by listening and learning from three different stories or conversations: 1) the stories people tell themselves and tell others, 2) the difference between the intent of the story and its effect, and 3) the way one's identity needs to be restored after important conflict.[12] These are identified by the Harvard Project as the Story Conversation, the Feelings Conversation, and the Identity Conversation. Each has questions associated with it that the authors encourage people to ask and answer as guidance and understanding before undertaking a difficult conversation.

Assessing the three conversations is particularly useful for confusing conflicts, and those in which feelings run high. As guides for better understanding, difficult conversations are facilitated by questions that generate information about a conflict. As a practice of conflict assessment and intervention, the difficult conversation guide is a useful tool that may be used by outside observers or by participants to transform interpersonal conflicts.

## THE VALUE OF EXPERIENTIAL EDUCATION FOR INTERPERSONAL CONFLICT TRANSFORMATION[13]

Experiential education is the medium through which PACS is actively taught. It provides opportunities for relationship development, and through relationships, conflicts are transformed. Experiential education is a form of teaching that is dynamic and lively, much like conflict and peace. Interpersonal conflict can be addressed through innovative interventions and experiences that are increasingly recognized in Peace and Conflict Studies. With the development of PACS into a multi-layered, multi-dimensional field with equal emphasis on research, theory, and practice, educating and equipping students to meaningfully address conflicts are vital to the growth of the field. The skills and techniques of peace and conflict work are internalized more readily in the context of practical application experiences.

Plato allegedly stated that one can discover more about a person in an hour of play than in a year of conversation. Activities, initiatives, play, and fun are words commonly used to describe experiential education methods. Experiential education methodology, however, is much more than play. Experiential education is about learning through the collaboration of teacher and student as they together experience and reflect. This experience is then translated to other circumstances in their lives. Experiential education is the opposite of rote memorization, in which authoritarian teachers require students to follow a rigid set of steps in order to learn what the teacher deems important or relevant. Conflict transformation requires flexibility, a broad repertoire of skill, immersion in practice, and application into real life. In this way, experiential learning is inextricably entwined with conflict transformation.

Experiential learning is a process that encodes understanding within the learner through physical activity. This is the kinesthetic encoding of experiential education, and empowers the learning process. Through engagement in creative activities, and in conjunction with reflection and the other elements of experiential education methodology, students understand and retain knowledge in a fundamentally different manner than formal instruction. Experiential education methods, including the use of role-play and other interactive strategies, are cutting edge strategies to build relationships and to increase positive interpersonal conflict transformation.

As an emerging and important instrument of conflict transformation, experiential education provides a relational foundation for interpersonal conflict transformation in particular. In this way, it provides a training ground for the skills required to address interpersonal conflict. This value is applicable to students of all ages. The principles of experiential education align with conflict transformation.

## SUMMARY

Peacebuilding practice demands that individuals be mindful of how they are communicating with others, and whether or not their conduct and behavior are affirming or demeaning. Resolving interpersonal conflict has long been the realm of psychology, but now transforming interpersonal conflict is an important skill for peacebuilding practice as well. Communication plays a critical role in conflict and conflict transformation. The literature of difficult conversations and experiential learning serve as guides and training ground for transformation of interpersonal conflict. Awareness of conflict styles, intervention styles, and languages of appreciation are important components of transformative processes. Relationships form the foundation of interpersonal conflicts and their effective transformation.

## QUESTIONS

1. Observe the behaviors of people you live with, work with, and two people that you socialize with. What are their languages of appreciation and what led you to these conclusions? What is your primary, secondary, and tertiary language of appreciation?
2. Consider each of the conflict styles and create a plausible exchange between the five styles over how to do a group project.
3. Discuss the representation of conflict styles as a cube and as a circle. Which do you prefer and why?

4. Engage in research regarding Mountaintop Removal as a coal re-
   trieval strategy in the Appalachian Mountains of the eastern United States, and identify three different conflicts. With attention to
   the interventions presented in this chapter, how might a resolution
   to the conflicts be achieved?

## NOTES

1. Lewis Carroll, *Through the Looking Glass, and What Alice Found There* (UK, Macmillan, 1871).

2. M. Roloff and D. Cloven, "The Chilling Effect in Interpersonal Relationships:
The Reluctance to Speak One's Mind." In D. Cahn, Editor, *Inmates in Conflict: A Communication Perspective* (Hillside, NJ: Lawrence Erlbaum Associates. 1990): 53.

3. Kenneth Thomas and Ralph Kilmann, "An Overview of the Thomas-Kilmann
Conflict Mode Instrument (TKI)," *Kilmann Diagnostics.* Accessed December 10, 2014.
http://www.kilmanndiagnostics.com/overview-thomas-kilmann-conflict-mode-
instrument-tki.

4. Neil H. Katz, John W. Lawyer, and Marcia Koppelman Sweedler. *Communication
and Conflict Resolution Skills* (2nd ed.) (Dubuque, IA: Kendall/Hunt Publishing Company, 2011): 5.

5. Paul Wallace, *The White Roots of Peace: Iroquois Book of Life.* (Santa Fe: Clear Light
Publishers, 1990).

6. Kenneth Cloke and Joan Goldsmith, *Resolving Conflicts at Work: Ten Strategies for
Everyone on the Job* 3rd ed. (San Fransisco, Jossey Bass, 2001).

7. Gary Chapman and Paul White. *The 5 Languages of Appreciation in the Workplace:
Empowering Organizations by Encouraging People* (Chicago, IL: Northfield Publishing,
2011).

8. Winston Churchill, "Their Finest Hour," June 18, 1940 (The Churchill Centre,
2015). Available at http://www.winstonchurchill.org/resources/speeches/1940-the-
finest-hour/their-finest-hour.

9. Gary Chapman, *The Five Love Languages: Singles Edition* (Chicago, Northfield
Publishing, 2009): 225.

10. Sam Mettler, Creator, *Intervention*, 2005.

11. Stone, Douglas, Bruce Patton, and Sheila Heen, *Difficult Conversations: How to
Discuss What Matters Most* (New York: Penguin, 2000).

12. William Wilmot and Joyce Hocker, *Interpersonal Conflict* (Sixth Ed.) (New York,
NY: McGrawHill, 2001): 241–242.

13. The Experiential Education section of this chapter was based on contributions
from Frannie Varker, Experiential Educator and Facilitator and graduate student in
Peace and Conflict Studies at the University of North Carolina Greensboro.

# SIX

# Negotiation

## LEARNING OUTCOMES

- To be able to describe the common stages in the process of negotiation
- To recognize the key points for successful negotiation
- To understand the difference between interests and positions in the negotiation process
- To learn the main criteria of principled negotiation

## OVERVIEW

There are three familiar models of negotiation: soft, distributive, and principled. Negotiation is a familiar process for many people, and so the chapter includes a fairy tale that brings the principled negotiation process to life. The tale of Knight Errant and the Bad, Bad Dragon represents an entire negotiation process: the characteristics of a dispute ideal for a negotiation intervention, the progress of the main characters through all the stages of negotiation, and the steps that lead to a final negotiated agreement. The chapter concludes with some of the common errors of negotiation, criticisms of principled negotiation, and a brief commentary about the role of negotiation in international conflict settings.

## INTRODUCTION

Negotiation is part of everyday life. People negotiate daily when talking to family, friends, or co-workers about how to accomplish something. Negotiation is "a process of voluntary problem solving or bargaining."[1]

In addition to the applicability of negotiation to ordinary people in everyday life, the vast number of civil, criminal, personal, and international conflicts are resolved following the same principles of negotiation.

In 1981, Roger Fisher and William Ury wrote a book entitled *Getting to Yes: Negotiating Agreement without Giving In.*[2] The book introduced "Principled Negotiation" into conflict resolution, a step-by-step proven strategy for working out mutually acceptable agreements for every sort of conflict. This book, which has added Bruce Patton as an author in later editions, has become the seminal book about negotiation. It is an accessible guide through the stages and purposes of negotiation, based on the work of the Harvard Negotiation Project of Harvard University. Under the leadership of professors Fisher and Ury, the Harvard Project developed a new paradigm for conflict resolution in the form of formalized negotiation. The familiar term "win-win" was popularized from *Getting to Yes*, and describes the process and goals of Principled Negotiation (which is expanded later in this chapter). Understanding some of the formal and fundamental skills and techniques of negotiation extends the everyday process of negotiation to the global application for peacebuilding, and provides important knowledge and training for practice in the field of PACS. According to Fisher, Ury, and Patton, "however unsavoury the other side . . . the question you face is not whether to negotiate, but how!"[3]

## NEGOTIATION PROCESS

One of the most appealing features of negotiation is that it is effectively a dialogue that leads people to reach agreements or compromises without disputes or becoming angry. Negotiation is a "back-and-forth communication."[4] People can negotiate for themselves or as representatives of a group, or have people negotiate on their behalf. Negotiations are common in relationships, in professional sports, in human resources and especially hiring, in collective bargaining, and in the business world. Negotiations are also part of international relations, and are often highlighted in the media when countries are seeking resolution to internal or interstate conflicts.

*Getting to Yes* identifies three measures of successful and wise negotiations. These criteria allow people to test the quality of their negotiated agreements and the process as it unfolds:

1. The process of negotiation should produce a wise agreement if agreement is possible.
2. The process should be efficient.
3. The process and agreement should improve or at least not damage the relationship between the parties.[5]

There are also specific situations that are most conducive to successful negotiation. These are identified as a time when two or more parties must make a decision about their interdependent goals and objectives, when the parties are committed to peaceful means for resolving their dispute, and where there is no other clear or established method or procedure for reaching the agreement that needs to be made.[6] Negotiations are characterized by these stages:

1. Preparation and planning
2. Discussion and exchanging information
3. Clarification of goals
4. Negotiation toward a Win-Win outcome through concession and compromise
5. Agreement
6. Implementation of a course of action[7]

In practice, a negotiation process is more fluid than the list indicates, and these phases may not progress definitely from one to the next because negotiation is about reaching an agreement, a process that often creates its own unique pattern. Importantly, these phases characterize any negotiation, no matter how briefly parties engage the phase.

There are other factors that influence the negotiation process, though they are not always positive influences. There are times during the negotiation that people behave defensively. It is wise to be mindful that negotiation is not about realizing personal achievements, although some parties will behave as though it is and try to manipulate the process for their own purposes. Another influence is that sometimes people in authority, especially in the workplace or in government, may be resentful of the need for negotiation because they hope their leadership is strong enough to overcome conflict. In fact, conflict is such a normal part of daily life, especially in the workplace, that attention to negotiation and the attendant skills are a human resource strength. Unexpected behaviors do not mean that the negotiation is not proceeding ultimately toward an agreement, but they do explain why the process may seem circular and does not always flow smoothly through the stages toward agreement.

## POSITIONS AND INTERESTS

Positions and interests are central concepts to negotiation that must be recognized and understood for effective conflict transformation with the negotiation intervention. In simple terms, the position is something that a party has decided upon; the interest is what caused them to make that decision.[8] Positions are usually concrete and explicitly expressed and so are very easy to identify. Interests, however, are difficult to discern because they are more likely to not be expressed, to be intangible, and are often inconsistent because they involve fears, hopes, and concerns. When entering negotiations, interests are most important because they are powerful human needs and contain the keys to a good, wise, satisfactory agreement.

The most common form of negotiation is positional negotiation. This is the successive giving and taking of positions until an agreement is reached. Positions often lead to arguing, which is inefficient and frequently endangers ongoing relationships. A contest of positional statements for example, are, "I want the car," "No, I want the car." Ury, Fisher, and Patton stress that arguing over positions usually produces unwise outcomes. In the international arena, focusing on positions has led to unnecessary bloodshed. Positional bargaining puts relationship and substantive interests in conflict. Positions[9] can be useful because they tell the other side clearly what is wanted, but the adversarial nature of positional bargaining is not the only route to achieving the purpose of an acceptable agreement.

Interests are the other central concept to negotiation, and the identification of interests is central to many conflict transformation interventions. According to Ury, Fisher, and Patton, "every negotiator wants to reach an agreement that satisfies his substantive interests," which is why they are negotiating in the first place.[10] Interests are critical to conflict transformation because they define the real problem and contain the genuine elements for resolution. Desires and concerns are interests. As Ury et al. state, "The basic problem in a negotiation lies not in conflicting positions, but in the conflict between each side's needs, desires, concerns, and fears . . . Interests motivate people; they are the silent movers behind the hubbub of positions."[11] For this reason, negotiating with the best interests of each party in mind leads to a better process and much better outcomes.

Most of the negotiation literature focuses on one of the interest or positional strategies, but there are a number of different names for them.[12] . Prior to the advent of Fisher and Ury's work, the general consensus about negotiation strategies was "interest-based (or integrative, or cooperative) bargaining, while the other was positional (or distributive or competitive) bargaining."[13] These are also described as "hard" and "soft" which are explained more in the next sections.

## SOFT NEGOTIATION

According to the literature, soft negotiation is integrative bargaining. Soft negotiation is so integrated in terms of satisfying the other party that the negotiator wants to avoid conflict if at all possible.[14] Although the parties bargain over positions, soft negotiators are usually highly relational and their efforts are directed toward preserving the relationship. They treat the other participant in the negotiation as a friend, trusting for a good outcome, and open about what they really need from the negotiation. Soft negotiators will make concessions, give in, and in general want agreement to come quickly and therefore will give up their own interests in an effort to satisfy the interests of the other party. The soft negotiator is vulnerable to competitive negotiators and often ends up feeling unsatisfied with the negotiation process.

Much of the literature contends that all negotiation processes are combinations of hard and soft approaches. *Beyond Intractability*, a well-used conflict resolution web resource, explains: "First negotiators try to 'create value' by enlarging the pie as much as they can. (This is the approach advocated by interest-based and principled negotiation.) But inevitably, the pie then needs to be divided up, which calls for distributive negotiation. So they claim that all negotiation is a combination of creating and claiming value, not one or the other as other theorists suggest."[15]

## HARD NEGOTIATION

Hard negotiation is essentially extremely competitive bargaining. This form of negotiation has many names including positional, power, adversarial, or hard-ball, but most often appears in the literature as distributive negotiation. It is a zero sum form of negotiation. The assumption is that only one side can win or achieve any level of satisfaction. Unlike interest-based bargaining, distributive negotiations pursue individual, rather than joint gain. The process is a contest of wills, so that the party that withholds agreement the longest is often considered to be the most successful.[16] The goal is maximum reward and minimal loss. The relationship often does not survive the negotiation.

In distributive negotiation, parties negotiate over positions. They may use intimidation or power. They make extreme demands, often only hoping to win a portion of what is at stake. Bargaining may go back and forth, moving towards a middle ground from outrageous beginnings. Negotiators in a distributive situation are cautioned against giving the first position and ever accepting the first offer. Keeping the other person involved for an extended period and feigning reluctance are tactics to sway a negotiation in favor of the power negotiator. When hard and soft negotiation styles are paired, the hard style almost always wins the negotiation but loses the relationship, which can be considered a "win-lose" agreement. When hard negotiation styles are paired, there is no guaranteed winner, and the outcome is usually considered "lose-lose." When soft styles are paired, an agreement is often reached quite quickly as both parties wish to preserve the relationship more than they wish to "win" their position, resulting in a "win-win" for both.

The story is told of President Jimmy Carter working with Prime Minister Menachem Begin of Israel and President Anwar Sadat of Egypt at Camp David. In an effort to persuade President Sadat of his conviction, Prime Minister Begin allegedly swore he would cut off his right hand if he gave up land in the Sinai desert. This is hard negotiation! Strong statements like this make negotiation difficult. President Carter recognized the interests behind the negotiations, and in order for Prime Minister Begin to maintain his dignity yet negotiate with President Sadat, President Carter moved the men away from their positions and suggested that the Israeli parliament could enact the necessary moves. This focused the process on mutual interests, and allowed the negotiation to proceed with the political relationship of both parties intact and their interests served. With the assistance and negotiation skills of President Carter, the initial positional and hard negotiation concluded as a soft, principled negotiation working to protect the interests of both parties.[17]

## PRINCIPLED NEGOTIATION

Principled negotiation is a method of negotiation developed at the Harvard Negotiation Project that guides people to decide issues based on their merits. The process of principled negotiation recognizes mutual gains wherever possible, rather than haggling through what each side says it will and will not do.[18] According to Fisher, Ury, and Patton, there are four simple but self-explanatory central guidelines for mutual gain during negotiations that are well explained in their book and repeated here:[19]

1. Separate the People from the Problem
2. Focus on Interests, Not Positions
3. Invent Options for Mutual Gain
4. Insist on Using Objective Criteria

This form of negotiation is also called integrative, problem-solving, or interest-based negotiation. It can be used with any number of people, any number of issues, and with people who do not have equal experience in negotiation. Parties' goals are not inevitably at odds with each other and mutual gain is possible. It does require active listening and assertion skills, as good communication is critical to satisfactory agreements. Principled Negotiation assumes that parties have both diverse as well as common interests.[20] There are no tricks and no posturing during a principled negotiation.[21] Negotiators get what they need in a way that also helps the other party obtain some of their goals.[22] This method requires a certain amount of trust, the recognition of interdependence, and full disclosure of necessary information, which are not present in a distributive negotiation.

## BATNAS AND EATNAS

The BATNA is simply the Best Alternative to Negotiated Agreement and forms a core tenet of principled negotiation, and was developed by Fisher and Ury.[23] BATNA is also a wise strategy for anyone involved in negotiation processes.[24]

Ultimately,[25] the basic test of any negotiated agreement is whether or not it produces a better outcome than both parties' alternative to a negotiated outcome. For example, a party who is assured of a swift win in the court system will choose a litigated win over a negotiated compromise. In situations involving international arms disputes, the best alternative to a negotiated agreement is to continue negotiating. In the world of professional sports, players with free agency may bargain for employment with any team that offers them the best deal, so the players have more alternatives.[26]

Negotiation practitioners and scholars Guy Burgess and Heidi Burgess adapted the concept of BATNA slightly to emphasize what they call "EATNAs—Estimated Alternatives To a Negotiated Agreement" instead of "best alternatives."[27] This means that even when disputants do not have good options outside of negotiations, they often think they do and that perception will motivate them to continue toward a negotiated agreement. According to EATNA principles, perceptions are all that matter. If a disputant thinks that they have a better option than the ones they are hearing, they will most likely pursue that option. EATNAs are considered critical to successfully negotiated agreements because they can often lead to last-minute breakdowns in the negotiation. According to principled negotiation, parties develop an agreement that truly meets their interests; knowing one's own EATNA and the EATNA of the other party works to complement the principled negotiation process and ultimately result in an agreement that meets the criteria of a successful negotiation.

## BRAINSTORMING

A critical feature of integrative negotiation is the process of brainstorming. Brainstorming takes place when people generate as many ideas as possible without judging those ideas as good or bad, possible or unworkable. This is an opportunity to be as creative as possible and to build on ideas as they come out. Quantity is important, quality is not. Participants have to keep in mind that judging an idea as good or bad can limit the length of the list as well as the creativity used. Once a list has been created, the ideas can be discussed, evaluated, narrowed down, combined, ranked, prioritized, and selected. There are multiple options for working with the list, some more positive and forward moving than others. Having the opportunity to expand the potential resolutions increases the likelihood of finding something that works for both parties.

An age-old example of principled (integrative) negotiation is the conflict over an orange. Two people want the same orange. There are a number of potential resolutions. Some conflict interveners would take the orange away from both people; others would try to find an additional orange. Many intermediaries choose to cut the orange in half and give each person half, which seems fair. However, all of these resolutions leave the parties feeling unsatisfied. Integrative negotiation, however, involves asking each party why he or she wants the orange. In this way, it may be discovered (for example) that one person is very hungry and needs the entire orange to fill up. The other person wants to bake a cake and needs the rind of the orange in order to make their special recipe. Both people will be satisfied if the orange is peeled and one is given the rind; the other the meat of the orange. In addition to both parties being satisfied, the relationship is preserved.

Of course this is simplistic, but the principle remains the same for more complex conflicts. A critical component is the conversation about why participants want what they want. A preferred method by peace professionals, principled negotiation allows people to leave the negotiation with the relationship intact and their interests served. The following fable was developed as an allegory by a graduate student to demonstrate the applicability of principled negotiation within a conflict situation. Within the fable, each of the elements of principled negotiation is evident.

## A NEGOTIATION FABLE [28]

This story tells of the age-old conflict between Knight Errant and the Bad, Bad Dragon. But contrary to popular assumption, in this story the Knight Errant and the Bad, Bad Dragon engage in negotiations in a way that a wise agreement is achieved for both of the protagonists.

The Classic Tale goes like this: A Bad, Bad Dragon terrorizes a farming village. One of the farmers is a Beautiful Maiden, which is surprising after years of working on a farm in the Middle Ages. Normally and for reasons unknown (because there are other Beautiful Maidens in the Land), this woman is regularly taken hostage by the Bad, Bad Dragon. But lo and behold, there is a hero to this story; immaculate in his suit of armor with a smile clearly stolen from a tooth-paste commercial. He engages the Bad, Bad Dragon in a battle, slaughters him and rescues the Beautiful Maiden. Still in his miraculously immaculate suit of armor, he rides back into the village and another ballad is written about him. But he does not marry the Beautiful Maiden, believing she is way below his economic and societal class. It seems the story ends here, the conflict has ended badly for everyone involved, relationships are ended, hearts are broken, the village and its Beautiful Maidens are left in fear once again, and the opportunities for negotiated agreements and conflict transformation are lost.

Important to our rendering of Principled Negotiation is the fact that the death of the Bad, Bad Dragon was not inevitable. In contrast to the Knight Errant, the Bad, Bad Dragon is selfless, intelligent, seeks to maintain his relationships, and has learned how to apply principled negotiation after reading the book *Getting to Yes*.[29] The assumption that a Bad, Bad Dragon can read and that he found in some way this book is as equally reasonable as the mere existence of a Bad, Bad Dragon. In our alternate fairy tale, and in order to achieve his goal, the Bad, Bad Dragon applies the four principles of (a) separating the people from the problem; (b) focusing on interests, not on positions; (c) inventing options for mutual gain; (d) insisting on using objective criteria in his conflict with the Knight Errant. Imagine this:

### *Separate the People/Mythical Creatures from the Problem*

After declaring to all villagers that he had come to their rescue, our heroic Knight Errant rode on to the cave where the Bad, Bad Dragon was hiding together with his hostage, the Beautiful Maiden. After arriving there, he challenged the Bad, Bad Dragon:

Knight Errant: 'Come out of your hide-out, you cowardly mythical creature!'

Bad, Bad Dragon: 'If I were mythical, I would not exist and therefore could not come out.'

Knight Errant: 'What?'

Bad, Bad Dragon: 'Never mind.'

Knight Errant: 'Come out here and get what you deserve!'

Bad, Bad Dragon: 'I sense a problem out there.'

Knight Errant: 'Problem? What are you talking about? You are evil, and therefore you'll die!'

Bad, Bad Dragon: 'I think there is a problem. The problem is that we see each other as adversaries, but that is not necessarily the case.'[30]

Knight Errant: 'Oh, really? I think otherwise. You are the Bad, Bad Dragon and I am the heroic Knight Errant. We are adversaries by definition.'

Bad, Bad Dragon: 'Well, only if we follow the classical storyline. But there might be another possible outcome?'

Knight Errant: 'Like?'

Bad, Bad Dragon: (Considering the role of identity)[31] 'I do not know yet. But I am only a Bad, Bad Dragon. Maybe you could help me with your self-declared paramount intelligence, and together we might be able to find that outcome.'

Knight Errant: 'Of course I am willing to use my supreme intelligence in order to find a better outcome. And we will do that together, in order that you can learn from me and maybe become a Good, Good Dragon.'

Bad, Bad Dragon: (Saying what the other wants to hear)[32] 'That was what I hoped for, that a heroic and intelligent person like you might be my teacher.'

Knight Errant: (Graciously) 'Of course.'

Bad, Bad Dragon: (Smiles and swallows his pride).

*Focus on Interests, not Positions*

Knight Errant: 'So, how should we go on, in your opinion?'

Bad, Bad Dragon: 'Maybe we should start with our positions. I want to kill you and live happily ever after. What is your position?'

Knight Errant: (Loudly)'What do you think I want? I want to exterminate you.'

Bad, Bad Dragon: (Not reacting to the emotional outburst)[33] 'Well, apparently our positions are not reconcilable. But maybe our interests are?'

Knight Errant: 'Of course I know the difference between positions and interests. But for the sake of your learning experience, can you restate the difference?'

Bad, Bad Dragon: 'A position is taken by a person in order to serve their interest. For example, a knight wants a new sword. This is his position. But he wants the sword in order to be able to fulfill his duties as a knight. This is his interest. A position is what the particular person decides upon. An interest is the cause that made him decide in the way he did.' [34]

Knight Errant: 'Very, very good, there is still hope for you. So, what do we do now?'

Bad, Bad Dragon: (Doing his best to restrain himself in order to help the Knight Errant retain his dignity)[35] 'Well, I propose we try to figure out what our particular interests are, as they are crucial in order to find common ground.'[36]

Knight Errant: 'And how do we do that?'

Bad, bad, dragon: 'We ask each other why we took our particular position.[37]

Knight Errant: 'So, why do you want to kill me, besides for being a Bad, Bad Dragon?'

Bad, Bad Dragon: (With notable coolness) 'Well, I want to stay alive. And due to your paramount reputation as a great and determined warrior, this is so far the only way I could think of. And why do you want to kill me?'

Knight Errant: 'As you already and correctly mentioned, I am a great and determined warrior with a paramount reputation as such. In order to uphold this prestige as well as my source of living, I have to travel the countryside, kill dragons, and save maidens.'

Bad, Bad Dragon: 'Seems both logical and reasonable to me.'

*Invent Options for Mutual Gain*

Knight Errant: 'Now we know the interests of one another. But what comes next?'

Bad, Bad Dragon: 'Now we can think about different solutions. But we should do that without deciding yet. It is important to separate inventing from deciding, as judgment prevents creativity and imagination. There should be no criticism at all during the inventing session.'[38]

Sitting side by side, the Bad, Bad Dragon and the Knight Errant began their brainstorming session outside the dragon's cave. After agreeing to the basic rules during the brainstorming session, especially the non-criticism rule, they ask the dragon's hostage (who is surprisingly able to read and write despite life in the Middle Ages) to jot down the different ideas which are about to be brought forward. She writes on the outside wall of the cave with chalk (which is also surprising).[39]

> Bad, Bad Dragon: 'I could disappear magically, enabling you to come triumphantly back to the village.'

> Knight Errant: 'You could flee from me so that anyone can see what a coward you really are.'

> Beautiful Maiden: (Quietly thinking to herself) 'Guys...'

> Bad, Bad Dragon: (Still being notably cool) 'Hm. There might be another option that is not only benefitting us in the short-term perspective, but also in the long-term perspective.'

> Knight Errant: 'What do you mean?'

> Bad, Bad Dragon: 'I want to survive. You want to gain prestige and secure a source of living. If we team up, I can survive. You will be able to get not only more prestige, but also long-term job security. We could go from village to village together. At first, I terrorize the village a little and, of course and for reasons unknown, take the most Beautiful Maiden as a hostage. Then you come in, in your immaculate suit of armor, we engage in a 'fight' that leads to my 'death', and we go on. This would lead to mutual gain.[40]

> Beautiful Maiden: (Thinking to herself) 'Seriously?'

> Knight Errant: 'Simply killing you is still an option.'

> Bad, Bad Dragon: 'Sure. As well as killing you is.'

> Knight Errant: 'Fair enough.'

> Bad, Bad Dragon: 'Let's think about the different options for a while.'

### Insist on using Objective Criteria

After Knight Errant and Bad, Bad Dragon separated for a while in order to think about the different options, they came back together and start talking again.

> Knight Errant: 'What now?'

> Bad, Bad Dragon: 'We need to find some objective criteria on which we can make our decision.'

Knight Errant: 'Why should we need objective criteria for that? And what defines an objective criterion?'

Bad, Bad Dragon: 'We need objective criteria because not using it as a basis for our decision is costly. It is costly as it costs time and is basically a competition over who is more stubborn. However, using objective criteria would allow us to decide independently of one another's will. An objective criterion has three characteristics: The already mentioned independence from our wills is the first one, the second one is that it is legitimate, and the third one is that it is practical.'[41]

Knight Errant: 'Makes sense. However, I still think that I need to kill you. My objective criterion is moral standards,[42] and lying is a necessary ingredient of your teaming-up solution. Consequentially, this option is out of the game for me.'

Bad, Bad Dragon: 'Well, my objective criterion would be efficiency.[43] And I think that the team proposal makes sense in the framework of this objective criterion.'

Knight Errant: 'Seems like we have an impasse here . . .'

Beautiful Maiden: (Who sneaked into the dragon's library during the night and also read *Getting to Yes*) 'Not necessarily. I think I have a solution for that.'

Knight Errant and Bad, Bad Dragon: 'Really? You? Do tell!'

Beautiful Maiden: (Inwardly rolling her eyes) 'Well, you guys could use fair procedures to decide upon which objective criteria you should use. Drawing lots would be an example for such a procedure. It is inherently fair and no one can complain afterwards.[44]

Knight Errant: 'That seems fair to me. What do you think?'

Bad, Bad Dragon: 'I am also okay with that. Let us draw lots.'

The Beautiful Maiden went out to the fields, accompanied by both the Bad, Bad Dragon and the Knight Errant. She collected two straws, one of them longer than the other. She put them in her fist and held them toward the Knight Errant and the Bad, Bad Dragon. In a moment of chivalry and grace, the Knight Errant let the Bad, Bad Dragon pull first; he got the long one. They decided to choose efficiency as their objective criterion. Consequently, they teamed up and lived happily ever after. The Beautiful Maiden, no longer a hostage, returned to her home, and continued the work on her farm, waiting for the next Bad, Bad Dragon (for there are many in the Land), and perhaps another Knight Errant. But the Knight Errant in our story gained an even greater reputation as a warrior and the Bad, Bad Dragon lived to be the last of his kind. This fine tale records the only negotiation between a Knight Errant and a Bad, Bad Dragon!

*Notes by the Minstrel*

Due to the character of the described conflict, it was not possible to take the BATNA (Best Alternative to a Negotiated Agreement) into account, as the BATNA on both sides would have been the fight. However, in other situations it is important that the parties develop a BATNA. A BATNA protects the negotiator from agreeing to a settlement that is in contrast to his own interests and it assures the efficient use of each side's asset in the sense that the best outcome is possible to be reached. It makes resisting pressure of any kind easier and is more flexible than a bottom line.[45]

Philip Allinger's creative and entertaining rendition of conflicts between the Bad, Bad Dragon, the Knight Errant, and the Beautiful Maiden demonstrates clearly the concepts and guiding principles that characterize the principled negotiation process. When the four stages of principled negotiation are engaged, the outcomes for all parties involved are favorable. This is one of the core distinctions of principled negotiation—conflicts are transformed well.

## CRITICISMS OF PRINCIPLED NEGOTIATION

Principled negotiation is most prominent in North America and despite its widespread use and application in a number of negotiation environments, it has been criticized for its Western origins. Some criticisms[46] claim that principled negotiation trivialises conflict, routinizes methods of negotiation, and undervalues the role that situation and context play in handling conflict.

William McCarthy has criticized the method for its lack of attention to the role and analysis of power in negotiation.[47] He suggests that the balance of power, more than the development of a BATNA, is the key element to determine the limits of an agreeable settlement. McCarthy also criticizes principled negotiation for assuming that the factors that make for successful negotiation work in all contexts, including in family quarrels, international negotiations, market haggling, and government regulation. For example, there are strong political and ideological components underlying the relationships within labor disputes and in the international conflict arena, and McCarthy suggests that the effects of differences among disputes require further study before a common model of negotiation can be claimed.

## NEGOTIATION ERRORS

David Lax and James Sebenius are negotiation scholars.[48] They claim that formal negotiators face a dilemma in deciding whether to pursue a cooperative or a competitive strategy, and this tension can produce a number of errors during negotiation, which in turn produce unwanted conflicts if not carefully recognized and approached.[49] In 2001, James Sebenius wrote a well-referenced article that summarized the most common errors of negotiators.[50] According to Sebenius, the way to avoid these common mistakes is to stay focused on solving the right problem.

At times, especially in business negotiations or international conflict negotiations where the stakes are very high, negotiators can endure intense pressure which can in turn lead to costly mistakes. Negotiators at all levels of conflict can become absorbed with following the correct stages of a conflict intervention, and lose sight of both the problem they are solving and of the larger goal, which is to transform conflict!

Sebenius suggests that bad habits result in common negotiation errors. These errors can prevent the establishment of good habits. The guiding principle to establishing good habits, and the guiding principle of good negotiating focus, is posited by Sebenius in the following way: "Your negotiation problem is to understand and shape your counterpart's perceived decision so that the other side chooses in its own interest what you want."[51] Although this may seem manipulative, shaping a decision so that both parties readily agree and feel that their own interests are met creates a sustainable agreement.

There are at least six errors of negotiation that commonly manifest while people are negotiating. These are the most common classes of errors and bad habits identified by Professor Sebenius, and are summarized and presented in Table 6.1.

The table compares behaviors and assumptions that intuitively appear during negotiation processes, but tend to become "bad habits." The literature recommends instead that negotiators practice "good habits," as habits, by their nature, guide any life process toward a positive or a negative conclusion. Negotiation is no exception. The errors of negotiation are common in any negotiated process.

## INTERNATIONAL NEGOTIATION

Negotiation is not uncommon in the international conflict arena. However, the vast majority of studies[52] on strategic international conflict management have concentrated in the area of interpersonal conflict. Accord-

**Table 6.1.   Six Common Bad (and Good) Habits of Negotiating**

| Bad Habit | Good Habit |
| --- | --- |
| 1. Neglect the other side's problem | 1. Solve the other side's problem as a means of solving one's own |
| 2. Let cost concerns in its many forms overtake other interests | 2. Work with the interests of the parties as a whole and focus on relationship |
| 3. Let positions drive out interests | 3. Recognize and balance the tension between cooperation and competition |
| 4. Search too hard for common ground and miss it | 4. Differences can also transform conflict |
| 5. Neglect BATNAs | 5. The potential deal and the BATNA work together like two blades on scissors |
| 6. Fail to correct for bias | 6. Prepare extensively, including research about the other party's interests |

Compiled from James K. Sebenius, "Six Habits of Merely Effective Negotiators" *Harvard Business Review* (April, 2001):87-95.

ing to William Zartman[53] certain conditions must exist for negotiation in the international arena.[54] These pre-conditions are articulated by Bercovitch and Jackson as:

1. A low or decreasing probability of attaining conflict goals through violent struggle, withdrawal, or avoidance
2. A decreasing value of the conflict goals, relative to the direct costs of pursuing those goals and relative to other goals
3. A set of common or compatible interests between the parties, or at least the possibility of a settlement offering mutual advantages over continued conflict; and
4. The flexibility by each leadership to consider negotiation

In these conditions, the skills and techniques of negotiation as presented in this chapter are the same as those that guide individuals tasked with international conflict transformation through negotiated agreements.

Although lengthy discussion of international negotiation is beyond the scope of this book, a myriad of negotiations take place each day on bilateral and multilateral levels. For example, one of the most notable international negotiations in recent years involved the ceasefire between Russia and Ukraine after the 2014 invasion of Ukraine by Russian troops. The talks took place on February 12, 2015 in Minsk, Belarus between the leaders of Russia, Ukraine, France, and Germany. The seventeen-hour negotiation resulted in a ceasefire agreement between Russia and Ukraine. The talks also covered future constitutional reform in Ukraine to reconsider the legitimate rights of Russian people who live in Donbas,

Ukraine and consider themselves Russians, along with the withdrawal of heavy weapons from the front line, border problems, and economic and humanitarian issues. Each of these was negotiated in the way that the negotiation process has been outlined in this chapter.

Another example of negotiations at the international level involves ongoing talks about the Iranian nuclear issue, which is a two-decade-long conflict. Iran has developed a range of technologies, including uranium enrichment, warhead design, and delivery systems. Although the Iranian government continues to insist that its nuclear activities are entirely peaceful, leading Western state officials in global affairs disagree with Iran's claims. As a result, several Western and non-Western states have made efforts over the years to negotiate a settlement with Iran to limit its nuclear program. In November 2013, Iran agreed upon a negotiated interim accord with Great Britain, France, the United States, China, and Germany. The agreement was reached through negotiating: Iran showed restraint and agreed to delicately balance the country's nuclear undertakings in return for alleviation from international sanctions that seriously destabilized the economy. The negotiating parties and Western diplomats extended the deadline several times in their pursuit of a final negotiated agreement.

Negotiations have been critical in ending war and establishing the terms of ceasefire around the world and throughout history. Once negotiated agreements are in place, post conflict nations and societies can begin the lengthy process of peacebuilding and restoration without the direct violence of guns and other forms of warfare.

## SUMMARY

Negotiation is an age-old process used to help people resolve an issue through conversation and bargaining. Negotiation can be accomplished without formal assistance, can be supported with some external third party assistance, or can be accomplished through professional negotiators on behalf of the conflicting parties. The negotiation process can sometimes damage relationships, and so people engaging in negotiations need to be wise regarding their choice of negotiation style and their conduct within those processes. Soft and distributive negotiation tends to injure relationships and leave parties (at least one party) unsatisfied, without their needs met. Peace professionals prefer to negotiate in a principled manner using interests as a basis for the process. Exploring the selected positions of parties in conflict can take negotiators at all levels of contest toward a satisfying conclusion.

## QUESTIONS

1. Think about a situation where you negotiated with another person to accomplish something that was important to you. How do you think the outcome could have been different now that you understand the various forms of negotiation?
2. Simulate a university group project negotiation. Identify five tasks that need to be accomplished and negotiate the completion of each by a different member of the group. Discuss the process by responding to the following questions:
    a. Were all the parties genuinely satisfied? (Did you recognize conflict styles?)
    b. Why was this outcome satisfactory or unsatisfactory?
    c. Were you able to identify the positions and interests?
3. Select a children's story and reinterpret to incorporate and highlight effective negotiation principles in a way similar to the story of The Bad, Bad Dragon.
4. Find a film or television show that portrays a successful principle-based negotiation. What principles were present that contributed to the resolution? What was missing, and how could it have gone better through negotiation?

## NOTES

1. William C. Warters, *Mediation in the Campus Community: Designing and Managing Effective Programs* (San Francisco, CA: Jossey-Bass, 2000): 6.
2. Roger Fisher and William Ury, *Getting to Yes!: Negotiating Agreement without Giving In* (London, UK: Penguin Group, 1981).
3. Roger Fisher, William Ury, and Bruce Patton, *Getting to Yes: Negotiating Agreement without Giving In*, 3rd ed., (New York: Penguin Books, 2011): 163.
4. Ibid., xxvii.
5. Ibid., 4.
6. Roy J. Lewicki, David M. Saunders, and John W. Minton, *Essentials of Negotiation* (Boston: McGraw Hill, 1999): 1.
7. Jacqueline M. Nolan-Haley, *Alternative Dispute Resolution in a Nutshell* (St. Paul, MN: West Publishing Company, 2013): 27.
8. Fisher, Ury, and Patton, 2011: 43.
9. Fisher, Ury, and Patton, 2011: 4, 5.
10. Ibid., 21.
11. Ibid., 43.
12. Heidi Burgess, "Negotiation Strategies" (*Beyond Intractability*: January, 2004). http://www.beyondintractability.org
13. Ibid.
14. Ibid.
15. Ibid.
16. Fisher, Ury, and Patton, 2011.
17. William Wilmot and Joyce Hocker, *Interpersonal Conflict* (New York: McGraw-Hill Companies, 2014).

18. Fisher, Ury, and Patton, 2011: xvii.

19. Ibid., 17–95.

20. Ibid., xvii.

21. Ibid.

22. Wilmot and Hocker, 2014.

23. Fisher and Ury, 1981

24. David Lax and James Sebenius, "The Power of Alternatives or the Limits to Negotiation," in *Negotiation Theory and Practice*, eds. J. William Breslin and Jeffery Z. Rubin, (Cambridge: The Program on Negotiation at Harvard Law School, 1991): 99.

25. Ibid., 112.

26. Tanya Glaser, *Conflict Research Consortium*, 2005: np. . . Book Review: David Lax and James Sebenius, "The Power of Alternatives or the Limits to Negotiation," in *Negotiation Theory and Practice*, J. William Breslin and Jeffery Z. Rubin, eds. (Cambridge: The Program on Negotiation at Harvard Law School, 1991), pp. 97–114. Available at David Lax and James Sebenius, "The Power of Alternatives or the Limits to Negotiation," in Negotiation Theory and Practice, eds. J. William Breslin and Jeffery Z. Rubin (Cambridge: The Program on Negotiation at Harvard Law School, 1991), pp. 97–114.

27. See Guy Burgess and Heidi Burgess, "Limits to Agreement: Better Alternatives," 1998. Available at Conflict Research Consortium http://www.colorado.edu/conflict/peace/problem/batna.htm.

28. By Philip Allinger. Used by permission. Philip Allinger was a graduate student at the University of North Carolina Greensboro studying for one year in the university's partnership study program with Konstanz University in Germany. Rather than writing an essay, Philip developed this story as an application of *Getting to YES!* in a skills and techniques of conflict transformation course developed by two of the book authors in 2014.

29. Ibid.

30. Fisher, Ury, and Patton, 2011: 40.

31. Ibid., 32.

32. Ibid., 28.

33. Ibid., 34.

34. Ibid., 42F.

35. Ibid., 30.

36. Ibid., 44.

37. Ibid., 42.

38. Ibid., 62.

39. Ibid., 63–64.

40. Ibid., 73.

41. Ibid., 83; 86.

42. Ibid., 86.

43. Ibid., 86.

44. Ibid., 87F.

45. Ibid., 99F.

46. Katja Funken, "The Pros and Cons of Getting to Yes-Shortcomings and Limitations of Principled Bargaining in Negotiation and Mediation." *Zeitschrift fur Konfliktmanagement* (2002): 3.

47. William McCarthy, "The Role of Power and Principle in Getting to Yes," in *Negotiation Theory and Practice*, eds. J. William Breslin and Jeffery Z. Rubin (Cambridge: The Program on Negotiation at Harvard Law School, 1991): 119.

48. See, for example Tanya Glaser of the Conflict Resolution Consortium at http://www.colorado.edu/conflict/peace/treatment/lax7543.htm.

49. Tanya Glaser, *Conflict Research Consortium* Book Review: David Lax and James Sebenius, "The Manager as Negotiator: The Negotiator's Dilemma: Creating and Claiming Value" in *Dispute Resolution*, 2nd ed., edited by Stephen Goldberg, Frank

Sander and Nancy Rogers (Boston: Little Brown and Co., 1992), pp. 49–62. Available at http://www.colorado.edu/conflict/peace/treatment/lax7543.htm.

50. See James K. Sebenius, "Six Habits of Merely Effective Negotiators." *Harvard Business Review* (April, 2001): 87–95.

51. Ibid., 88.

52. See Jacob Bercovitch and Richard Jackson, 2001: 3. "Negotiation or Mediation?: An Exploration of Factors Affecting the Choice of Conflict Management in International Conflict." *Negotiation Journal*, Article first published online: July 7, 2007. DOI: 10.1111/j.1571-9979.2001.tb00227.x.

53. William Zartman, "Explaining disengagement." In *Dynamics of Third Party Intervention: Kissinger in the Middle East*, edited by J. Rubin (New York: Praeger, 1981).

54. Bercovitch and Jackson, 2001: 2.

# SEVEN

# Facilitating Group Processes for Transformative Change

LEARNING OUTCOMES

- To explain the role of group dynamics in the transformation of conflict
- To analyze the basic skills and role of a facilitator in engaging group processes
- To explore how experiential education promotes community and peacebuilding
- To demonstrate the application of facilitation processes and skills to the broader purposes of conflict transformation

OVERVIEW

Groups struggle to find ways to balance conflict with the need for unity and cohesion while still respecting the differences that characterize groups. The tensions are often expressed as differences in the goals of the group, ideas of other members, behaviors and roles of members, or group procedures.[1] There are three types of conflicts common to groups that reflect an imbalance in the relationship between unity and change. This tension can be managed and transformed through the implementation of facilitated or educational processes. In this way, people have the opportunity to resolve real conflicts through collective engagement. Facilitation can be a formal or informal process during which the group proceeds through established processes toward the goal of managing and transforming group conflict situations.

## INTRODUCTION

As individuals struggle to live and work within the context of familial, neighborhood, community, and broader socio-political systems, they grapple with both productive and hurtful mechanisms for dealing with conflict. Globalization, diversity, competition, and new technology further contribute to the complexity. Because people are always interconnected through collective contexts, understanding group dynamics is essential to the change process and the goals of community building and peacebuilding. Peace and conflict practitioners employ a number of skills to manage and transform the challenges that arise in groups.

Conflict is a normal part of group interaction. Some interactions are more stressful and entrenched than others, for a number of different reasons. Many groups struggle to deal with difficult changes that result from cut backs, mergers, changes in composition or personnel, changes in management, re-engineering, and more everyday events. Managing group conflict requires "a delicate balancing act, like that of a tightrope walker, or a rock climber who must find just the right handholds."[2] Groups often lose their focus on their goals, especially in the context of managing and transforming divisive situations. Too often, people do not have answers to what they are experiencing, but know it is painful and that their workplace, community, neighborhood, or places of worship are not comfortable anymore. Although this discomfort might feel personal, it is often a shared, or group, experience. The process of facilitation (both formal and informal) can help groups find a constructive and collective path toward change.

## DYNAMICS OF GROUP PROCESS

Groups are the context for human activity, but the dynamics of group processes means that they are also agents of change. Working within the context of small (families and neighborhoods), medium (organizations and communities), or large group settings (social systems), formal and informal groups are an effective way to approach and overcome conflict. The facilitation of groups through conflict transformation utilizes the dynamics of group processes. This refers to the way that people in groups interact and ultimately process change together. The first and most immediate small group within which people learn to interact is the family, but groups are also found in neighbourhoods, organizations, and communities. In these, members learn to be together, to belong, and to help each other. This process of interaction means that groups are a place for socialization and change.

The recognition of groups as environments for facilitating positive change is a global phenomenon.[3] Groups have been used in multicultural contexts in Europe to meaningfully combat social exclusion and to strengthen people's sense of community and belonging.[4] In South Africa,[5] groups have served as sites of personal and interpersonal change. During times of great upheaval, groups have served as the locale for social change. Groups also provide a backdrop for transforming relationships across differences and provide opportunities for linking groups with the Indigenous models for change that are most meaningful to them.[6] In groups, people find meaning, healing, and connection.[7]

There are a number of factors at work in group dynamics that influence group processes. Groups promote interpersonal and social change[8] but they can also reinforce negative interactions and worldviews.[9] PACS workers, knowledgeable about how to facilitate change in groups, can work with natural and formed groups for productive and creative processes. Groups then work through their conflicts productively to promote and affirm collective action and socialization.

A group facilitator is most productive when they respectfully listen to and observe group members, asking gentle questions rather than telling people what to do. The process is one of using basic communication skills to join with groups in order to work toward positive change. Facilitating change focuses on identifying local strengths as a base for capacity building, goal setting, and finding solutions.[10] At the same time, the facilitator pays attention to building relationships within the group and patiently reinforcing the development of interpersonal connections. These relationships can serve as bridges during the change process from negative conflict.[11] The skills used for facilitating change within small groups are the same basic skills used in larger contexts, from extended families to global organizations.

## Facilitation as a Process

Facilitation is a process used formally and informally to assist in the use of groups as agents of change. In addition to basic group skills, the facilitator may use a variety of practices and tools to help the group move through their concerns to their goal. These may include brainstorming, differentiating between interests and positions, needs identification, and consensus building.

Formal literature identifies two primary facilitator roles. One role is called a basic role, and the other is called a developmental role, based on which tasks the facilitator provides.[12] A basic facilitator helps a group solve a problem by using process skills. This means that the facilitator carefully guides a group through formal stages, or a process, toward their intended goal. A developmental facilitator not only helps the group solve a problem in this way, but also helps them improve their process skills at the same time. This is a longer term commitment than a basic facilitation. The facilitator is not only facilitating but teaching as well.

A facilitator works to help create a group climate, designs the agenda (as appropriate), analyzes information gained through observation, intervenes in group dynamics, navigates decision processes, and ensures follow up. These responsibilities may be more or less formal depending on the context. Ingrid Bens defines a facilitator as, "One who contributes structure and process to interactions so groups are able to function effectively and make high-quality decisions. A helper and enabler, whose goal is to support others as they pursue their objectives,"[13] the facilitator might also act as a coach, teacher, or mentor. Content is the domain of the group (what), while the process (how) is the facilitator's job.[14]

In general, effective facilitators develop a broad repertoire of skills, often acquired through a combination of formal training, seminars, and experience. Facilitation of groups is a conflict intervention that seems to be increasing in demand. There are formal associations that train, develop, and assign facilitators, including the International Association of Facilitators.[15] Facilitators are skilled in dealing with disruptive behavior, providing and receiving feedback in a way that progresses individuals and groups forward, and asking questions. They are also familiar with group dynamics, including when to listen, be assertive, build consensus, and distinguish between positions and interests.

Establishing ground rules for group processes is another critical skill of facilitators. Sometimes ground rules are called agreements or guidelines. The purpose of ground rules is to resolve conflicts as they arise, and work toward group goals. The facilitator can offer ground rules for the group to suggest as members work through their task. Ideally, members would help craft their own agreements. The advantage of starting with a prepared list is that it can be well thought out and a facilitator's experience can contribute to discussion of a broad range of considerations. Groups that develop their own guidelines tend to demonstrate increased commitment to resolving their issues and often adopt the ground rules for future work together. Ground rules provide an objective standard for interaction whenever the group is off task or headed in a non-productive direction. At other times, the ground rules can provide a framework for affirmation. Facilitators can express appreciation or commendation to the group when members have moved through the process and abided by their agreements.

*Group Cohesion and Groupthink*

Groups demonstrate two common characteristics and behaviors: group cohesion and group think. These are opposites; the one represents a transformative state, the other a conflict state enforced by silencing all dissenting opinions. Group cohesion refers to the mutual attraction that bonds the group together and gives members pride in their unity. Cohesion also ensures a commitment to the work and tasks of the group.

There are effective ways for all members of the group, especially the leader or facilitator, to establish group cohesion. Effective ways to ensure cohesion are to establish a group identity (like matching shirts, hats, or uniforms), group traditions (like badges, songs, or a membership card), recognizing contributions (awards), and stressing the value of teamwork while acknowledging and respecting the needs of individual members through careful and frequent meaningful communication.[16]

Cohesive groups are characterized by satisfied group members who display high levels of interaction. Members have a desire to conform to the expectations of the group, discover creative and productive approaches to achieve their goals, and function in a friendly and supportive environment.[17] Cohesion is a strong deterrent to negative conflict, and by its nature, facilitates improved group problem solving, enhances creativity, and encourages the respectful and inclusive expression of differences of opinion.

A conflict inherent in highly cohesive groups is a vulnerability to a behavior recognized as groupthink. Groupthink is a common group conflict that rarely manifests in the ways most often associated with conflict. That is, instead of arguing or fighting, there is a shocking level of agreement. In situations of groupthink, group members value consensus so highly they fail to think critically about the outcomes of decisions they are responsible to undertake and all agree with one another, regardless of what they really think. Often groups who have fallen into groupthink behaviors describe themselves as highly consensual as though consensus is the paramount value.

## GROUPS AND CONFLICT

There is a common misconception that effective groups never have conflicts. Group conflict is inevitable, but conflict does not always connote negative interaction. Conflict in groups can be recognized as the expression of legitimate differences of opinion, as opportunities to improve group problem solving, increase the cohesiveness of the group, and enhance creativity. The primary purpose of group interaction is usually to promote and achieve a goal.

People commonly recognize conflict expressions; these are frequently disagreements associated with anger and hostility. There are three types of group conflict that can be converted into cohesion through the facilitation of group processes. In this way group dynamics can change and conflict can be transformed. These are substantive conflict, affective conflict, and procedural conflict.

Substantive conflict happens when members of a group disagree about ideas, issues, decisions, actions, or goals. In these situations, private motives and hidden agendas become much more important than the stated goals of the group; and they subtly or overtly influence and derail conversations and discussions. Substantive conflicts interfere with the goals of the group.

Affective conflict is the result of interpersonal differences in personality, styles, and what they need to feel appreciated by the group. In addition members may feel threatened by the group or engage in a power struggle with one or more members. Affective conflict involves the way people feel and relate to others, and so is more difficult to resolve than substantive conflict. Substantive and affective conflicts often appear together in group dynamics.

Procedural conflict is disagreement among group members about the process or procedure to be chosen by the group to accomplish a goal. Often procedural conflicts arise when groups have not resolved substantive or affective conflicts. It then becomes simpler or preferable to some group members to argue over process, procedures, agendas, and topics for discussion, than it is to engage with the deeper issues and resolve the deeper affective or substantive conflicts.

*Power*

There is a common perception that power is an individual attribute.[18] Power, however, is also an issue for groups. Power can be used against people and not for the mutual and collective benefit of a group. In interpersonal relationships, especially in group settings, power is really a function of relationship. This is called the "relational theory of power."[19] According to this theory, power is a relational concept that resides in the relationship of a person to the environment, or situation they are in.[20] Kenneth Boulding, one of the early peace and conflict scholars, stated that "integrative power [which he defines as the most basic form of power][21] depends very much on the power of language and communication, especially on powers of persuasion."[22]

*The Attribution of Blame*

One of the central tendencies among group members is to attribute negative motives and negative consequences to the behaviors of others. Accordingly, one member may blame group problems on the other members, but then assume credit for group successes. This is called Attribution Theory and is a significant contribution toward examining and understanding the causes of group conflict.[23] There are three primary attributions that prompt conflict in groups: if one feels constrained by what other group members want; if one feels that other group members tend to harm oneself or others; and if what other group members want to do seems abnormal or illegal. In this way, attribution theory is relevant to conflict transformation because it addresses the origins of conflict in groups as judgements about the motives and characteristics of other group members.

*Culture*

Conflict becomes more complex in diverse groups, where conflicts can originate in matters related to culture, gender, and power. Different cultures approach conflict directly or indirectly and either in an expressive or subtle manner. When a culture places a high value on the individual and on individualism, members of that culture are more are likely to express disagreement in terms of their own needs. If, conversely, a member comes from a more collectivist culture, they place a higher value on cooperation and therefore will be less likely to express conflict directly.

Cultural diversity brings strength and creativity to group processes. It can also be a source of conflict when there is diversity across ethnoracial identity, national origin, income, geography, gender/sex, sexual orientation, and religion.[24] Some conflict comes from unexamined assumptions by participants in the group who attribute negative qualities to members from other identity groups.[25] Values differ across diverse groups. "Competent group practice must always rest on a respectful, sensitive attitude to others, whether culturally or personally, and must aim to create harmony and understanding, racially, ethnically and culturally."[26]

Cultural definitions of gender lie at the heart of much conflict, including group conflict.[27] The International Committee of the Red Cross describes gender in terms of learned behaviors that are culturally expected and ascribed roles, attitudes, and values. Sex refers to biology.[28] Although there is a large literature base exploring the potential effects of gender on conflict and conflict styles, there is other research that suggests that men and women may respond to conflict more in alignment with their habitual conflict styles than with responses attributable to their sex.[29] In 2006, Ann Nicotera and Laura Dorsey determined that "conflict style is not driven by biological sex, regardless of how many studies try to find the effect, it's simply not there."[30] However, studies of people that have been in war have demonstrated that although men, women, boys, and girls experience similar phenomena during and after conflict, their experiences and levels of vulnerability are influenced by cultural definitions of their sex.[31] Although this is an area still being researched, it would appear that in matters of conflict, gender is more relevant than biological sex, suggesting that conflict and responses to conflict are culturally based rather than gender based.

## GROUPS WITHIN ORGANIZATIONS

Groups are the building blocks of organizations.[32] They link the individual with collective goals and functions, and engage with the overall dynamics of the organization. The process can engage both formal and informal leadership and groups. Groups can be a negative influence, particularly when they work to enforce terror through bullying and mobbing and/or silencing voices. They can contribute positively to creativity and healing as they work to create space for multiple voices and encourage respectful dialogue.[33]

The leadership provided through transformative facilitation skills has become increasingly important within organizations confronted with managing change environments and the associated conflicts. Four principles of facilitation are integral to group conflict resolution, especially in organizations and large groups:[34]

1. Everyone must actively participate.
2. Teams generally perform better than individuals (if they work effectively).
3. Process (how something is done) affects outcome (what is accomplished).
4. The requirement for additional facilitators and greater facilitation expertise increases with the size of the group.

### Transforming Group Meetings

One of the primary group conflicts in today's organizations comes from the practice of group meetings. As organizations enlarge and expand and struggle with a number of different conflicts, there are many reasons for groups of people to meet in person or electronically. As the number of meetings continues to increase in most organizations, the practice of formal meetings has become a source of individual and group conflict. Poorly conducted meetings are a source of conflict that is relatively simply resolved or transformed through good chairperson skills. These are international principles and skills applicable to purposeful collections of people all around the globe, from informal group interactions to global level interactions among state leaders.

Meetings need a purpose, which can be focused on a product or a process. At the end of the meeting, members ought to know that that purpose was achieved, or that they are meeting again until it is. This is a skill that is applicable in almost any formal group context, from a family meeting to the United Nations. When the purpose of a meeting is clear to all members of a group, managing conflicts and differences is not usually difficult because the common goal encourages people to work collectively toward positive change. However, many meetings do not have a purpose that warrants collecting the group in one location; others have meetings simply out of habit. In these situations, people are frustrated, goals are rarely achieved because they are unclear, and ordinary group dynamics and dialectics are unmanaged. Consequently, conflict escalates.

In the situation of organizational meetings, often someone in a hierarchical position of authority establishes the time, place, composition, and purpose of the meeting, and then chairs the meeting as well. However, chairing meetings is a skill; poorly chaired meetings are a source of group conflict. Well chaired meetings are a form of positive group processes, and a means of managing the synergy of conflicts that naturally indwell group meetings. The person chairing the meeting ought to ensure that the purpose of the meeting is clear to all participants and they have an achievable agenda that was developed collaboratively and is then followed. Good chairs also make sure that the meeting goals can be achieved in the time allocated, and they ensure that everyone that wants to participate has an opportunity to do so. These behaviors create group cohesion and transform ordinary conflict dynamics into productive action, while often strengthening the relationships of the people attending the meeting.

Collaboration is a common part of PACS practice. Collaboration is an approach to group conflict that emphasizes the search for solutions that satisfy all members of the group, while achieving the group's common goal. Collaborative leadership can be transformative. This works when culturally appropriate. There is a common and conflict-inducing misunderstanding that collaboration means that all members of the group speak. When meetings work collaboratively, they are an effective group process in which relationships are strengthened and goals are achieved.

*Large Group Conflict Transformation*

When difficult events are shared by a large number of people, PACS practitioners can provide meaningful assistance through the facilitation of a group that is larger than typical. Large group facilitation is conducted with the same procedures and principles as small group facilitation, but on a larger scale. The conflict the group members are struggling with, the time frame involved, and the final goal of the group are additional dynamics that influence the process. Sometimes large groups will be subdivided into smaller work groups and then (but not always) reconvened as one group toward the end of the process so the large group can evaluate progress toward the overall intended goal.

Large group transformation is a process that is effective for disputes among members of a large family. It is also a positive tool for business settings and any other settings in which large groups of people recognize that they can resolve their conflicts through a positive process that will not harm relationships. It is also very useful in advance of a potential conflict, like organizational succession planning or estate planning. Facilitators guide the formal large group transformation process in five phases: entrance into the conflict, individual interviews, mediation, reunion, and action.

The first phase begins when the facilitator enters into the conflict. The facilitator begins by interviewing the party who requested assistance to transform the group conflict. During the interview, the facilitator asks questions about who is involved in the conflict, how these people may be contacts, who has tried to resolve the issues and how. During the entrance phase, the facilitator also determines which facilities are available for a large group conflict resolution process, and how that person would describe the situation if it was resolved. During this first phase, the facilitator may also meet with the larger group to talk about their role and describe the conflict transformation process. During this phase, the group process has officially been entered into by all parties. Questions can be answered and preparation can begin for the next phase.

The second phase involves an interview with each individual identified in the initial meeting. This is a confidential meeting where the participant has an opportunity to vent, examine their role in the conflict, explore what they would like to see happen, discuss what they might be able to do to help transform the conflict, and identify other people they think are part of the conflict and need to be interviewed. Parties are also asked if they want to resolve individual issues with anyone or if they think mediation would help mitigate the conflict. If the group is very large, there may be a necessity for multiple interviewers.

The third phase is a mediation phase. Mediation takes place with people who agreed that mediation would be helpful during the interview phase. These group members are given the opportunity to sit together confidentially with an impartial mediator (or several), depending on the size of the group in order to discuss their issues and to consider possible resolution. Mediation is a voluntary process, and if parties do not wish to participate in mediation, the fourth phase can be more difficult, but the process will continue.

Members meet together as one large group for the fourth phase. Depending on the size of the group there may need to be more than one facilitator. This phase varies in characteristics depending on the group and their concerns. The fourth phase is the reunion of the large group. Usually, issues and potential resolutions are identified and recorded so that they can be used in the next phase of the facilitation.

The fifth phase is the action phase. During this phase, the lead facilitator collects and prioritizes the recorded and identified issues and possible resolutions, according to the will of the group. It is a common practice for facilitators to post these on paper on a wall or other surface so that the entire group can visually acknowledge the identified issues and possible resolutions, and move them around as they see best in order to develop an action plan. During this phase, the large group can reconfigure back into small groups once again to brainstorm and discuss. An action plan is then developed that includes dates and responsible parties, which is shared with the large group and the process continues until everyone is satisfied. A good action plan includes a strategy for follow up. In this way, the trained facilitator is a guide for the large group as they work through conflict and transform it together.

*Appreciative Inquiry (AI)*

Appreciative Inquiry (AI) is both a philosophy and a process and has gained significant popularity among PACS practitioners because of its positive and powerful transformative qualities.[35] Appreciate Inquiry provides a strong paradigm for making decisions, creating strategic change, and providing analysis, based on what is done well. In 1996, David Cooperrider facilitated AI as the foundation for a global organization dedicated to promoting grassroots interfaith cooperation for peace, justice, and healing.[36]

Appreciative Inquiry is an asset-based approach that leverages cooperation; it is time consuming but is reputed to be thorough and transformative. Appreciative Inquiry was developed as an alternative to more traditional problem solving approaches that may limit analysis and understanding, due to the focus on problems rather than solutions. It is another way to transform conflict in large groups by encouraging people to talk about what they really think and why. Appreciative Inquiry is popular because it uses a holistic approach to conflicts by including a more positive perspective on a transformed future, instead of focusing on existing problems. Appreciate Inquiry recognizes that when encountering group conflict, members of organizations talk to each other about what they are experiencing. Appreciative Inquiry "appreciates" what is being said and encourages further inquiry, acknowledging that the kernels of transformation are already in the people who are in the organization or group. People know what they are experiencing and why it is a conflict for them. In addition, they have established group relationships as they work toward an imagined future together.

There are five underlying principles of AI that guide facilitations.[37] The language of AI processes is positive, inspiring, and focuses discussions and interactions toward a desired group future. Appreciative Inquiry I is based on questions and attention to the things people say and talk about. The five principles are identified as the constructionist principle, the principle of simultaneity, the poetic principle, the anticipatory principle, and the positive principle, but these are guiding principles rather than formal stages.

Briefly, the constructionist principle asserts that people construct the organizations they inhabit through the relationships, language, and the day to day interactions they share. The constructionist principle means that the inquiry constructs or stimulates new ideas, stories, and images that generate new possibilities for action. The principle of simultaneity rests in the recognition that social systems move in the direction of the topics people discuss, what they think about, and what they ask about. The seeds of change are located simultaneously in social systems, groups, and organizations within the conversations, inquiries, and questions of people in those systems. The poetic principle recognizes that organizational life is depicted poetically in the stories people tell about their group, so that the story of the organization is constantly being co-authored. The words and topics of the poetic principle construct meaning beyond the actual topic and words so that the genuine goals and interests of group members may be recognized. The final two principles are the anticipatory principle and the positive principle. The anticipatory principle is important because it captures, or anticipates the ideal future group members talk about, together. The conflict situation is transformed in part by the anticipation of what tomorrow could be like. The positive principle proposes that sustainable change comes from positive social bonding and sentiments like hope, excitement, inspiration, and camaraderie, which promote the strong connections and relationships among groups in conflict.

The central principle of AI is that when all members of a group are motivated to recognize the most positive qualities of their group and organizational culture, change is rapid and simple. This is achieved through attention to and appreciating the responses to what is inquired. Organizational change and group change, then, are only limited by people's imaginations, not by problems. Facilitators and consultants popularly implement the five principles into a cycle of five processes. These processes[38] are Definition (What is the focus of the inquiry); Discovery (What gives life to our organization or team); Dream (What might be?); Design (What should be?); and Destiny /Deliver (How can the dream be realized?).[39]

## EDUCATION AS A FACILITATED CHANGE

Education is a source of transformative change.[40] Group work can provide transformative learning in an educational environment.[41] As a transformative tool the educational process can challenge structures of oppression, and their underlying values.[42] There are different forms of education, which are different kinds of group processes, but each one provides a perspective and practice for conflict transformation.

Critical education is a form of praxis and learning. Paulo Freire defines praxis as "the action and reflection of men and women upon their world in order to transform it."[43] Freire argues that the educator's role in a participant's learning "must coincide with those of the students to engage in critical thinking and the quest for mutual humanization."[44] David Kolb, another educator who greatly influenced experiential education philosophy, describes learning "as the process whereby knowledge is created through the transformation of experience."[45] Experiential education is a collaborative process, which relies on group processes, which are increasingly used as a change process within organizations and communities.[46]

## COMMUNITIES AS GROUPS

Communities are a form of collective action. This makes them an ideal tool for community change. Groups can be effective in community because of their transformative potential.[47] These groups can build capacity within themselves and their area of influence; they can develop empowerment strategies and engage in community peace-brokering. These and other community development and conflict resolution interventions are essentially "peacebuilding from below."[48] In these ways, groups are the building blocks for community action and the dismantling of intolerance.[49] Groups support the healing process because they encourage collective reflection, social action, restoration, restitution, and social healing,[50] and are the framework for community work, community development, and the advancement of a civil society.[51] The same "issues that we struggle with in the wider world, such as power, prejudice, an intolerance of difference, totalitarianism, democracy, conflict and hostility are also found in the microcosm of groups."[52] There are many community based projects building on the collective nature of groups that have been used to support empowering and transformative change. These include neighborhood gardens, community policing, sports, and safety. Such "peacebuilding from below" is transformative, sustainable, and enjoyable.

## SUMMARY

Group dynamics, processes of facilitation, and the dynamics of collective action are all processes that can effectively facilitate positive change. Facilitation can be used by PACS workers to manage and transform conflict in many settings through large and small, formal and informal groups. These processes are versatile and work to transform group conflicts among families, neighborhoods, organizations, and global organizations. Group problem solving, large group conflict transformation, Appreciative Inquiry, and experiential education are facilitation processes that help people in groups to work through complex issues and conflict.

## QUESTIONS

1. What are the skills and characteristics of an effective facilitator? Which of these skills do you have? Which do you need to grow?
2. Describe the core principles of Appreciative Inquiry. AI has occasionally been an effective organizational practice at the highest levels of American and Canadian government. Why? In what contexts would AI be particularly useful?
3. What is experiential education and how is it useful in the process of transforming conflict?
4. Explain how community change can be fostered by group dynamics. What is harmful and beneficial to groups and their growth?

## NOTES

1. Isa N. Engelberg and Dianna R. Wynn, *Working in Groups* (Sixth Edition) (Upper Saddle River: Pearson, 2011): 173.

2. William Wilmot and Joyce Hocker, *Interpersonal Conflict* (Eighth Edition) (New York: McGrawHill, 2011): 51.

3. Lily Becker, ed., *Working with Groups* (Cape Town, South Africa: Oxford University Press, 2005); Lordan, Nuala and Mary Wilson, "Groupwork in Europe: Tools to combat social exclusion in a multicultural environment," in *Social Work with Groups: Mining the Gold*, ed. Sue Henry, Jean East, and Cathryne Schmitz (New York: The Haworth Press, 2002): 9–21.

4. Ibid.

5. Becker, 2005.

6. Ibid.

7. Lily Becker, "Groups and Organizational Life," in *Working with Groups*, ed. Lily Becker (Cape Town, South Africa: Oxford University Press, 2005): 66–81.

8. Ibid.

9. Lily Becker, "An Overview of Groups and Groupwork," in *Working with Groups*, ed. Lily Becker (Cape Town, South Africa: Oxford University Press, 2005): 7–30.

10. Ibid.

11. Ibid.

12. Roger Schwarz, *The Skilled Facilitator : A Comprehensive Resource for Consultants, Facilitators, Managers, Trainers, and Coaches* (San Francisco, CA: Jossey-Bass, 2002).

13. Ingrid Bens, *Facilitating with Ease!: Core Skills for Facilitators, Team Leaders and Members, Managers, Consultants, and Trainers* (San Francisco, CA: Jossey-Bass, 2005): 5.

14. Ibid.

15. For more information, see http://www.iaf-world.org/index.aspx.

16. Engelberg and Wynn, 2011: 190.

17. Ibid., 186.

18. Ibid., 115.

19. See Ibid., 115ff.

20. Morton Deutsch, "Conflicts: Productive and Destructive," in *Conflict Resolution Through Communication*, ed. Fred Jandt (New York: Harper & Row, 1973): 15.

21. Maire Dugan, 2003.

22. Kenneth Boulding, *Three Faces of Power* (Newbury Park: Sage, 1989).

23. Attribution Theory is credited to Psychologist Fritz Heider, who originally applied it to human interactions in general. See Engelberg and Wynn, 2011: 175.

24. Jose Sisneros, Catherine Stakeman, Mildred Joyner and Cathryne L. Schmitz, *Critical Multicultural Social Work* (Chicago, IL: Lyceum Books, Inc., 2008).

25. Lordan and Wilson, 2002.

26. Lily Becker, "An Overview of Groups and Groupwork," in *Working with Groups*, ed. Lily Becker (Cape Town, South Africa: Oxford University Press, 2005): 23.

27. Dyan Mazurana and Keith Proctor, "Gender, Conflict and Peace" Occasional paper (Somerville: World Peace Foundation at the Fletcher School, 2013): 3. Available at http://fletcher.tufts.edu/~/media/Fletcher/Microsites/World%20Peace%20Foundation/Gender%20Conflict%20and%20Peace.pdf.

28. International Committee of the Red Cross (ICRC), *Addressing the Needs of Women Affected by Armed Conflict*, (ICRC: Geneva, 2004): 7.

29. Ibid., 186.

30. Ann M. Nicotera and Laura K. Dorsey, "Individual and Interactive Processes in Organizational Conflict," in *The Sage Handbook of Conflict Communication*, eds. John Oetzel and Stella Ting-Toomey (Thousand Oaks: Sage, 2006): 312.

31. Mazurana and Proctor, 2013: 4.

32. Andre de V Smit, "Groups and Organizational Life," in *Working with Groups*, ed. Lily Becker (Cape Town, South Africa: Oxford University Press, 2005): 66–81.

33. Ibid.

34. Adapted from Thomas Justice and David W. Jamieson, *The Facilitator's Fieldbook* (New York: American Management Association, 2012): 3.

35. The term "Appreciative Inquiry" was developed for organizational development by David Coperrider in his 1986 doctoral thesis at Case Western Reserve University in Cleveland, Ohio. To learn more about AI and Dr. Cooperrider, see *David Coooperrider and Associates*, at http://www.davidcooperrider.com/tag/dissertation/.

36. This is chronicled in by Canon Charles Gibbs and Sally Mahé, *Birth of a Global Community: Appreciative Inquiry in Action* (Brunswick: Crown Custom Publishing, 2003).

37. D.L. Cooperrider and S. Srivastva, "Appreciative Inquiry in Organizational Life," in *Research in Organizational Change and Development, Vol. 1*, eds. R.W Woodman and W.A. Pasmore (Stamford, CT: JAI Press, 1987): 129–169.

38. Jane N. Watkins and Bernard J. Mohr, *Appreciative Inquiry: Change at the Speed of Imagination* (San Francisco, CA: Jossey, 2001).

39. This was changed from Delivery to Destiny by Cooperrider because "delivery" connoted traditional managerial change mechanisms, which deflated the spirit of AI. See Gervase R. Bushe, "Appreciative Inquiry: Theory and Critique," in *The Routledge Companion to Organizational Change*, eds. D. Boje, B. Burnes, and J. Hassard (Oxford, UK: Routledge, 2011): 3.

40. Lordan and Wilson.

41. Ibid.

42. Ibid.

43. Paul Friere, *Pedagogy of the Oppressed* (New York: Continuum, 1970): 36.

44. Ibid: 75.

45. David Kolb, *Experiential Learning: Experience as the Source of Learning and Development* (Englewood Cliffs: Prentice Hall, 1984): 41.

46. The Experiential Education section of this chapter is based on contributions from Frannie Varker, an Experiential Educator and Facilitator. See About the Contributors.

47. Lily Becker, Willem de Jager, Madeleine Duncan, and Monica Spiro, "Conclusion: Groupwork—A unifying language," in *Working with Groups*, ed. Lily Becker (Cape Town, South Africa: Oxford University Press, 2005): 216–219.

48. Connie O'Brien, "Community Groups and 'Peacebuilding from Below,'" in *Working with Groups*, ed. Lily Becker (Cape Town, South Africa: Oxford University Press, 2005): 53.

49. Lily Becker, *Working with Groups*, 2005.

50. Becker, de Jager, Duncan, and Spiro, "Conclusion," in *Working with Groups*, 2005.

51. Ibid.

52.  Becker, *Working With Groups,* 2005: 7.

# EIGHT

# Mediation

LEARNING OUTCOMES

- To learn the key principles and basic phases of mediation
- To identify the role of the mediator
- To identify those conflicts for which mediation is an appropriate intervention
- To recognize those situations for which mediation is not appropriate, safe, or transformative

OVERVIEW

Mediation is introduced as a tool for change. Its basic and distinguishing principles are presented and appropriate interventions are reviewed. Three models are exploded: facilitative, narrative, and transformative mediation. The chapter also expands into different forms of application, including conflict coaching and international mediation.

INTRODUCTION

Mediation is possibly the most recognized form of conflict transformation. However, it is a specific intervention for specific situations and therefore limited in its scope. Mediation is a confidential process in which a trained mediator facilitates a discussion between two or more participants and empowers them to explore a resolution of their own design. In mediation, roles are very clear and participants have control over the outcome. The role of the mediator is to control and guide the process. One of the common initial ways people become familiar with mediation is through peer mediation in the public school system. There, students have the opportunity to learn about the strengths of mediation through co-mediation.

## THE GROWTH OF MEDIATION FOR CONFLICT TRANSFORMATION

In the United States and Canada, mediation was relatively unknown in the public arena before 1965. Prior to the mid-1960s, labor and management negotiations tended to be the primary arena for mediation. One of the outcomes of the rise in grass roots movements, including the Civil Rights Movement, the Women's Movement, and other indicators that people could take charge of their own lives, was an increase in the use and popularity of mediation outside of the labor movement for resolving conflict. Mediation developed because it is a tool that ordinary people can engage relatively easily in order to resolve conflicts without having to first approach the court system, which prior to the introduction of public mediation, had been primarily the only other option for disputes.

During the early days, mediation was envisioned to be a system of justice parallel to the courts. Community conflicts and issues not addressed by the courts could be mediated by ordinary people, guided by trained mediators. Most of the early cases primarily involved state-related issues like minor traffic violations and property damages. Arenas and opportunities for Mediation have grown over the years and today mediation is used to prevent ongoing conflict in government, business, and family matters around the globe, including international relations.

The popularity of the mediation concept is evident in the fact that more than five hundred communities in the United States and Canada have a formal community mediation center, housed in local government or existing as a non-profit agency. The people working in these centers are formally trained and certified Mediators; most are highly experienced. Mediation continues to be well recognized as a conflict transformation methodology and trained mediators have many different backgrounds. Because mediation has provided some relief to the often backlogged legal systems, many law schools have begun to train attorneys in directive or facilitative forms of mediation. However, it is important to note that the advocacy and adversarial nature of legal training can create some cognitive dissonance. There is also a caution in the field and a perceived conflict of interest for lawyers to practice mediation, because they are remunerated by billing clients by the hour.

Mediation is a widespread and formal process today and highly applicable to a number of conflict settings. There are many organizations across the country and around the world that offer training, support, and direct mediation services. Formal mediation training is useful and helpful in the workplace and at home. It is a fine opportunity for students to develop their conflict transformation skillset. There are principles of mediation that assist students of Peace and Conflict Studies (PACS) to understand the best situations for mediation intervention.

## BASIC PRINCIPLES OF MEDIATION

There are five basic principles and characteristics of formal mediation that are important for understanding how mediation works. These basic principles distinguish mediation processes from other forms of conflict interventions. These are:

- Formal training and/or Certification in mediation
- Mediator neutrality
- Voluntary participation
- Self-determination of agreement
- Confidentiality

One of the central and primary principles of mediation is the necessity for engaging formally trained Mediators to lead the session(s). This is partly because mediation operates on counterintuitive principles and so formal training and the experience acquired through that training are critical for success. For example, mediators are supposed to remain neutral and not give advice; the conflicting parties are supposed to work together to determine the best resolution for their conflict. As a result, mediation training and certification requires that mediators spend time learning the principles, process, and techniques. The accepted standard for mediation training is forty hours. Because mediation is relationship based, its outcomes do affect the relationships between conflicting parties.

It cannot be stressed enough that mediation is a skill that requires formal and on-going training and practice. An increasing number of jurisdictions in Canada and the United States are requiring formal mediation education and certification for mediators. Striving for professionalism and quality of practice, three organizations, the American Bar Association, the American Arbitration Association, and the Association for Conflict Resolution, have collaborated to develop a set of standards that reflect the tenets for mediation and mediators. The document was drafted first in 1994, and was then revised and ratified in 2005.[1]

The requirements for mediation certification are not standardized and there are a number of views regarding the best qualifications. The legal community suggests that only lawyers be trained as mediators, while others view this as a conflict of interest that does not truly protect the neutrality and integrity of mediation. Another view is that certified mediators should have a university degree. Yet another group believes that a great deal of skill and talent would be wasted if people were to be required to be lawyers or hold a university degree before they could serve ly.

as mediators. Most mediators are volunteers or paid nominally. Restricting access to formal training excludes members of marginalized groups and reduces many opportunities for mediation peacebuilding.

Neutrality, or impartiality, is another principle of mediation. The term neutrality has come under attack in recent years because in reality no one can truly be neutral. Yet in mediation, the mediator must demonstrate no vested interest in either party or the outcome. In mainstream settings, this typically means that the mediator is unknown to the participants to ensure there is no bias toward either participant or their issues. Mediators are careful to give the appearance of balance, not favoring one participant or the other. Should participants have a concern about the impartiality of the mediator, it could derail the mediation.

With organizations or governmental agencies that have an on-going mediation program, the mediator may be known to some participants. For example, in the United States Postal Service REDRESS mediation program, a small cadre of mediators are used for all discrimination cases. It is not unusual for a mediator to mediate with the same supervisor multiple times. It is incumbent on these mediators to maintain a distance and follow process to assure the integrity of the mediation process.

While the tenet of impartiality remains central to mediation, within many cultures a trusted elder or community member who is a formally trained mediator would be preferable to someone neither party knew. For the parties, comfort levels increase as they feel that the mediator understands their issues and has the best interests of their community at heart. As with all mediations, the mediator would still be aware of and monitor their own biases and work to help the parties resolve their differences without taking sides.

Another area where neutrality varies is in social justice mediation. Here, the term "multi-partial" is used to explain the role of the mediator. In this model of mediation the mediator is not detached, but partial toward all parties collectively. The mediator does not advocate for either party, but their goal is to give all participants the means and opportunity to tell their story and to be heard.

Through training and practice mediators learn to recognize and control their biases so that they are able to help participants self-determine their outcomes. It is critical that parties feel like the mediator is impartial and open to hearing and exploring their issues. Adherence to the process and principles is key to maintaining that sense of neutrality or impartiality.

A hallmark of mediation is voluntary participation by conflicting parties. The voluntary nature of mediation participation is one of its distinct features. Sometimes, people refuse; other times, they are reluctant, and it is important that the difference be recognized. There are times when a reluctant party can be encouraged to participate in mediation. Hesitation or resistance can be rooted in a lack of knowledge. When people familiar with mediation take the time to explain the intent and process of mediation, attitudes shift and the process of building trust and the early stages of conflict transformation begin. Once people are assured that they will have guidance and will be making their own decisions, and that they will not be required to agree to anything they do not want, many try the process. Voluntary participation, or consent to participate, is important because when people are forced into mediation by the courts or by some other persuasive people, conflicts are usually not truly transformed.

An additional principle is self-determination. One of the core principles of mediation is that under the guidance of a mediator, the parties determine the resolution of the conflict. Mediators do not have any authority to impose a decision and must guide the parties in the mediation to make their own decision regarding agreement. It is important for participants to understand this clearly. While the delay can sometimes be frustrating for participants who struggle to make decisions and frustrating for participants who make decisions easily, it is critical that mediators comply with their mediation training and not tell parties what to do or how to resolve their dispute. In this way, the principle of self-determination relates to the principle of neutrality, or impartiality, of the mediator.

Confidentiality is the last tenet. Unlike court involvement, mediation is offered privately behind closed doors, where parties' issues are not aired and discussed before the public. During the opening moments of a mediation session, mediators carefully explain the importance of confidentiality on their part and on the part of the parties. This further encourages the conflicting parties to feel relaxed and to trust the process, knowing that they can struggle through the conflict and mediation process without concern of their words or views being distorted later.

The confidentiality aspect of mediation is so important that typically all those involved in the mediation sign an agreement or consent to mediate. For example, this agreement specifies that notes from the mediation will be destroyed and the mediator cannot be called to testify on behalf of any party, under any circumstances. At the end of many mediations a discussion takes place among the people in the room identifying what can or cannot be shared outside of the mediation room.

The tenets of mediation are critical to the process of successful mediation. In summary, these are: formal mediator training and/or certification in mediation; neutral and impartial behavior on the part of the mediator; voluntary, informed and non-coerced participation by the parties; a self-determined signed agreement between the parties at the end of the mediation; and the assurance of absolute confidentiality that what has transpired in the room will not be shared outside, including that the mediator will not be called to testify in favor or against the parties to the mediation.

## CASES APPROPRIATE FOR MEDIATION

Mediation is a practical way to manage many disputes. The process is flexible and can accommodate a variety of situations, but it is important to recognize when mediation is and is not a suitable intervention. Disputes about tangible issues (such as money, property, behaviour, rights, and licenses) are easier to mediate than disputes based on personal values or beliefs. There are no fixed rules for determining which situations are best for mediation, but there are some important factors to consider. The affirmative answer to the following three questions provide a simple guide to determining the appropriateness of a dispute for mediation:

1. Is there a negotiable issue in dispute, or is the conflict over something else?
2. Will all the people involved commit to meeting together to work toward an agreement?
3. Is this a problem that demands intervention, cannot be ignored, and will not go away?

When the answer to all of these is affirmative, the dispute has the potential to be resolved positively through mediation. It is important to mediate as quickly as possible because the earlier a dispute goes to mediation, the greater the potential for settlement. When disputes are prolonged, the parties tend to become more entrenched in their positions and are less willing to consider another point of view, which is necessary for successful mediation.

In addition to an effective means to resolve disputes, mediation is also an effective means of preventing conflict. It has become more common for a group to proactively work with a mediator to write agreements together in anticipation of future conflicts. As a tool for resolving conflict, mediation has expanded from court-based small claims cases and family court-mandated divorce mediation to the business arena, and beyond. Today mediation is used to resolve a broad spectrum of conflicts in settings as diverse as business, the legal system, the community, and the international setting, as presented in Table 8.1, Settings for Mediation.

## CASES THAT ARE NOT APPROPRIATE FOR MEDIATION

While mediation does offer potential resolution for conflicts that are seemingly too difficult, it is not a panacea. There are parties and issues that are not conducive to mediation, and forcing mediation under these circumstances can exacerbate the conflict and lead to other and greater problems. For example, when one party does not want to participate but is forced to do so, mediation is virtually impossible, which is why court-mandated mediation is often not successful. In disputes that involve pub-

**Table 8.1.   Settings for Mediation**

| Business | Legal System | Community | International |
|---|---|---|---|
| Workplace human resource conflicts | Civil court disputes | Cultural and ethnic issues | Diplomatic conflict |
| Discrimination | Criminal court cases | Neighborhood issues | International conflict |
| Successor issues | Divorce | Domestic issues | Peace accords |
| Labor issues | Custody | School disputes | Resource disputes |
| Contract disputes | Juvenile court issues | Re-integration of offenders into the community | Identity conflicts |
| Workplace complaints | Eviction | Individual Education Plans | Intractable conflicts |

lic record, such as the setting of a legal precedent, or recognizing oral history as a legitimate record, mediation is a poor conflict intervention choice because it is a private and confidential process. These cases need to be resolved in court for several reasons, including the need for public education and documentation of the judicial decision.

Most criminal and domestic violence cases are not appropriate for mediation. Safety of both parties is a paramount concern, and the likelihood of re-victimizing a victim is a critical consideration in determining whether or not to use mediation to transform a conflict. There have been an increasing number of successful victim-offender mediations in recent years, and so victims ought to be provided this opportunity, but for their own safety, must never be forced. One of the reasons why these situations often do not result in effective mediation is because the victim is required to face their offender throughout the process, which can be extremely difficult. Likewise, offenders need to be screened carefully to ensure that they will not re-victimize the victim and to ensure that they are participating voluntarily and motivated by a genuine desire to transform the situation. Mediation is relational, and so when mediation is not helpful for transforming conflict, it is damaging. Mediators are formally trained and expected to be wise and discerning regarding mediation in criminal and domestic violence cases.

There are other situations that are not appropriate for mediation but sometimes these are not immediately recognizable, even for trained mediators. For example, if parties are out for retribution or only want to participate in formal mediation in order to understand the perspective of the other party and manipulate them for preconceived ends, mediation has a reduced likelihood of success. As the actual mediation process moves forward, a mediator may become aware of a situation like this. In

mediations like these, formal training in mediator techniques and strategies is required to complete or end the mediation.

Trained mediators can sometimes determine that cases which might
seem inappropriate at first are actually good candidates for mediation.
While a party with severely diminished capacity is not typically a good
candidate for mediation, with the support of an advocate during the
mediation, the process may be doable. Severely violent cases, especially
those involving incest, rape, and murder are not usually good candidates
for mediation, yet there are now documented successes with some of
these cases. Mediations provide an opportunity for victims to receive
answers, confront the offender, and express the harm inflicted. For offenders it is an opportunity to offer remorse, make amends, and promote
healing for the victim. However, in those circumstances in which mediation is not the appropriate model, a different conflict intervention is required.

## MEDIATION MODELS

The field of mediation is diverse and pluralistic. There is no consensus on
how to depict the practice. Mediation can be best examined from the
perspective of a continuum—directive, transformative, and facilitative.
By definition, the intention of mediation is to empower people to make
their own decisions and resolve their conflicts in a manner that fits with
their lives and experiences. This is true across the continuum. Although
new models of mediation are emerging, the core principles have not
changed and remain valid characteristics in each of the different models
practiced. Where models differ is primarily within the tasks of the mediator and which strategies are sanctioned by that particular model.

On one end of the continuum are directive or evaluative processes.
This model is typically practiced by lawyers who may offer their opinion
about how a judge might rule a dispute, or what might be a viable option
for resolution. On the other end are transformative processes in which
mediation can "foster and support positive human interaction" through
the process of empowerment and recognition.[2] In the middle of the continuum are models which are facilitative in nature. In all models, the
mediator assists parties so they can clarifying their conflict and explore
options for resolution.

## COMMONALITIES

All of the models have characteristics and process in common. In each,
mediators begin with an opening statement outlining what mediation is,
the structures and limits, and the mediator's role. Next, most models ask
the participants to talk about what brought them to the mediation and

what they would like to accomplish. Many models use a caucus phase in which the mediator meets privately and confidentially with parties in turn. Typically there is a negotiation step, although this may differ in how this is accomplished based on the particular model. Finally there is an ending, which may be the crafting of an agreement or if there is no agreement, a discussion about where to go from the point the mediation was stalled. The intensity and longevity of these steps are dependent on the model.

In addition to the tenets and process, all models are built on a framework of respect, trust, curiosity, and reflective listening. All those in the mediation room are to uphold the principle of respect for each other and to recognize each other's conflict as important. Mediators trust and expect the parties to be capable and competent and to know what works best for them individually. Mediators approach the conflict from a position of curiosity and an effort to help parties explore how the conflict came about, how the conflict impacts those involved, and how each party envisions their future after the conflict is transformed. This is all accomplished through active or reflective listening. Nonjudgmental, active listening assures that what parties share is heard and understood and is a very important part of the mediation process for all parties.

## FACILITATIVE MEDIATION

A crucial element to facilitative mediation is the establishment of a safe and private environment. Parties are often uncomfortable sitting across a table from someone they have a dispute with. Mediators attempt to develop instant rapport with the parties while remaining neutral or impartial. The key skills used in this model are active listing and questioning. Active listening helps sort out positions and interests and helps parties hear each other. There is a great deal of paraphrasing and reframing that takes place in the process of working toward the core issues and possible resolutions.

Most mediation centers use the Facilitative or Transformative model. The National Association for Community Mediation and many law schools advocate the Facilitative model. There are five parts to the Facilitative Mediation Model:[3]

1. Open the mediation. This phase sets the stage for what is to come. Introductions are made, expectations are shared, ground rules are created, the process is outlined, roles are discussed, and any necessary paperwork is completed, such as an agreement or consent to mediate.
2. Focus on the past. This second part is typically where parties have an uninterrupted opportunity to share what brought them to the mediation and what they would like to have happen. A discussion

may follow parties' statements if they have questions, suggestions, or additional comments they would like to make. This segment focuses on the harm that has been caused and how parties have been impacted.

3. Focus on the present. The present phase can take place with parties together or with parties in private meetings with the mediator. Participants talk about how things are presently and the associated feelings. This phase may include venting about the situation. When parties are ready to discuss what they need for the relationship and situation to be improved they are ready to move forward and focus on the future.

4. Focus on the future. Focusing on the future can again take place with parties together or in private meetings. But, it's essential for this phase to end with the parties together. Here they share options for resolution, negotiate, and develop a plan.

5. Close the mediation. If there is a resolution agreed upon by the parties, this phase would memorialize that agreement. Often the agreement is written and signed by all parties. The mediator congratulates the parties, reminds them of their accomplishments and the confidentiality of the mediation, and escorts them out.

In Facilitative Mediation, mediators are careful to ask questions rather than telling parties what to do. They avoid making suggestions or providing solutions. Mediators question assumptions, probe for specifics, and demonstrate patience while parties collect their thoughts. One of the roles of the mediator is to encourage people to feel comfortable so that they will talk.

In summary, Facilitative Mediation is the mediation of issues and relationships based on the understanding of the conflict by each party. The mediator's role is to facilitate a conversation between the parties about the conflict, its effects, and possible resolutions. Parties are encouraged to look beyond their positions to create a resolution that meets everyone's interests and that is satisfactory to all involved.

## NARRATIVE MEDIATION

Narrative Mediation is an approach to mediation that is premised on the idea that how we perceive and talk about conflict and how we talk about our reactions to social conflict provide clues to how people want to end conflict. Like other forms of mediation, the practice of narrative mediation is built on a framework of trust, curiosity, respect, and reflective listening. While many of the techniques are similar to other forms of mediation, the Narrative Mediation model has been developed as its own model because it is designed to encourage parties to respond narratively, and to tell stories.

The role of the mediator in Narrative Mediation is ultimately to facilitate a new narrative, relationship, or story between the conflicting parties. The primary purpose of the narrative form of mediation is to hear the story, or narrative of each party, and to find the common ground for reconciliation. The first chapter of this book introduced positions and interests in conflict transformation. Narrative mediation is one way that these are heard, explored, and then transformed. In their book *Narrative Mediation*, Winslade and Monk (2000) explain that people have an established social construct before they enter any conflict. This means that they already have ideas about the world around them that shape the mediation. These deeply held values, interests, and desires, which take place in a social and cultural context, cause people to prioritize certain values and goals over the values and goals that caused the conflict.

Narrative Mediation is developed on the assumption that conflicts are socially constructed as language, discourse, or narrative. The language people use when hearing or telling a narrative plays a central role in constructing who we are or how we engage or behave with others, and focuses on how complex social contexts shape the multiple facets of social conflict. When people tell the story of a conflict during Narrative Mediation, they use words and language they are familiar with to reflect much about their own thoughts. This in turn provides insight for the mediator into how that person experiences and perceives conflicts. The narrative also reveals the values, beliefs, perceptions, interpretations, and understandings of conflict. In this way, narratives about conflict highlight social constructs but also reveal potential transformation through the commonalities revealed through the narratives.

In the way that narratives can provide opportunities to resolve conflict, how people talk about social conflict can also limit opportunities for resolution, and so the mediator must work skillfully to convert the limitations into opportunities. This provides a way of understanding the biases that people hold about conflict or one conflict in particular, which in turn can provide alternative approaches or solutions to the conflict. This is particularly useful for mediation. At the end of the process, the agreement becomes the basis for a different relationship among the parties.

Strategic questions from the mediator are critical to Narrative Mediation. Typically these can be categorized as open-ended questions, closed questions, leading questions, and probing questions. Open-ended questions are particularly important for mediation and for Narrative Mediation in particular. An example of an open-ended question is "Please tell us your story." Closed questions, which can be answered in a word or a phrase, are also important to the process because they provide a tool for the mediator to return parties to the topic or issue at hand. For example, "How long have you worked there?" would be a closed question which focuses a participant who is talking off topic. Leading questions are another tool for mediators to use. Through the use of leading questions, the mediator states what is true or obvious in order to lead the participant toward resolving the dispute. Leading questions are purposeful; for example, "You do want to transform relationships at work, don't you?" The fourth type, probing questions, involve some form of "Why?" or "Please tell us more." The probing question asks for more information. Learning to develop strategic questions and posing them is an important skill for mediators.

In practical terms, there are three phases of Narrative Mediation. These are unique to Narrative Mediation and are not usually part of the other, more linear models:

1. Engagement. This is the storytelling phase. During this phase, the mediator listens to the version of the conflict or story of each party while listening for embedded needs and interests, and for how the conflict has affected each party, according to their story. During this phase, the mediator also probes for earlier attempts at resolution that are perhaps not offered in the story.
2. Deconstruction. During this phase, the mediator stresses that the conflict or the dispute is the problem and that together, the people must control it. Neither of the parties are the problem. As a means of doing so, the mediator challenges assumptions the parties make about each other, about themselves, and about the conflict, according to their narratives.
3. Construction. The construction phase assumes that cooperation and transformation already exist, but must be uncovered during the mediation. This is achieved through questions. The role of the mediator is to uncover, support, and extend the new narrative/story/relationship, between the parties.

In summary, Narrative Mediation is the mediation of a conflict story based on the selected story materials of each party. The mediator's role is primarily to encourage talking in the form of a narration or story. Parties are encouraged to deconstruct, or take apart, the conflict narrative and construct, or create, a new description in which cooperation and conflict transformation are the central themes of the story they can tell together.

## TRANSFORMATIVE MEDIATION

Over the last decade, the transformative approach to mediation has increased in popularity. Multiple mediation centers that were founded on the Facilitative Model have shifted to the Transformative Model. During the processes of Transformative Mediation, parties have more control over the process and outcome than they do in the other models of mediation.

Transformative Mediation was initially introduced in Bush and Folger's 1995 book, *The Promise of Mediation*. The model is built on the assumption that conflict is a crisis in human interaction. Mediation has the potential to do much more than merely resolve a particular contest; it can and does support positive human interaction and transforming relationships between conflicting parties.

The foundation of Transformative Mediation is to move people from a position of weakness to strength, and change the quality of conflict interactions from self-absorption to clarity and openness. Mediators work to encourage and support empowerment and recognition. "[E]mpowerment means the restoration to individuals of a sense of their value and strength and their own capacity to make decisions and handle life's problems. Recognition means the evocation in individuals of acknowledgment, understanding, or empathy for the situation and the views of the other."[4] The mediator's responsibility is to refrain from guiding the conversation and instead follow it, capturing opportunities for empowerment and recognition. They do this through restatement or paraphrasing.

A difference between Facilitative and Transformative Mediation is the use of reframing. A Transformative Mediator does not soften or reframe a negative or derogatory statement made by one or more the parties into a more positive, future oriented statement as they do in Facilitative Mediation. Transformative Mediation is more concerned with the quality of the interaction than a resulting agreement. After multiple incidences of violence across the country at a number of different stations, the US Postal Service adopted the Transformative Mediation model. The REDRESS program has served to mediate disputes, especially discrimination, among postal employees before the conflicts escalate and lead to violence.

In summary, Transformative Mediation is focused on how people interact in the conflict so that parties engage their personal strengths and improve the relationship between them. The mediator's role is primarily to capture and nurture opportunities for such empowerment and recognition.

## CO-MEDIATION

All mediation models may be conducted with one or more mediators. This increases the potential for understanding and expands the possibilities for resolution. Some mediators find co-mediation difficult to practice. It does require an ability to be self-aware and share the workload. Some mediators do not like to share control of the process. For a successful co-mediation, mediators need to look like partners, be in-tune to cues, and supplement each other's practice. Parties benefit from different styles, perspectives, and questions. Mediators benefit from the ability to periodically sit back, observe, and reflect. Most parties prefer co-mediation because it potentially doubles their chances of being understood.

There are times that co-mediation cannot be practiced due to logistical concerns. For example, private mediators have to coordinate with someone, maybe someone they are not familiar with, and have to share the remuneration. In government or non-profit agencies, budgets often prohibit co-mediation. However, in school peer mediation programs, mediators always work in pairs.

PEER MEDIATION

Peer mediation programs are a common introduction to the mediation process. Qualified organizations, such as the San Francisco Community Boards,[5] have designed peer mediation programs for public adoption that can be offered in public schools at all grade levels. Founded in 1976, it is the oldest public mediation center in the United States. A typical peer mediation program for an elementary or secondary school might follow steps similar to these for implementation:

1. Meet with school administration to describe and receive approval for a program.
2. Meet with school personnel to describe the program, offer curriculum materials, and solicit people to operate the program.
3. Train personnel in conflict resolution and peer mediation, according to a trusted and qualified authority.
4. Meet with students to describe the program and solicit peer mediators.
5. Train selected students to mediate.
6. Meet with peer mediators and faculty/staff regularly to support the program.

Institutionalized programming can ensure the viability and survival of peer mediation. Selecting faculty, staff, and students who want to participate is preferable to assigning those who would prefer not to be involved.

The peer mediation process is similar to the adult process, although simplified. In elementary school, mediators typically wear identifying sashes and work in pairs on the playground to intervene in conflicts they see taking place. Peer mediators ask if there is a problem and if the students would like help resolving it. They offer ground rules then ask to hear each person's story. Mediators repeat the story using active listening skills and ask how each student feels about the conflict. Next, mediators help the students brainstorm possible solutions to the problem. From the generated choices, the mediators encourage the students to select something that will work for them. They conclude the process with a restatement of the resolution and congratulations.

In secondary school, the mediation process looks much more like the adult facilitative process described previously. While students do not work on the playground they do work in pairs and are available to mediate based on the particular school's design and schedule. Students can search out mediators or affiliated faculty/staff or they can be referred by other school personnel.

In both elementary and secondary schools, mediation programs improve students' communication skills and train them in leadership, decision-making, and anger management skills. Other benefits to using a Peer Mediation Program include:

- The ability to prevent low-level conflicts from escalating.
- The provision of a safe environment for young people to solve their problems.
- The ability to improve communication between students and school personnel.
- The promotion of citizenship qualities.
- The opportunities to learn about consequences.
- The opportunities for students to talk with someone their own age, rather than only authority figures.
- The development of practical conflict resolution skills for a multicultural and diverse world.[6]

Peer Mediation programs result in decreased incidents and suspensions in schools and most mediations result in agreements. In these ways, peer mediation programs can benefit and broaden the learning potential of students in our schools.

## CONFLICT COACHING

Mediation is a highly successful model for conflict transformation. But, when all parties cannot or do not get to the mediation session, mediators may use conflict coaching, a model that has proved helpful and is gaining favor. With this model, someone in conflict can be aided to work through their issues without the other party being present. An opportunity presents itself whenever a person learns of conflict coaching and selects to participate, one party wants to mediate but the other party refuses, or a mediation was scheduled and one participant did not show up for a scheduled mediation.

Conflict coaching is similar to mediation although one-sided. The mediator meets with the party. They conduct a brief opening, explaining confidentiality and their role, then the mediator asks the person to share what circumstances persuaded them to seek mediation. The mediator helps the party explore their situation and determine what they would like to have happen at the session and what they feel they need to have happen. Once the problem has been considered, the mediator assists the party in discussing options for resolution. Alternatives can be brainstormed and evaluated. The mediator can assist by role-playing possible interactions. By the conclusion of the session, with the help of the coach, the party will have selected a plan for addressing their issues, and developed a back-up plan should the first plan be unsuccessful. A follow-up session can also be scheduled if the party would like to check back in to either celebrate their success or rethink the issue.

An advantage of conflict coaching is its nonthreatening nature. It is just the person with the problem and a coach talking in private. The session is kept confidential and the party maintains their self-determination. Conflict coaching is an effective way to increase a party's conflict skills and confidence, while addressing an issue plaguing them.

## INTERNATIONAL MEDIATION[7]

In the arena of international conflict, mediation is an appropriate and effective conflict resolution tool. It is employed by government or nongovernment actors external to the conflict to bring opposing and sometimes obstinate political elites to the negotiation table. Unlike interpersonal mediators, international mediators have their own interests and outcomes, and are not expected to be neutral.

Conflict resolution processes and techniques that include mediation are often perceived as building negative peace (the absence of war) rather than building positive peace (social justice).[8] Although mediation is often an important way to contain and manage conflict, stop wars and prevent the further loss of life and bloodshed, international mediation, as a conflict transformation instrument, does not build equitable peace unless it is partnered with other peacebuilding processes that can transform relationships and structures for sustained peace.

Also important to international mediation practice is the recognition of Indigenous processes of mediation, which have been an integral part of traditional restorative processes for many years.[9] Traditional mediation approaches have evolved from their own cultural contexts and because of this internal strength must be front-and-center in peacemaking and peacebuilding processes with or within these communities.[10] Many of the aspects of mediation explained earlier in this chapter have their origins in Indigenous practices and teachings from around the world.

To better understand the role and impact of international mediation, Marieke Kleiboer[11] has identified four conceptual frames or models that identify motivation and facilitate effective mediation in international disputes. These models also serve as useful conceptual lenses to understand the long-term consequences of mediation.[12] The four models for understanding the rather complicated world of international mediation are these:

- Power-brokerage Model
- Problem-solving Model
- Domination Model
- Humanist Restructuring Relationships Model

The power brokerage model assumes that states are rational unitary actors operating in an anarchic global arena in which the balance of power alone prevents war.[13] The power brokerage model acknowledges the grave realities of power politics and the role of state political power on the world stage, and thereby encourages conflict intervention. In the context of power brokering, states use mediation to secure their own national interests and to provide stability in the global system. Since it is a model that recognizes the brokering of power, disputing parties usually agree and are motivated to mediation to save face, seek favorable settlements, and improve relations. Power brokerage mediation enhances inter-state relationships while settling disputes and encouraging states to pursue their national interests.

The problem-solving model has similarities to interpersonal problem-solving models. Problem-solving improves communications between state leaders and encourages them to analyze conflict, to change perceptions of the other, and to manage conflict. The role of the mediator is to explore each dispute individually to fully grasp the underlying dynamics in order to facilitate a sustainable agreement among the leaders.[14]

The domination model allows core states to resolve both manifest and latent conflicts through mediation but dependent core-periphery relationships are not altered. In this model, there is no advocacy for a New International Economic Order (NIEO).[15] The primary purpose of mediation according to the domination model is to settle manifest conflicts in peripheral states while ignoring the deeper structural roots of global inequalities between core and peripheral states, and within core states.

The third model, the humanist restructuring relationships model, engages a mediator to ensure several processes and goals, including the empowerment of states and ethnic groups to pursue their basic human needs. The mediator role is one of analysis of the deep underlying roots of conflicts while leading a fair process focused on long-term change. The mediators create a balanced process that is empowering, fair, and respectful for all of the parties. In this way, the mediators ensure that all parties influence procedures and decisions together.[16]

Mediation is often voluntary and nonbinding, but it is embraced at the international level to pursue conflict transformation. Notably, mediation, like all conflict resolution strategies, is contingent on several factors. The escalation or de-escalation nature of the conflict, the parties involved in the conflict and their relationship to each other, and the tangible and intangible issues involved greatly influence and shape the prospects for successful and effective international mediation.

With regard to international mediation, Byrne encourages peacebuilders to "bear in mind that mediation efforts form an integral part of a much needed, multilevel, multi-modal, and multi-track coordinated and complementary integrated and holistic peacebuilding system."[17] Mediation, he reminds us, is a process that crosses levels while it simultaneously and sequentially engages participants and actors in activities that deal with both tangible and intangible issues.

## CONCLUSION

This chapter surveyed Directive, Facilitative, Narrative, Transformative and International mediation. To summarize these, directive mediation expands the role of the mediator to include offering judgments about resolution and potential outcomes. The Facilitative Model restricts the mediator role to helping parties discuss their conflict and negotiate resolution. During Narrative Mediation, there are three phases, and the mediator uses four types of questions to guide the parties through the conflict into a new narrative of the relationship between them. Transformative Mediation seeks to use empowerment and recognition for parties to gain strength and clarity to transform their relationship. Co-mediation can be used with any model and international mediation does not require mediator neutrality. Mediation is an immediate, low-cost, and effective means of conflict transformation at all levels of conflict.

## QUESTIONS

1. What are the basic principles of the models of mediation, and what are the three determining questions?
2. Think about conflicts you have been involved in that would have benefitted from mediation. What makes these conflicts suitable for mediation as the intervention?
3. Role-play a mediation between a youth and their parent. Designate people to be the mediator or co-mediators. The parent is concerned about the youth abiding by house rules, respecting their parents, and getting good grades in school. The youth is concerned about their parents running their life, not trusting them, and restricting their activity with peers. Evaluate your experience:

      a. What about this process was difficult and easy for you?

    b. What did the mediator(s) do that worked or did not work for you?

    c. Are you satisfied with the outcome?

4. Research a current world conflict. Apply the four models of mediation and determine which, if any, might be the most effective way to end the fighting.

## NOTES

1. American Arbitration Association, American Bar Association, Association for Conflict Resolution, "The Model Standards of Conduct for Mediators." This document can be found at http://www.americanbar.org/content/dam/aba/migrated/2011_build/dispute_resolution/model_standards_conduct_april2007.authcheckdam.pdf.

2. Robert A. Baruch Bush and Joseph P. Folger, *The Promise of Mediation: The Transformative Approach to Conflict* (San Francisco, CA, 2005), 1.

3. William C. Warters, *Mediation in the Campus Community: Designing and Managing Effective Programs* (San Francisco, CA: Jossey-Bass, 1999).

4. Baruch Bush and Folger, The Promise of Mediation: The Transformative Approach to Conflict (San Francisco, CA: Jossey-Bass), 22.

5. See the comprehensive website *Community Boards: Building Community Through Conflict Resolution,* available at http://communityboards.org.

6. "Peer Mediation Programs: Facts and Statistics," https://sites.google.com/site/peerMediationprograms/home/facts-and-statistics.

7. The authors gratefully acknowledge Dr. Sean Byrne for his guidance and contributions for this section. Readers are encouraged to consult his full chapter, "International Mediation: Observation and Reflections" in Alexia Georgakopoulos (Editor) *The Handbook of Mediation: Theory, Research and Practice,* (Routledge, NY: forthcoming 2016).

8. David Barash and Charles Webel, *Peace and Conflict Studies* (Thousand Oaks, CA: Sage, 2002).

9. Brian Rice, "Relationships with Humans and Non-Humans Species and How They Apply toward Peace-Building and Leadership in Indigenous Societies." In Thomas Maytók, Jessica Senehi and Sean Byrne (Editors.) *Critical Issues in Peace and Conflict Studies: Theory, Practice, and Pedagogy,* Lanham: Lexington, 2011: 199–277.

10. Byrne, 2016: 11.

11. See Marieke Kleiboer, *The Multiple Realities of International Mediation* (Boulder: Lynne Rienner, 1998).

12. Byrne, 2016: 4.

13. Kleiboer, 1998: 42.

14. Ibid., 57.

15. Ibid., 64.

16. Kreisberg, 416.

17. Byrne, 2016: 11.

# NINE

## Multi-Door Courthouse

### LEARNING OUTCOMES

- To learn how Alternative Dispute Resolution (ADR) options contribute to the conflict transformation practices
- To understand that multi-door courthouse options do not offer as much control in decision making to parties as other conflict transformation practices
- To recognize the key characteristics of ADR options, including self-help centers, fact-finding, arbitration, neutral evaluation, collaborative practices, settlement conference, and short trials

### OVERVIEW

The multi-door courthouse concept is the collective recognition of Alternative Dispute Resolution (ADR) practices. Ideally, when someone has a conflict or dispute, they have access to what is referred to as the multi-door courthouse, which means there are multiple alternatives for resolution. The traditional courthouse offers the public only one door for resolving disputes: the litigation process. Unlike most PACS practices, which are collaborative and include the disputing parties, the interventions outlined below are often restricted to practice by attorneys, judges, and members of the legal profession, so disputing parties have less influence in the outcome of their conflicts.

## INTRODUCTION

The concept of the multi-door courthouse was first suggested in 1976 by Harvard Law Professor Frank E. A. Sander at the Conference on the Causes of Popular Dissatisfaction with the Administration of Justice (commonly referred to as the Pound Conference). His idea was that disputants be screened and offered an alternative to litigation. Litigation is an action brought to court to enforce a particular right or to resolve a particular conflict. Since 1976, many jurisdictions around the world have established a multi-door courthouse so that citizens in dispute have input into the method used to resolve their dispute. The goal is to offer parties different paths to dispute settlement that avoid the stress and expenses inherent in litigation. At the same time, courts face serious backlogs which result in delays of months or years for parties to have cases heard by a judge or a jury. These alternative methods are quicker and less expensive to clients and courts than litigation.

The multi-door courthouse uses Alternative Dispute Resolution (ADR) processes. ADR (alled appropriate dispute resolution by some) is a term used to describe a variety of different methods of resolving legal disputes without going to court. Jurisdictions may vary with regards to which ADR options are offered. Options may include a self-help center, fact-finding, arbitration (binding and nonbinding), case evaluation, and short trial.

The goal of ADR options is to obtain a determination regarding the dispute without requiring a judge or jury. In some options, court personnel can be appointed to assist the parties in selecting a process and contacting appropriate assistance. In other areas, rosters or lists of neutral facilitators are given to the parties to select from. A neutral is an individual who facilitates an ADR process in an impartial manner in an effort to settle a dispute. They do not act as an advocate or attorney for either party. Most ADR proceedings are less formally structured, which is intended to allow parties to feel more comfortable presenting their case. In the following section, seven ADR options are presented.

## SELF-HELP CENTERS

Self-help centers are being implemented around the United States in both family courts and justice courts. Most self-help centers have a mission to increase informed access to the legal system by providing education, information, legal forms, community referrals (legal and non-legal), and other support services for individuals who wish to represent themselves rather than have an attorney. In these centers, assistance is usually available to walk-in customers.

People staffing these centers are required to be neutral. Neutral means that they assist with the identification and completion of legal forms, but are not allowed to give legal advice or opinions about what parties should do. They cannot tell someone if they should file a case with the court, how a judge might rule, or how to fill out the paperwork. They cannot recommend attorneys. They may provide information or training on court rules and procedure. Typically a website is available with court related topics and information about how to resolve issues through the court or other ADR options. Many centers offer a regularly scheduled ask-an-attorney program. Attorneys are available for brief individual consultation or group questions. Many people benefit from this opportunity to discuss their case or to ask questions of someone in the legal profession before deciding how to proceed to resolve their issues.

## FACT-FINDING

Fact-finding is a third-party conflict intervention that is particularly effective when parties or their attorneys encounter a difficult decision due to incomplete or contradictory information. This can be any kind of decision, by any disputing parties, that requires factual clarification before proceeding. Fact-finding is usually initiated by a written agreement between disputing parties and an official neutral fact-finder or team of fact-finders as recommended by the American Arbitration Association. The final appointment is made either by the parties, or if they choose, by the organization. Since a difficult decision with conflicting information is invloved, it is important that the fact-finder be neutral and have the skills and expertise required to deal with difficult issues of fact. A final report is submitted to the parties, who can then usually make the decision.

When assigned teams investigate to find facts of a case, it is called joint fact-finding. These teams may be representatives from the groups in conflict or disinterested experts. In both cases, the teams are selected by the parties that are seeking to clarify the facts that will inform their pending decision. The team is given the task of working together to research, collect, discuss, and debate facts. This kind of forum results in interaction and communication that would probably not occur under other circumstances. This can be helpful in resolving a factual dispute. It is a shift from the traditional adversarial discovery process.

Information and resources are shared. This is contrary to withholding information, which often happens when a case moves to litigation. Team members and adversaries gain access to each other's point of view and expertise. The result is a more objective, fair, and balanced inquiry process. In addition, there is the potential benefit of discovering unrecognized opportunities for balancing competing interests. If still not able to resolve the case, parties can often narrow issues down and then send the case to a neutral to make a decision.

Neutral fact-finding is similar to joint fact-finding except that a neutral is used to make active inquiries instead of selected teams. The fact-finder may also be authorized to provide a recommendation for possible resolution. The results of this process can significantly impact any additional process used. The fact-finder can provide actual data or numbers to inform a negotiation between disputing parties.

## ARBITRATION

Arbitration has characteristics of mediation as well as litigation. It has long been used in the labor field to provide expedient resolution of disputes at a lower cost. Fundamentally, arbitration is much like a trial, in that the neutral, called an arbitrator, has been given the authority to make a decision for the parties. Parties can call witnesses, present evidence, and argue the merits of their case to a neutral decision maker. In some jurisdictions, parties may select this method of dispute resolution. In others, depending on the amount of the claim, disputants may be court ordered to participate in arbitration.

An arbitrator may be an individual or a panel (a group of two to three) acting as a neutral. The arbitrator may be an attorney, a judge, or someone who has been formally trained in the expertise of neutrality, or a combination of all three. Sometimes these people are called a neutral.

Arbitration typically requires more time than mediation but less time than court. The value of arbitration is the decreased time and expense involved. Parties can decide whether the outcome is to be binding or final, or if it will be advisory only. In a nonbinding case, parties can proceed to court whereas with a binding outcome, parties have agreed to accept the arbitrator's decision.

In addition to binding and nonbinding arbitration, there are other forms: med-arb and final offer arbitration. The most widely recognized is med-arb, which is a combination of mediation and arbitration. The process begins as mediation. If the parties they are not able to resolve the issues with the help of the mediator despite their best efforts, then the process shifts to arbitration. The mediator changes roles during the process and makes a decision for the parties as an arbitrator. An advantage of med-arb is that the arbitrator is exposed to parties' issues in more depth than a typical arbitrator.

During the mediation portion, the perspectives of each party are explored in order to inform the decision soon to be made by the arbitrator. It is also expedient; it does not require time to schedule sessions or to find another neutral to assist the parties. Using the dual process assures the case is settled. A disadvantage of the med-arb process is a lack of assurance that the arbitrator will be impartial since they have already heard the case as a mediation and have been exposed to more information than they would be in a typical arbitration. It is also extremely difficult to shift between the competing roles of mediator and arbitrator.

Final offer or baseball arbitration is another variation. Final offer arbitration, or baseball arbitration, is most helpful when there are only money issues to be determined. It is sometimes called baseball arbitration because the process is similar to a pitching exercise in baseball: one party submits a demand and the other party makes a counter offer. Both sides try to convince the arbitrator of the merits of their case and the reasonableness of their offer. The arbitrator may only select one offer or the other. Arbitration contributes to dispute resolution as an alternative to litigation.

## CASE EVALUATION

Case evaluation as ADR originates with an individual's attorney. An individual consults with a lawyer and the lawyer explains the likely result if the case was taken to court. In recent years, there has been a movement to incorporate independent outside parties such as a retired judge or attorney panel to provide the evaluation more objectivity. In some jurisdictions, parties must agree on the neutral evaluator to be used. In others, this neutral evaluation has become part of the litigation process. The responsibility of the neutral or evaluation panel is to review a case and provide an informed opinion as to how a judge might rule. The outcome gives participants a better appreciation of the strengths and weaknesses of their case and can enable them to return to negotiation.

Early neutral evaluation, is similar to case evaluation. The intent is to provide insight into the merits of a case and the likelihood that it will succeed in court. The principle of early neutral evaluation is based in a recognition that faster conflict resolution is desirable to all parties. Early neutral evaluation can be really helpful if both parties' attorneys are providing them with significantly different projected outcomes. In other words, attorneys for both sides are telling their clients that their case is strong and the outcome is likely to be in their favor. These evaluations contribute importantly to the process by preventing lawsuits that lack substance from going to court. This is a benefit for the parties and the overburdened legal system.

## COLLABORATIVE PRACTICES

Collaborative practices empower participants to resolve legal disputes without judges, magistrates, or court personnel making the decisions for them. Specially trained collaborative lawyers work with other experts such as mental health professionals, financial professionals, family coun-selors, or social workers to educate, support, and guide parties in reach-ing balanced, respectful, and lasting agreements. This method strives to remove the "win-lose" mentality so often found in litigated cases.

Collaborative processes are most effective for divorce cases. In a safe and dignified environment, often over a series of group sessions, the parties discuss and reach agreement on issues such as child custody and visitation, asset division, and spousal support. The process is intended to reduce the conflict and minimize its impact on the parties, their children, and their lives.

## SETTLEMENT CONFERENCE

A settlement conference is an ADR that may be mandatory or it may be selected by the parties in a dispute. Parties and their attorneys meet prior to a trial with a judge, who might be a selected neutral, commissioner, or magistrate, to determine if the matter can be settled. At the conference, each side makes offers. The judge makes observations on the validity and fairness of offers. While the judge has no official power to make parties settle, they can strongly encourage resolution through their evaluation of the parties' positions and indicate how another judge might be likely to rule during a trial. A conference is often conducted like an evaluative mediation, but is different from mediation in that conferences usually have lower participation by the parties and less consideration of non-legal interests. Like processes previously discussed, the settlement con-ference process is intended to resolve conflict outside of the traditional litigation process and to reduce the inherent adversarial nature of resolv-ing conflict.

## SHORT TRIAL

A short trial (also called a short cause trial) is exactly what it sounds like. As ADR, it is designed to fast track a case through the system toward a quick settlement. Whereas some hearings can take days and even weeks, a short trial is time limited. As well, the time for the requested award to be determined is limited.

A short trial may run from two to six hours for the presentation of the case, with a half hour for jury selection. In Nevada, each side has just fifteen minutes to question and select a jury or panel of four to eight members. This is followed by three hours for each side to present open-ing and closing statements as well as call, question, and cross examine witnesses. The jury retires to deliberate when both sides have completed their presentations. While jury time is not usually limited, most cases are completed within the day. The short trial is presided over by a judge selected from a panel. The judge oversees the process, instructs the jury, administers oaths, responds to points of order, and monitors the time.

A recent case that provides a typical example of a short trial involved an insurance agency and a family who was in a car accident. The mother and daughter were in their car and another driver collided with their vehicle. They were injured and spent several months seeing a chiropractor. Their assumption was that the insurance company would cover the medical bills. But, it did not and so they had a problem. They engaged the short trial process to be reimbursed for the cost. The insurance company claimed the family had cancelled part of their insurance before the accident in order to reduce their insurance costs.

Had this case gone to a traditional court, it would have been delayed considerably and been more adversarial. As it was, the discussion and presentations were made in a conciliatory manner. Information was shared on both sides and the decision then went to the jury. They deliberated for less than an hour and returned to share their decision with the parties. Everyone was thanked for their participation and the short trial concluded. The total time involved was eight hours. While parties had less input than they would with other processes, the short trial still afforded them an opportunity to resolve the conflict in less time, with less cost, and without the typical adversarial process of litigation.

## LITIGATION

Litigation remains an option at all times for disputing parties. The choice is never relinquished by using one of the other doors of the courthouse. Litigation means that disputes are settled in court. All parties must agree to litigation as the dispute resolution process and meet guidelines for specific processes. Often the guidelines are simple and limit only the amount of money in question. Courts recognize that the use of ADR processes for reaching settlement may be faster, more satisfying, and more likely to be successful for disputing parties than actual litigation.

## SUMMARY

Alternative Dispute Resolution (ADR) options are intended to resolve legal disputes outside of the court system. Providing different options allows parties to choose a route to dispute resolution that works best for them. Options vary with regard to the extent to which parties have a say in the final decision, according to the ADR forms. Though offerings vary across jurisdictions, ADR is increasingly encouraged by court systems and used by disputing parties because they are less expensive, tend to be resolved relatively quickly, are less stressful on individuals, and reduce strain on relationships.

## QUESTIONS

1. Most court hearings are open to the public. Sit in on a local hearing and discuss your thoughts in a journal. What were parties saying they wanted? What were their interests? Would a more transformative process have worked better?
2. Describe the advantages of arbitration and why it is a popular form of ADR for labour relations.
3. Compare what you learned in this chapter to portrayals of dispute resolution in popular television courthouse dramas or films and highlight any differences.
4. Locate a PACS journal article on the concept of ADR. Discuss the findings in a short reflection paper.

# TEN

## Storytelling as Peacebuilding

LEARNING OUTCOMES

- To understand the origins of storytelling
- To understand the contributions of storytelling as a primary peace-building instrument for peace and conflict praxis.
- To learn about storytelling festivals
- To learn about oral tradition, allegories, myths, and Truth and Reconciliation Commissions as conflict transformation

OVERVIEW

Stories engage and captivate the imagination and play an important role in conflict transformation, as this chapter explains. Through the telling of stories we learn about life, our history, other cultures, and even find belonging. Many kinds of stories are told but those studying peace and conflict are particularly interested in stories that tell about conflict and its transformation. In turn, our understanding of how people make sense of the conflicts they encounter during their lives is expanded. Storytelling is a practice that is has effected social change for as many generations, but is now advancing peacebuilding on the world stage.

INTRODUCTION

People like to talk with one another about their experiences, their adventures, their challenges, and their triumphs. The practice of telling stories is practiced as families and friends gather around the dining table, the campfire, or collect in the local coffee shop. Stories are also told by elders to youth, and by professional storytellers to large and small audiences. Storytelling encodes the culture of a community in its language and in its contents as people listen and learn about shared understandings of identity, of power, of history, of values, and of hopes for the future.[1] Storytelling is a tradition as old as the human story, and is an important means of cultural production.[2] Storytelling is a subtype of a larger oral category recognized as "narrative," and is the focus of this chapter because of the strength and distinction it brings to the study and advancement of Peace and Conflict Studies (PACS) globally. More than general narrative, stories unite us, invite us, and bind us together at local, national, regional, and global levels.

In the movie *Saving Mr. Banks*,[3] Walt Disney states "George Banks and all he stands for will be saved. Maybe not in life, but in imagination. Because that's what we storytellers do. We restore order with imagination. We instill hope again and again and again." This thread of hope connects storytelling to peacebuilding and to PACS. Through stories, we are able to understand how people make meaning of conflict, and how they envision peace. It is one of the critical tools of community engaged research, and of Indigenous culture.

The power of stories has long been recognized in societies with oral traditions, but for those societies that have relied heavily on the written traditions of bureaucratic organization, recognition has been slower. Storytelling is the way that we entertain one another, but it is also often how we instruct others or make sense of our own experiences. For much of the world's history, stories have been converted into written history from the perspective of one party, but not the other. In the world of organizational change for example, storytelling is increasingly being recognized as an important way to manage knowledge, to understand resistance to change, and to understand what has worked well.[4]

While storytelling is something we may all be familiar with, the recognition of its power to heal and transform has been pioneered in PACS through the work of Dr. Jessica Senehi.[5] Storytelling is explored as peacebuilding in the traditions of oral history, allegories, and myths. The growing paradigm of constructive storytelling, and the common evaluations of storytelling as the heart of peacebuilding are explained. The global trend toward formal storytelling festivals, the value of Truth and Reconciliation Commissions, and the Canadian Indian Residential School Legacy Truth and Reconciliation Commission, are examples and models of storytelling for peace.

## WHAT IS STORYTELLING?

The written word is an important part of western cultures, which are built upon the rule of law. As a result, the written word has been the dominant form of record keeping and until recently, oral societies have been considered to be peoples without history. The study of storytelling has helped us to understand that this could not be further from the truth. Both oral and written methods have their own strengths and meanings for the context and society in which it is dominant. Rather than having no historical record, research has learned that oral societies record and document their histories not just with the spoken word, but also often include dancing and drumming. Although most oral societies have now adopted the written word as a tool for documentation, expression and communication, many still greatly value the oral transmission of knowledge as an intrinsic aspect of their cultures and societies.[6]

Despite the familiarity of most people with the concept of telling stories, defining storytelling is more challenging. There are a number of appropriate descriptions emerging in the peace and conflict literature. There is a general consensus that storytelling is an interaction of words and activity between a storyteller and at least one other person as audience. Ryan[7] has described storytelling simply as the art of telling a story. In the world of peace and conflict, storytelling is also a powerful communication that increases understanding, knowledge, and builds relationships. This includes all forms of shared oral or signed narrative, whatever the circumstances of the telling. Storytelling, deep storytelling, in which one's own story is listened to and heard, has also been described in as the "deeply affective process of locating, articulating and communicating personal stories."[8]

Storytelling provides tellers with both agency and voice, which is especially important for people who may have been silenced for years at the individual or the community levels. Importantly, no one can argue against another's personal story. Flaherty has stated that "a story cannot be contested when it is 'my' story, 'my' experience. Nothing but honesty and openness is required in this offering and nothing but openness is required in the receiving."[9] Senehi[10] observes that as a connector and builder, storytelling is easily accessible and inclusive; stories require no special equipment or training, and can be understood by people of all ages, social strata, and cultures.

In its narrative form, storytelling is rapidly gaining popularity as a research method and an important peacebuilding methodology. However, there are other reasons for the engagement of storytelling in peace and conflict research. Experiences are shared, but research is finding that for people who have endured trauma and violence, storytelling is healing for the teller. This is a way for us to understand how people have experienced conflict, which provides potential for the design and implementation of meaningful interventions. Storytelling is more than a method; it is a means of building peace for individuals and for groups.

Increasingly, narrative methods like storytelling are found in research literature and recognized as a way to construct knowledge and conduct research. Storytelling provides understanding into the ways people live with their losses and feelings and help people to understand one another. The telling of these stories in turn can have tremendous practical implications to promote peacebuilding and social justice, and for research because in many ways, research is storytelling and forms the basis of alternative ways of doing things.

Through stories, people communicate and express how they make sense of their lives and their experiences. They also express how they see their past, what they are doing in the present, and how they think about the future. Stories connect people with their lives and with the lives of other people. Senehi et al. maintain that in the story is an "integrity of self and a vision to our lives and our work . . . to recognize the ways in which we have been resilient and strong can be a move toward de-colonization, de-silencing, self-respect, dignity, a sense of truth and justice, and a de-atomization of our lives and our aims."[11] In this interpretation of storytelling, one shares one's personal experiences. But storytelling is much more than just the sharing of experiences:

> . . . stories are not discrete objects transferred uncritically from person to person. They are selected, framed, and constructed by individuals in a particular context and with particular considerations. . . . The narratives are interpretive and often unverifiable, but they also reference actual events, for example, wars, social conflicts, and geographic relocations that have affected people's lives. While interpretive, these narratives reveal how people make sense of their experiences, history, and identity.

By being invited to tell their stories, especially for peacebuilding work, people can make sense of their lives, perceptions, and experiences, both in the past and in the future.

Stories complement written histories, which is relevant for the transformation of identity conflicts. Stories can provide valuable material to supplement written records and can assist researchers to identify aspects of the research area that were not apparent in written sources—like motivations, relationships, the construction of cultural meaning. Storytelling allows for study of the recent past through the perceptions of participants with firsthand experience. Storytelling is a powerful way of understanding how people experience identity conflict because it allows people to tell and hear personal stories.

Stories can also provide seeds of hope, make sense of what people have been feeling, and generate an avenue for change or for conflict transformation. Seeing that people do not easily or spontaneously open up about their past pains or traumas, storytelling provides opportunities for people to express their experiences and make sense or work through them. In this way, storytelling in its broadest form encourages and facilitates conflict transformation.

## FOUR FORMS OF STORYTELLING AS CONFLICT
## TRANSFORMATION

There are many stories and many styles of stories, but four particularly related to conflict transformation are explained here: oral tradition (also called oral history in many societies), allegories, myths, and narrative. Language is possibly the most complex symbolic system of any culture and encodes the way that people see the world. In turn, language gives life to stories, which are interpretation of real events.[12] Each have their own effect on the peacebuilding process for those that tell and hear the stories.

## ORAL TRADITION

One very common and well known type of storytelling is the oral tradition, or oral history, which despite its title is much more than the recounting of historical events. Oral traditions are more than genealogies or entertainment; they are stories that emphasize details and thereby transfer knowledge about circumstances, battles, migrations, and other significant events and people across the generations. These stories are usually transferred verbatim from one storyteller generation to the next and are highly reliable sources for understanding the traditions and histories of people groups.

For example, in ancient societies, especially Indigenous societies around the globe, the values, histories, and main markers of culture have been and are communicated through stories. These are oral traditions that are often kept by elders[13] and are carefully guarded and repeated from one generation to another through many generations. Oral traditions are found among the story keepers of Jewish traditions, Chinese traditions, Native American traditions, and Canadian Indigenous (Aboriginal) traditions, for example. The keepers are usually recognized in the community as Elders, senior members of society whose primary responsibility in the community is the protection and transmission of history and values through the oral stories. In these societies, for which there are typically no written records, storytelling is a process of cultural production and negotiates meaning for all those who tell and hear the stories.[14] Storytelling—written or oral—helps foster the collective identity of a people, no matter where they are situated.[15]

Stephen J. Augustine, Hereditary Chief and Keptin of the Mi'kmaq Grand Council, whose traditional territory lies along the north eastern coast of the United States and into Ontario, Canada, describes the role of storytelling among the Elders this way:

> The Elders would serve as mnemonic pegs to each other . . . speaking individually uninterrupted in a circle one after another. When each

Elder spoke they were conscious that other Elders would serve as "peer reviewer" [and so] they did not delve into subject matter that would be questionable. They did joke with each other and they told stories, some true and some a bit exaggerated but in the end the result was a collective memory.[16]

These collective memories are more than stories; they are intergenerational cultural transmissions of history, values, and identity.

In 1997, the Canadian Supreme Court ruled that oral traditions are acceptable legal renditions of events. In his ruling, Chief Justice Lamar stated, "The laws of evidence must be adapted in order that [oral] evidence can be accommodated and placed on an equal footing with the types of historical evidence that courts are familiar with, which largely consists of historical documents. . . . This process must be undertaken on a case-by-case basis." With this ruling, oral history, at least in Canada, is now recognized with the authority and credibility of written history, adding another dimension to making sense of past and current conflicts and conflict transformation in societies with oral traditions.

## ALLEGORIES

Allegories are stories with two meanings. The first story is the story itself, which is the surface story containing characters, a plot, and a setting. The second story is symbolic, and provides a deeper meaning to the surface story and presents principles or sometimes commentary. Allegories are a form of metaphor that often tell stories of conflict transformation. On the surface known children's stories, contain allegories within the stories are religious, historical, philosophical, or political messages intended for adults. Modern Western culture recognizes these as myths, legends, or fables; some are fairy tales, but they all communicate principles. Although allegories are an important form of narrative, their relevance to PACS has to do with the way they allow people to experience entire conflict cycles vicariously. In this way, people can recognize conflict, observe how it is detected, and how different people respond; they have opportunities to witness positive conflict transformation, and they also watch negative responses to conflict. Significantly, there are allegories with which people have related over years, decades, and even centuries, learning and observing as others experience conflict and as different conflicts are resolved in a number of different ways, with varying degrees of effective transformation.

Allegories can be recognized in examples throughout history. Around 380 BCE, Plato wrote *Allegory of the Cave* in Book 7 of *The Republic. The Cave* is the story of people who were chained to the wall of a cave and mistake appearance for reality. Although the story is thousands of years old, it is an exploration of the sometimes limited perceptions of people about the world around them. *The Pilgrim's Progress* by John Bunyan, first published in 1678, tells the tale of one man's journey from one place to another as a story of hazards and encouragements, but allegorically, it is a spiritual journey of a soul's path from earth to heaven. *Pilgrim's Progress* may be the western world's first printed allegory, written when Bunyan was in jail for violations against the Church of England. The popular seven books written by C. S. Lewis, *The Chronicles of Narnia,* are a religious (Christian) allegory. The series covers many central human themes and explores a number of conflicts surrounding the central figure, Aslan the Lion. The books were written between 1949 and 1956 and have now been made into allegorical movies. The *Narnia* series provide a rich landscape of conflict types and styles, and the many relationships between people, land, time, and the animal world. Although *Narnia* is a wonderful story, it is also a powerful example of the relationship between conflict transformation and allegory.

Some allegories are more political and offer commentary about world events and especially political change. In 1945, George Orwell wrote a famous political and historical allegory entitled *Animal Farm,* a novel that tells the story of the rise of the Communist Party in Russia between 1917 and 1943. Although the main characters in this important book are animals, the allegory presents the ideologies and personalities of real people. Another social commentary with which many people are familiar is *The Lord of the Flies*, written in 1954 by William Golding. The book tells the story of a group of British boys left alone on a deserted island without social structures or authorities, but the book is more than a story of their time together; it is an allegory about human nature. Through literature and now in movies there are a number of allegories that explore conflict. More recent allegories include the movie *Avatar*, which explores colonialism, and most of the popular *Zombie* movies are allegories about cultural values. In all of these, conflicts are presented, explored, and then resolved.

Although allegories are stories that communicate or comment on social values through stories, conflicts are often presented, explored, and transformed within the allegories. Since allegories incorporate many levels of social organization within interpersonal, local, regional, and global settings, they represent relevant and useful forms of expressing conflict and exploring conflict transformation.

## MYTHS

Myths are stories that gain wide acceptance because they communicate a fundamental truth about life, reflect the most important concerns of a people, and help to preserve the integrity of that same people's culture.[17] In fact, the word Mythos simply means historical story. Today, the popular connotation has assumed fantastic and superhuman dimensions; myths are generally conceived to be epic stories of heroes and monsters. Homer's *Illiad* and the *Odyssey* are well-known examples of myths. Although there is no historical proof that any of the events within the myths occurred, for the people of the time and for readers in modern times, the stories have preserved ancient Greek culture, which is another important purpose of myths for conflict transformation; they provide cultural context. For those cultures that have endured ethno-political conflict, myths can elevate nationalism beyond a sense of belonging, sometimes to levels of danger and violence. Information about cultural preservation and identity are some of the additional main ways that myths contribute to PACS.

Myths provide information about cultures that assist in conflict analysis and intervention. Since myths usually reflect the most important concerns of a group, they contain archetypal symbols that help make us conscious of and curious about our origins and destiny and they capture a society's basic psychological, sociological, cosmological, and metaphysical truths. Myths are interesting stories that also reflect social values and transfer these values across the generations. Stories told about contemporary issues such as climate change fit the deeper meaning of the word myth, since they connect visible daily experience to invisible social, geological, and economic forces that influence our lives.[18] The importance of mythical stories to conflict transformation is in the concepts and principles they convey, rather than actual events.

## NARRATIVES

When people talk about their own experiences, and how they have made sense of events, circumstances, and people in their lives, they are telling their own story. In other words, the content of a story is dependent on the interpretation of the narrator. This form of storytelling has taken on a significant dimension in PACS, and is also a form of research and refers to the more formal telling of a story, often in response to a question. When we tell and listen to others stories we receive valuable information about underlying core concerns and accompanying emotions. Increasingly, scholars in the field of PACS are developing research projects based on narrative methods.[19]

In these types of studies, people are asked to tell their own story in their own words and language, which is sharing their narrative. During the telling of a narrative, the researcher listens and records the story, and then looks for common themes in a number of stories. In this way, conflicts may be analyzed and better understood. When appropriate, researchers can design conflict interventions that will best transform the conflicts evident in the narratives of others, by collecting these stories.

This is becoming a powerful tool for building peace, transforming conflict, and informing public policy.

Storytelling and narratives have been used since the 1990s to reduce and transform conflicts among Catholics and Protestants in Northern Ireland, blacks and whites in South Africa, Palestinians and Israelis, and between descendants of Holocaust survivors and Nazi perpetrators.[20] In Northern Ireland, where one in four people have been personally affected by "The Troubles," an organization named *Towards Understanding and Healing* has embraced narrative and storytelling with great success. Among other peacebuilding initiatives, facilitators work with people to share their story.

Narratives can simply be someone relating a story about something that happened or that they observed or experienced, and they may relate events or be explicitly fictional. Narratives are never pure fact or pure fiction, though a fictional narrative may be used to persuasively express an idea that the narrative sees as true. Narratives can also extend beyond interpersonal communication and be related in a number of media, though access to narrative expression in media is restricted and difficult.

## CONSTRUCTIVE STORYTELLING[21]

Constructive storytelling is simply a means for constructing community through storytelling and includes all kinds of shared narrative.[22] Since the process of listening to a story involves "walking in the narrators' shoes" and because stories translate well across culture, when people listen to each other's stories they recognize what they have in common, despite the context of social conflicts, and even across cultural divides.[23] Constructive storytelling recognizes that storytelling can be and must be a significant part of conflict transformation, and in particular, of peacebuilding.[24] Through storytelling spaces are created for people to participate in order to define their communities, to voice their experiences to one another, to build trust and to heal from past conflict, and to shape their individual and collective futures. Storytelling requires an element of trust and a desire on the part of all parties to recognize the dignity and experiences of the other.[25] Through constructive storytelling, "groups and societies create, recreate, and alter social identities, power relations, knowledge, memory, and emotions."[26] In this way, storytelling controls social meaning and is a means through which community is constructed.

## EVALUATING STORYTELLING

The evaluation of storytelling as a peacebuilding methodology and as a research method is controversial because of the highly subjective nature of a story. However, one of the greatest challenges to evaluating storytelling as a peacebuilding method is the need to develop new kinds of evaluators and new kinds of approaches to evaluation.[27] To date, there are no accepted standards for evaluating stories, though the "Empowering People through Praxis" chapter of this book explored some of the more recognized methodologies. Ironically, this subjectivity is also the greatest strength of storytelling both for peacebuilding and for inquiry and discovery. When people tell their stories, new information is recovered and often cultural factors, belief systems, values, and other matters that are rarely uncovered through quantitative research or through archaeological research percolate to the surface.

## STORYTELLING FESTIVALS

Before the advent of electronics people depended on stories for education and entertainment, but almost more importantly, for cultural transmission. The Greek Amphitheatre, Shakespearean England and The Globe Theatre, and contemporary movies that bring the past alive provide many opportunities to see how popular storytelling festivals have been with people across the generations. However, with changes in technology and culture, and especially the fast-paced consumerism of western society, storytelling as a broad social form fell out of prominence but did not vanish. Storytelling in festival form in Canada and the United States has been experiencing a revival and is being recognized as a powerful tool to help people make sense of conflict and other life experiences. As a result, storytelling festivals are more widespread.

Professional storytellers from around the world gather at festivals and tell stories, allegories, myths, and narratives. These types of storytellers are often called Tellers, which distinguishes them from the Elders of Indigenous oral traditions. Storytellers are less restricted than other artists when choosing material that is meaningful to them.[28] A number of people have initiated storytelling opportunities for peacebuilding and these are readily discovered through internet searches. Story-based workshops and programs have been established to address race relations, to emphasize cultural traditions, and to interpret communal histories through video, dance, photography, and story.[29] As Senehi concludes, the storytelling is relevant for the transformation of intercommunal conflicts, and it brings attention to the important projects of contemporary storytellers, which "may provide important models for ways in which intercommunal relationships can be improved from the grassroots level."[30] Beginning in Jonesborough, Tennessee more than forty years ago, storytelling festivals have been increasing in number and size, and renewing our appreciation of the art of storytelling.

In 2007, Dr. Senehi initiated one of North America's larger annual International Storytelling Festivals. Situated at the University of Manitoba in Canada, the Festival has won several prestigious awards for its work with youth and peacebuilding. The goals of the Festival are to nurture the art of storytelling in its central Canadian host city; to promote youth voice as a critical skill for global citizenship, and also to promote the use of story-based approaches for peacemaking. According to the Festival's website, "If we tell each other our stories, we can never again be enemies. Storytelling is a bridge between people, a bridge between cultures, and a bridge between worlds."[31] The Winnipeg International Storytelling Festival features regional, national, and international tellers. The Festival includes a School Program, Peace-building Workshops, and Public Events, and is distinguished by its inclusion of Aboriginal, Deaf, French, and human rights programming. The festival, attended by a steadily increasing population of kindergarten to grade twelve students and the general adult public, is based on the belief that storytelling builds community and nurtures the development of young people.[32] Storytelling, especially in the festival context, influences possibilities for conflict identification, and for collaboration between the teller and the listener, and for conflict transformation.

## TRUTH AND RECONCILIATION COMMISSIONS

The Honorable Justice Murray Sinclair is a Canadian-Ojibway judge who served as chair of the three person Canadian Truth and Reconciliation Commission (TRC). The TRC was a comprehensive response to the Indian Residential School Legacy for First Nations children, resulting from Canada's national assimilation policy from pre-Confederation until the 1960s. The Commission engaged personal storytelling to listen to the accounts of over 6,700 survivors of Canada's Residential Schools[33] in an effort to heal, rebuild, and renew Aboriginal[34] (Indigenous) relationships and the relationship between Aboriginal and non-Aboriginal Canadians. Justice Sinclair, whose Ojibway name is Mizanay Gheezhik (which means "the One Who Speaks of Pictures in the Sky") stated, "If you think truth is hard, try reconciliation."[35]

During the five year Commission process, seven national events were held during which any people, especially Aboriginal people, who had been effected by Canada's Indian Residential School policy were invited to share their story with the Commissioners. This is called Statement Gathering and establishes an historical record through testimony while people talk through and make sense of what has happened to them, which also helps individuals to heal. Through this, the Canadian government has established and recognized storytelling in the form of Statement Gathering as an alternative dispute resolution process.

One of the primary goals of the Canadian TRC was to achieve reconciliation through activities such as public education and engagement, commemoration, and recommendations. Justice Sinclair is quoted as stating, "Reconciliation is about forging and maintaining respectful relationships. There are no shortcuts." The TRC was part of the Government of Canada's Residential Schools Settlement, which overlapped the National Apology delivered by Canadian Prime Minister Stephen Harper on June 11, 2008 on behalf of all Canadians to everyone who had been abused, whose lives had been damaged by the policy. Importantly, this meant that although people had an opportunity to share their own stories with Commissioners who would listen and counsel them, they also heard the words "We were wrong," from the head of government, who represented all the wrongdoers.[36] Together, the apology, the responsibility acknowledged by the political leader of the state, and the chance to share one's own experiences are important elements of healing and reconciliation.[37]

Possibly the most well-known TRC was established in South Africa in 1995, as an effort toward healing and reconciliation from the Apartheid years.[38] The South African Justice Minister stated, " . . . a commission is a necessary exercise to enable South Africans to come to terms with their past on a morally accepted basis and to advance the cause of reconciliation."[39] In South Africa, three committees were also established for all members of the conflict in an effort to encourage healing and reconciliation individually and collectively, and to give "members of the public a chance to express their regret at failing to prevent human rights violations and to demonstrate their commitment to reconciliation."[40] Public storytelling was the main vehicle.

Truth and reconciliation commissions are established by governments to discover and address wrongdoing. Often the wrongdoing is extreme and involves severe human rights abuses committed by a government in the past. Although the process is formal, people are invited to voluntarily share their experiences in the form of telling their story. In 1991, Chile established the first TRC in order to document deaths and disappearances under the military dictator Augusto Pinochet. Truth and Reconciliation Commissions enhance peacebuilding and reduce inter-group, inter personal, and intra personal conflict. The TRC has been used in a number of contexts around the world, though the measure of their success toward individual and collective healing and reconciliation has not been studied comprehensively.

## SUMMARY

In summary, storytelling takes several forms, all of which make up an important part of the practices of Peace and Conflict Studies. Stories convey information, morals, and feats, and do so in a number of forms, including through oral traditions, allegories, and myths. Cultures and societies maintain their histories and identities through the oral traditions of Elders. Social and cultural values and principles are communicated intergenerationally and internationally through Tellers at Storytelling Festivals. Individuals sharing their personal story are a third form of storyteller, and these stories help people and groups of people make sense of events and experiences in their lives.

Together, the forms and practices of storytelling are expanding academic research, and also our understanding of other people and cultures, healing, and reconciling, while potentially informing policy makers and the democratic processes of living together peaceably. Storytelling is also a powerful force because it draws attention to the web of interconnections that make up our global community, and to the momentous challenges coming to future generations.[41] The human voice requires no special equipment or training and can be used in all situations to communicate. Storytelling in its multiple forms is a way of reporting experiences, conflictions, and the transformation of conflict that might otherwise be lost, denied, or dismissed.

## QUESTIONS

1. How would you describe storytelling and why is it important to understand the different types of stories? In what ways are they fundamentally different, or the same?
2. Attend a meeting in your community that is designed to address a conflict. Note how people share stories and what kind of stories they share in an effort to communicate their interests and perspectives.
3. Attend a local Storytelling Festival (or watch a recording) and enjoy the many types of stories and the ways they are told. What makes the stories compelling?
4. Watch the international news and see what stories are told about other nations. How do these stories compare to stories told about your nation?

## NOTES

1. Jessica Senehi, "Constructive Storytelling, A Peace Process," *Peace and Conflict Studies*, 9, No. 2 (2002): 43.

2. Ibid.

3. *Saving Mr. Banks*, Directed by John Lee Hancock. United States: Walt Disney Pictures, 2013. DVD, 125 min.

4. See Stephen Denning, *The Springboard: How Storytelling Ignites Action in Knowledge-era Organizations*. (New York, NY: Routledge, 2011).

5. See for example Jessica Senehi, "Constructive Storytelling in Inter-communal Conflicts: Building Community, Building Peace," in S. Byrne, C. Irvin, P. Dixon, B. Polkinghorn, and J. Senehi (Eds.), *Reconcilable Differences: Turning Points in Ethno-political Conflict* (West Hartford: Kumarian Press, 2000): 96–114; "Language, Culture and

Conflict: Storytelling as a Matter of Life and Death," *Mind and Human Interaction* (1998) 7, No. 3: 150–164; "Building peace: Storytelling to Transform Conflicts Constructively," in Dennis Sandole, Sean Byrne, Ingrid Sandole-Staroste, and Jessica Senehi (Eds.) *Handbook of Conflict Analysis and Resolution.* (New York, NY: Routledge, 2008): 199–212.

6. Erin Hanson, "Oral Traditions" (Indigenous Foundations, 2009). Available at http://indigenousfoundations.arts.ubc.ca/home/culture/oral-traditions.html.

7. Pat Ryan, *Storytelling in Ireland: A Re-Awakening.* (Londonderry, NI: the Verbal Arts Center, 1995).

8. Barbara Ganley, "Foreword," in Joe Lambert, *Digital Storytelling: Capturing Lives, Creating Community* (4th Edition), (Centre for Digital Storytelling, New York, NY: Routledge, 2013): ix.

9. Maureen Flaherty, *Peacebuilding with Women in Ukraine: Using Personal Stories to Envision a Common Future.* (Lanham: Lexington, 2012): 50.

10. Senehi, 2002: 50.

11. Jessica Senehi, Maureen Flaherty, Cindy Kirupakaran, Lloyd Kornelsen, Mavis Matenge, and Olga Skarlato, "Dreams of Our Grandmothers: Discovering the Call for Social Justice Through Storytelling," *Storytelling, Self, Society, 5,* no.2, (2009): 91.

12. Senehi, 2000: 106.

13. Shawn Wilson, *Research is Ceremony.* (Halifax, Fernwood, 2008).

14. Jessica Senehi "Constructive Storytelling: A Peace Process." *Peace and Conflict Studies,* 9, No. 2, 2002: 41–63.

15. Jeffrey Walter Decontie, "Indigenous Identities and Nation-Building within Canadian Urban Centres: Relevance for Algonquin Nationhood." (Unpublished Master's Thesis, University of Winnipeg, 2013): 14.

16. Stephen J. Augustine, "Oral Histories and Oral Traditions," in *Aboriginal Oral Traditions: Theory, Practice, Ethics* in Renée Hulan and Renate Eigenbrod, Editors. (Halifax: Fernwood Publishing, 2008), 2–3.

17. Julia Chaitin, "Narratives and Storytelling," in *Beyond Intractability,* Guy Burgess and Heidi Burgess, Editors. Conflict Information Consortium, University of Colorado, Boulder. Posted: July 2003. Accessed at http://www.beyondintractability.org/essay/narratives.

18. Ibid.

19. See Maureen Flaherty, *Peacebuilding with Women in Ukraine: Using Personal Stories to Envision a Common Future.* (Lanham: Lexington, 2012); and Laura E. Reimer, PhD Dissertation. *Dropping out of School: Exploring the Narratives of Aboriginal People in One Manitoba Community through Lederach's Conflict Transformation Framework.* (University of Manitoba, August 21, 2013). Available at http://mspace.lib.umanitoba.ca/handle/1993/22052.

20. Chaitin, 2003.

21. This is a term originated by Jessica Senehi, PhD and found in much of her work. The term is defined and presented comprehensively in "Constructive Storytelling, A Peace Process," *Peace and Conflict Studies,* 9, No. 2 (2002): 41–63.

22. Jessica Senehi, "Constructive Storytelling in Intercommunal Conflicts: Building Community, Building Peace," in Sean Byrne and Cynthia Irvin, Editors, *Reconcilable Differences: Turning Points in Ethnopolitical Conflict.* (West Hartford, Kumarian, 2000: 96).

23. Ibid.

24. Ibid.

25. Senehi, 2002: 49.

26. Senehi, 2000: 97.

27. Kenneth Bush, "What We Have Learned about Storytelling: On Story, Culture, and Evaluation," in Irish Peace Centres, *The Evaluation of Storytelling as a Peace-building Methodology.* (Belfast, NI: International Conflict Research Institute, 2011): 69.

28. Senehi, 2000:109.

29. Ibid

30. Ibid., 110.

31. University of Manitoba. Arthur V. Mauro Centre. *Winnipeg International Storytelling Festival,* 2014. Accessed at http://umanitoba.ca/storytelling/.

32. Ibid.

33. For a deeper understanding of the actions and contributions of Canada's Truth and Reconciliation Commission and the role of Residential Schools in Canadian history and Canadian reconciliation, see http://www.trc.ca.

34. The Indigenous people of Canada bear a number of different names because there are a number of different Indigenous peoples. Aboriginal is the Constitutional designation that replaced the term "Indian" in 1982, and is the most common and agreed upon name. Aboriginal people are also also recognized as First Nations or Métis, or by their tribe names, such as Cree, Ojibway/Anishinaabe, or Mohawk/Kahniakenhaka, to name three. The Inuit live in the far north and although they are Indigenous people, do not consider themselves Aboriginal. For more information about Canada's diverse Indigenous people, please see Government of Canada, *Aboriginal Peoples and Communities,* 2013, available at https://www.aadnc-aandc.gc.ca/eng/1100100013785/1304467449155.

35. The Honorable Justice Murray Sinclair, personal communication during introduction to Sol Kannee Lecture, "What Do We Do About the Legacy of Indian Residential Schools?" University of Manitoba, September 29, 2014. Full lecture available for viewing on You Tube at https://www.youtube.com/watch?v=qTiB13H0tic.

36. The full apology may be read or watched on video at http://www.aadnc-aandc.gc.ca/eng/1100100015677/1100100015680, or on the Canadian Prime Minister's website, at http://www.pm.gc.ca/eng/news/2008/06/11/pm-offers-full-apology-behalf-canadians-indian-residential-schools-system.

37. Laura Reimer, "Conflict Transformation: Canadian Democracy and Aboriginal Relations," *Global Journal of Peace Research and Praxis,* 1 (2014, 2015): 41. Available at http://www.partnershipsjournal.org/index.php/prp/issue/view/74.

38. For the mandate and purpose, see *Truth & Reconciliation Commission.* Available at http://www.doj.gov.za/trc.

39. Mr. Dullah Omar, former Minister of Justice, "Welcome to the Official Truth and Reconciliation Commission Website," Available at http://www.justice.gov.za/trc/, 2009.

40. Ibid.

41. Chaitin, 2003.

# ELEVEN

## Restorative Processes

### LEARNING OUTCOMES

- To recognize that the application of the principles of restorative practices require skill and insight
- To explore the difference between punishment and repairing harm
- To compare restorative justice to retributive or criminal justice
- To understand how restorative processes contribute to healing and peacebuilding

### OVERVIEW

In his book about changing the lenses through which we approach justice, Dr. Howard Zehr states that "crime is a violation of people and relationships. It creates obligations to make things right. Justice involves the victim, the offender, and the community in a search for solutions which promote repair, reconciliation, and reassurance."[1] This perspective, which focuses on repairing harm rather than determining blame, is now recognized as a restorative perspective, and is at the center of the restorative justice, or restorative practices, movement. Restorative practices are integral to the study of peace and conflict, and provide a new path for addressing harm and justice issues within conflict.[2]

### INTRODUCTION

The restorative processes movement has emerged into prominence relatively recently but the principles upon which it stands are not new. Originating in the practices of earlier cultures concerned with human dignity and the reintegration of people into communities after wrongdoing, specifically, restorative processes are an alternative for addressing harm in a timely and caring way. This is possible when all parties involved are committed to the restoration of relationships, trust, and community that have been harmed by someone's actions. Restorative justice is based on more collective understanding of wrongdoing and has been most common to traditional societies. In situations where people have been violated, criminal justice or retributive justice turns to the court systems to apprehend and incarcerate a convicted offender. However, having a criminal or offender does not necessarily mean that people are healed and relationships are restored, or that all is returned to the state it was prior to the violation. One form of justice has been served, but injustice remains and requires some form of address. Although restorative processes do not replace the current court justice system, they are increasing in popularity as a meaningful way to address injustice and the attendant harms. In this way many people, and by extension, many areas of civil society experience the transformation of conflict and restoration in ways they did not anticipate. In addition to criminal behavior and to other violations, restorative practices have been particularly effective in addressing the harm experienced among school communities and neighborhoods by the conduct of bullying.[3]

Everyone needs compassion, and the fundamental premises of restorative practices are based on the timeless principles that people respond favorably to being treated with kindness and understanding. For decades, research in the United States and Canada has shown that people are more cooperative, happier, and more likely to make positive changes when those in authority do things with them, rather than to them or for them.[4] Restorative practices reinforce this finding and respect all the people involved in a wrongdoing, especially those at the core of the wrongdoing—who are identified as the victim and offender. The restorative processes movement addresses the heart and soul of peacebuilding, seeking to provide compassionate principles for the transformation of conflict in all of the areas into which wrongdoing has intruded.

The core principles of restorative justice provide a foundation, guidance, and framework that have significant implications for families, schools, classrooms, prisons, organizations, workplaces, and governments. It is critical that students of peace and conflict studies learn the core principles in order to analyze practices and processes that bear the restorative label. The central principles of restorative practices are restoration, accountability, and engagement. These principles are explored and explained throughout the remainder of this chapter.

Scholar and practitioner Dr. Howard Zehr, the acknowledged founder of the modern restorative practices movement, cautions that although there is good intent and much good work taking place around the globe, practices or programs calling themselves restorative are not necessarily so. Although there is no clear agreement on a definition, restorative justice is described by Zehr as a process designed "to involve, to the extent possible, those who have a stake in a specific offense, and to collectively identify and address harms, needs and obligations, in order to heal and put things as right as possible."[5]

## THE UNITED NATIONS AND RESTORATIVE JUSTICE

In a continually globalizing world with its attendant conflicts, large international bodies like the United Nations have recognized the powerful potential of restorative practices for conflict transformation around the world. In July 2002, the United Nations Economic and Social Council adopted a resolution containing guidance for member states to encourage restorative justice policy and practice. UNICEF has provided an international definition of Restorative Justice as a way of responding to criminal behavior which emphasizes repairing harm caused by the crime, and restoring harmony as much as possible between offender, victim/survivor, and society.[6] Like community engagement, Indigenous research principles, and some of the other concepts we have explored in this book, restorative justice builds upon the interconnectedness of humanity. Restorative practices focus on relationships, and include the restoration of individuals and communities that might have been affected by wrongdoing.

## THE FOCUS AND PRACTICE OF RESTORATIVE JUSTICE

There is a book entitled *Changing Lenses*[7] by Howard Zehr, the title of which captures the shift offered by the restorative justice movement to the paradigm underlying and framing current pursuits of justice. Within this model the concept of punishment itself is questioned. Since the focus or goal of restorative justice is restoration, the process and practice stress the identification and remedy of harm. This is a departure from the focus and goal of legislated processes of justice, which determine blame and suitable punishment.

While the formal legal system typically identifies one victim and one perpetrator in the pursuit of justice, restorative justice processes include all the people who have been harmed by an event and can help restore justice. The process is described as restorative because during the intervention, it is clear to the offender that the behavior which caused harm is not condoned within the community. The community, however, is still supportive and even respectful of that individual, while not condoning the behavior. This is important because some critics of restorative practices claim that offenders get away with their crime. Restorative practices do not replace the legal process or the consequences of breaking the law by an offender, but they do heal the other people, and in many ways, the offender themselves, so that reoccurrences of the same harm are rare.

The actual practice of restorative justice is often called an intervention, and it takes place in the form of a group meeting in order to explore who has been harmed beyond the identified victim and perpetrator. Importantly, these meetings do not take place until the perpetrator has acknowledged their role in the harm. A central consideration to determine which people should be in attendance is which people respect and care the most for the people involved.[8] There are five critical questions to be posed to assist in the planning of a restorative justice process:

1. Who has been hurt?
2. What are their needs?
3. Whose obligations are these?
4. Who has a stake in the situation?
5. What is the appropriate process to involve stakeholders in an effort to put things right?

The responses to these questions help to identify who ought to be invited to participate in the restorative process in addition to the people who have been identified as offender and victim.

Sometimes, the question process leads to somewhat surprising inclusions; these people are included because they have been touched by the harm in some way. This is often referred to as the harmed community, and intervention is called a restorative conference.[9] The contrast between a harmed community seeking restoration and the state seeking blame and punishment is readily evident.

There are additional advantages to the selection or identification of community members through the careful pondering of the five questions. Invited individuals also form a support system for the offender(s) and for the victim(s). For example, students embarking on a restorative justice process after a bullying incident in their school can choose a support person within the school with whom they have positive relations, such as a teacher or bus driver; or, they can choose someone in the wider community such as someone from their faith community such as a sports coach or a public librarian. As with all restorative processes, the goal within the intervention is to provide support and positive mentorship while also helping as a guide. The wider definition of harmed community members also creates the flexibility needed during the follow up processes. The available resources for all members of the community are widened. In this way, the greater community is engaged, which helps to foster a more holistic society. Experience has shown that this decreases (and in some cases eliminates) future incidences of behaviors such as bullying.

Repairing harm and rebuilding trust are at the core of restorative justice. Throughout his work Zehr stresses the importance of respect as a paramount principle. The principles of restorative processes and of restorative justice contribute strongly to individual and collective healing from wrongdoing, hurt, trauma, and loss.[10]

## A BRIEF HISTORY OF THE JUSTICE SYSTEM

Knowledge of the development of the complicated court system in the United States and Canada is instrumental to understanding the growth of and/or return to restorative processes, including the contributions of many faith-based systems and Indigenous societies. The restorative justice movement, as the main subset of restorative practices, grew out of dissatisfaction with the hierarchical and coercive structures of the current criminal justice system. Although it is highly punitive now, the current system grew out of the prison system initiated two centuries ago by the Quakers, a faith-based group of people devoted to kindness, peace, and non-violence. The justice systems in the early colonies of the United States (and later Canada) were established as a more humane alternative to the severe corporal and capital punishments practiced in British and European prisons.

The justice system of the 1700s was designed to be very different from the large bureaucratic institutions of today. Although each prison reform since the 1700s was intended to be a more humanitarian response to human violations and wrongdoing, each ultimately evolved into a system that is arguably dehumanizing for both the victim(s) and the offender(s). Criminal justice often seems unjust and most certainly is not structured to restore relationships or to repair harm.

The quest for sound and restorative justice has dominated other cultures and most of Western history, and it is important to note that the search for the suitable administration of human justice did not originate in the early Americas. In fact, restorative practices are not new to transforming human conflict. According to written and oral history, they are and have been exercised by multiple populations around the world for many generations. In cultures of restoration, wrongdoing is regarded as a misbehavior which requires teaching, or as an illness which requires healing; it is not about assigning blame and meting out punishment. In Quaker and Amish communities, restorative practices find their roots in New Testament faith-based teachings of forgiveness and love rather than in the harsh rules and permissions often associated with religions. In Indigenous communities, including but not limited to the Maori of New Zealand, the Navajo of the United States, and some First Nations (Indigenous populations) in Canada, restorative processes guided traditional social practices for centuries. At times, especially in some of the First Nations of Canada, restorative justice has not meant a happy ending for all parties, but it has moved everyone involved toward healing and restoration because harm has been adequately addressed for all people concerned.

There are a number of alternatives to the criminal justice system, and in some jurisdictions, restorative practices have been partially implemented. These practices are, however, highly criticized by most restorative practitioners. According to restorative principles, intermediate rehabilitations like house arrest, community service, and electronic monitoring are not restorative. They are alternative forms of punishment that strengthen the net of social control over perpetrators. Although these practices are more humane than prison, they are not restorative, despite the names developed for many of these programs. In fact, in many ways these monitored and supervised programs strengthen the adversarial and punitive system they are allegedly replacing. Restorative justice questions the paradigms beneath such rehabilitation strategies, and recognizes that the foundational premises are about crime and punishment.

## RETRIBUTIVE JUSTICE

The current paradigm of criminal justice is one of retributive justice. In a retributive justice system, the focus is on the offender, and so it is often characterized as punitive, neglectful of victims, and lacking true offender accountability.[11] The central component of retributive justice is particularly dehumanizing—crime does not take place between people. Rather, crime violates the state (the country) and its jurisdictional laws. This is further realized in the courts with prosecuting lawyers titled Crown Attorneys and State Attorneys. Their job is to prosecute and blame an offender against the state to assure punishment; if victims are part of the process, it is not for restorative purposes for them or for the offender.

There are six main components of retributive justice:

1. Focus on adversarial conflict.
2. Establish blame and guilt.
3. Administration of punishment (usually pain).
4. Establish that the offender is in opposition to the State.
5. Show that intentions of the law are more important in the determination of justice than outcomes.
6. Justice is framed as as two sided—one side wins, one side loses.

As Zehr explains and summarizes, the retributive justice paradigm is a foundation that "builds upon the extraordinary and the bizarre, assuming an adversarial process based on a battle model."[12] Table 11-1 compares the restorative and retributive justice paradigms, simplifying the identification of which social values and assumptions underlie each paradigm.

In addition to the foundational, or paradigmatic, differences between retributive and restorative justice, another major difference can be best understood in terms of how crime is conceptualized. As clearly presented in Table 11-1, crime in the retributive model is an offense against the state, but in a restorative justice framework, crime is a violation of people and relationships. Restorative justice looks to the past to understand how things came to be as they are and to the future to create measures to make things the best for everyone involved.

**Table 11.1.   Restorative and Retributive Justice Comparison**

| Restorative Justice | Retributive Justice |
| --- | --- |
| Crime is an act against another person and the community | Crime is an act against the state, a violation of a law, an abstract idea |
| Crime control lies primarily in the community | The criminal justice system controls crime |
| Accountability defined as assuming responsibility and taking action to repair harm | Offender accountability defined as taking punishment |
| Crime has both individual and social dimensions of responsibility | Crime is an individual act with individual responsibility |
| Punishment alone is not effective in changing behavior and is disruptive to community harmony and good relationships | Punishment is effective<br>1.  Threat of punishment deters crime<br>2.  Punishment changes behavior |
| Victims are central to the process of resolving a crime | Victims are peripheral to the process |
| The offender is defined by capacity to make reparation | The offender is defined by deficits |
| Focus on problem solving, on liabilities/ obligations, on the future (what should be done?) | Focus on establishing blame or guilt; on the past (did he/she do it?) |
| Emphasis on dialogue and negotiation | Emphasis on adversarial relationship |
| Restitution as a means of restoring both parties; goal of reconciliation/restoration | Imposition of pain to punish and deter/ prevent |
| Community as facilitator in restorative process | Community on sideline, represented abstractly by state |
| Response focused on harmful consequences of offender's behavior, emphasis on the future | Response focused on offender's past behavior |
| Direct involvement by participants | Dependence upon proxy professionals |

Adapted from Zehr, 2002; 2003.

## THE STRENGTHS OF THE RESTORATIVE PARADIGM

Restorative justice is one of the best known alternatives and complements to retributive justice, and forms a ready comparison to increase people's understanding of the important differences between the two approaches. The restorative justice paradigm regards people differently. Rather than seeing "the accused" or "the offender," the restorative justice perspectives strive to respect a whole, complex person and the multiple roles and relationships that characterize them, rather than just in their role as an offender. Howard Zehr's *Changing Lenses* was groundbreaking for restorative practices. By changing the lenses through which we approach crime, Zehr encourages people to look at the "human tragedy involving real people" (p. 18), and to remind people that victims are also in need of justice after a crime. Until there is a replacement for the current justice system, restorative justice and restorative practices offer alternatives and complements to criminal justice.

Acknowledged as one of the founders of the modern restorative practices movement, Howard Zehr has researched, practiced, and written extensively about restorative justice. He continues to be an important voice as the field of conflict transformation continues to expand with the framing of restorative processes. In the field, these practices may be recognized by different names, including "peacemaking circles," VORP (victim offender reconciliation program), VOM (victim offender mediation), VOD (victim offender dialogue), "dialogues," and "restorative conferencing."

Restorative justice is a way of addressing wrongdoing. As a simpler way for people to remember the core principles and practices of restoration, Dr. Zehr has developed a summary of this in a series of threes (see Table 11-2). We are grateful to Dr. Zehr for his permission for this typology to be reproduced in this text. [13]

**Table 11.2.   Howard Zehr's *Three's of Restorative Justice*[1]**

| | |
| --- | --- |
| **Three Assumptions** underlie restorative justice: | When people and relationships are harmed, needs are created |
| | The needs created by harms lead to obligations |
| | The obligation is to heal and "put right" the harms; this is a just response. |
| **Three Principles** of restorative justice reflect these assumptions: | A just response acknowledges and repairs the harm caused by, and revealed by, wrongdoing (restoration); |
| | A just response encourages appropriate responsibility for addressing needs and repairing the harm (accountability); |

| | A just response involves those impacted, including the community, in the resolution (engagement). |
|---|---|
| **Three Underlying Values** provide the foundation: | Respect |
| | Responsibility |
| | Relationship |
| **Three Questions** are central to restorative justice: | Who has been hurt? |
| | What are their needs? |
| | Who has the obligation to address the needs, to put right the harms, to restore relationships? (As opposed to: What rules were broken? Who did it? What do they deserve?) |
| **Three Stakeholder Groups** should be considered and/or involved: | Those who have been harmed, and their families |
| | Those who have caused harm, and their families |
| | Community |
| **Three Aspirations** guide restorative justice: | The desire to live in right relationship with one another |
| | The desire to live in right relationship with the creation |
| | The desire to live in right relationship with the Creator |
| **Three Elements of Wrongdoing** to be addressed through restorative justice: | crime is a violation of people and of interpersonal relationships |
| | violations create obligations |
| | the central obligation is to put right the wrongs.[2] |

1. These are taken, by permission in personal correspondence, February 27, 2015, from Dr. Zehr's blog, The Zehr Institute for Restorative Justice at Eastern Mennonite University, Harrisburg, Virginia, April 20, 2009. Available at http://emu.edu/now/restorative-justice/2009/04/20/restorative-justice-and-peacebuilding/
2. Zehr, 2005: 19

This short list of threes provides a simple yet portable toolkit for remembering the core principles of restorative justice.

## TEACHING AND HEALING: INDIGENOUS PRACTICES

Before the court system arrived in North America, Indigenous stories tell us that many systems were set up so that people who committed an offense against their community were counseled toward reintegration with the community, rather than punished. In relation to this in Indigenous communities, leadership, religion, education, and socialization were tightly intertwined so restorative processes, and the circle mechanisms that guided the processes, reflected the relational accountability[14] that characterizes the Canadian Indigenous worldview.

The healing focus and relational aspect of restorative practices in the original and historical Indigenous communities in Canada have also meant that in traditional times, solitary offenders were not punished for past deeds. This is very important for the healing of Canadian Indigenous people, who have endured and survived generations of assimilation policies and colonization. In conflict situations that require intervention, many of Canada's Indigenous communities are engaging with restorative justice practices. Restoratively, when there is wrongdoing, the focus of the practices is toward the teaching and healing of all parties involved. Seated together in Circles, members of the harm community (selected as they are described above) tell their version of events without interruption from the others. In this respectful way, people, and especially the offender, are able to gain new perspectives and understandings about how the event was experienced by others.

As with other forms of conflict transformation, the past is included in the process, and explored through storytelling. The stories help everyone to better understand how the conflict came to be. The stories also include hopes and dreams as a base for designing plans for going forward into that future in ways that will be the healthiest for all concerned. Indigenous restorative justice is being resurrected by a growing number of rural and urban communities and is typically conducted as a Circle Process, involving all members of the community affected by the harm.

## RESTORATIVE PROCESSES

### Circle Processes

Although they emerged from small and homogenous settings, circles are now used for peacebuilding in a number of contexts, including neighborhoods, workplaces, schools, and within the criminal justice system. Quite literally people arrange themselves in a circle and pass a talking piece, which controls the process; only the person holding the stick can speak. The composition of the circle is constructed around who is required to repair harm. Today there are a number of different circle processes, named according to their purpose. The primary purpose of all circles, however, is to develop a consensus on how to repair the harmful results of an offence.[15] Circles may be identified by their function.[16] The types of circles have expanded, and now include Healing Circles, Workplace Conflict Circles, Teaching Circles, and Community Dialogue Circles.

## Peacemaking Circles

Peacemaking Circles are one form of restorative processes that emerged in Canada quite recently when a First Nations community asked to implement restorative practices into the courtroom of Judge Barry Stuart during the trial of one of their community members. In his legal ruling, the Judge formally titled the form a "Peacemaking Circle."[17] The primary goal of Peacemaking Circles is for all stakeholders to have a chance to talk about their perspectives and feelings about a particular incident, or wrongdoing, and how it affected them. Peacemaking Circles provide opportunities for all members of the conflict to listen to others in hopes of understanding, not responding. Through dialogue and understanding, people can begin to heal and repair the relationships that were harmed.

## Restorative Practices and Schools

School communities need restoration after they have endured wrongdoing. Recent efforts by an expanding number of trained Restorative Justice personnel have found schools, including colleges and universities, to be highly responsive to restorative justice and restorative practices. Restorative practices help students learn from their mistakes and restore people and relationships to a healthy place within the community. Purposefully implementing the basic principles of restorative practices to address the harms caused by bullying within the school system allows schools the flexibility and creativity needed in order to focus on harmed relationships rather than punishment.

As research has shown, punishment does not take into account the different developmental levels. Negative feelings and behaviors are often created because punishment does not teach accountability or responsibility and can contribute to the development of an individualistic society that alienates the bully. Canadian psychologists Gordon Neufeld and Gabor Mate[18] have evidence-based literature indicating that bullies themselves are harmed individuals, bearing pain that is too much to bear and lashing out at others in an effort to protect themselves from further pain. Traditional psychology literature and most efforts in schools indicate that there is a widespread belief that bullying is a learned behavior that can be unlearned. This behavioral analysis, however, seems to be losing strength in the light of more recent research[19] and the ineffective behavior modification programs established in schools over the past decade. Regardless of who is right, restorative practices can bring hope and healing to school communities seeking to transform the pain and conflicts that result from bullying.

Across the United States, Canada, Australia, and United Kingdom, literally hundreds of schools are implementing restorative justice programs as a tool to heal their school communities. Restorative practices and techniques, taught by trained leaders, are easily learned by students and educators alike. Restorative practices implemented in schools are addressing a number of different conflicts. The results are impressive. Schools report safer buildings and yards, reduced vandalism, fewer conflicts, and fewer bullying incidents. Restorative practices are also resulting in community building, better grades and school attendance, higher graduation rates, and improved conflict resolution skills among the members of school communities.

And, while the uses of restorative processes are primarily explored on the micro and meso levels here, they are also important to the transformation of conflicts on macro and mega levels. This is especially true for people who have collectively endured a shocking or traumatic event like the terrorist attacks in the United States on September 11, 2001; prolonged conflict or war as in many African countries, Serbia, or Bosnia; or horrific environmental anomalies involving severe flooding, ice storms, life-threatening heat waves, or catastrophic events such as Hurricane Katrina. In all of these situations, restorative processes address the harm that has been done in an effort to acknowledge the pain and harm that perhaps has not been acknowledged or recognized, in order to provide more wholistic conflict transformation.

## SUMMARY

Restorative practices, including restorative justice, have distinct qualities that focus on repair and restoration after harm. The primary aim of restorative programs is the redressing of harm and the reintegration of those who have been affected by wrongdoing back into the community as resilient and responsible members of the community. There are five questions that provide a guide to careful selection of a harm community, and together, the intervention often take place in a circle, which is an important part of the way restorative practices actually take place. Circles are used for many purposes, but the common bond is that they are all established by a harm community to heal and restore broken people, relationships, and communities.

## QUESTIONS

1.  Consider examples of situations that are usually resolved by the court. What are some of the outcomes that might be differently

resolved with restorative practices? How would these take place in a Peacemaking Circle?

2. How do the main differences between restorative justice and retributive justice paradigms affect the way we respond to random acts of violence or family conflict?

3. Look through the local newspaper for articles about human conflict that would be strong candidates for restorative processes. Write a second fictitious newspaper article as though the conflict has been addressed restoratively.

4. Write a short paper exploring a national conflict event, such as the 1995 bombing of the Alfred P. Murrah Federal Building in Oklahoma City, Oklahoma, or the reign of Hurricane Katrina in New Orleans, Louisiana. Perhaps consider an international event such as the tsunami and the subsequent Fukushima nuclear plant explosions in Japan in 2011. Give a brief factual account of what happened, then explore the harm that has taken place as a result of that event, which may not have been covered or considered in the media.

## NOTES

1. Howard Zehr, *Changing Lenses: A New Focus for Crime and Justice.* (Scottsdale, PA: Herald Press, 1990): 271.

2. Howard Zehr, *The Little Book of Restorative Justice.* (Intercourse, PA: Good Books, 2002): 43.

3. Susan Duncan, "Restorative Justice and Bullying: A Missing Solution in the Anti-Bullying Laws." *New England Journal on Criminal & Civil Confinement,* Vol. 37, (2011): 701. 2011 University of Louisville School of Law Legal Studies Research Paper Series No. 2011–09

4. Domènec Melé and Josep M Rosanas Power, Freedom and Authority in Management: Mary Parker Follett's "Power-With" *Philosophy of Management.*

5. Zehr, 37.

6. UNICEF, "Alternative Discipline." (n.d.) Accessed January 5, 2015 at http://www.unicef.org.

7. Howard Zehr, *Changing Lenses: A New Focus for Crime and Justice,* 3rd Edition. (Scottdale: Herald Press, 2005).

8. Brenda Morrison, "Bullying and Victimization in Schools: A Restorative Justice Approach." *Trends and Issues in Criminal Justice.* No. 219 (February, 2002). Available at http://aic.gov.au/documents/0/B/7/%7B0B70E4C9-D631-40D2-B1FA-622D4E25BA57%7Dti219.pdf.

9. Ted Wachtel, "What is Restorative Practices?" *International Institute for Restorative Practices,* (2012). Accessed March 10, 2015 at http://www.iirp.edu/what-is-restorative-practices.php.

10. Howard Zehr, "Doing Justice, Healing Trauma: The Role of Restorative Justice in Peacebuilding." *Peace Prints South Asian Journal of Peacebuilding* 1, no. 1 (Spring 2008): 3.

11. Zehr, 2002: 2005.

12. Zehr, 2005: 413.

13. Howard Zehr, personal correspondence, February 27, 2015.

14. Shawn Wilson, *Research is Ceremony.* (Halifax: Fernwood, 2008).

15. See Kay Pranis, Barry Stuart and Mark Wedge, *Peacemaking Circles: From Crime to Community.* (St. Paul, MN: Living Justice Press, 2003).

16. Kay Pranis, *The Little Book of Circle Processes: A New/Old Approach to Peacemaking.* (Intercourse, PA: Good Books, 2005): 14.

17. Zehr, 2002: 51.

18. See Gordon Neufeld and Gabor Mate, *Hold On to Your Kids: Why Parents Need to Matter More than Peers.* (Toronto: Random House, 2004).

19. See many educational reviews and websites, and in particular Gordon Neufeld, *Hold On To Your Kids,* 2004 and *Bullies: Their Making and Unmaking* available at http://neufeldinstitute.com/courses.

# TWELVE

# Exploring Transformative Change through Artistic Expression

LEARNING OUTCOMES

- To recognize that conflict comes in many forms
- To acquire an introduction to alternative and creative ways to make sense of conflict
- To learn about artistic expressions of individual and group conflict transformation
- To introduce the transformative influences of theatre, Improv, music, and photography

OVERVIEW

For much of history, people have used alternative mediums to reflect their understandings of conflict and conflict transformation, though those expressions have not been recognized. Improvisational Theatre, American folk music and protest songs, theatre, and photography are important alternative prisms that contribute to understandings of conflict and conflict transformation. Creative alternatives increase awareness of what forms of conflict people encounter, and how their interpretation of conflict is made plain for others through the alternative ways they have found to express those understandings.

The following sections are contributed by students in the Peace and Conflict Studies (PACS) field. The students have identified patterns of conflict transformation in the development and practice of their chosen passions. Artistic expressions have contributed to conflict transformation since their origins, but have only recently been recognized as important contributions to peacebuilding. This is an exciting development in the field that relates personal experiences and areas of creative expertise to PACS theory, research, and practice.

## INTRODUCTION

Art provides a different way of seeing the world, and it provides a way for emotions and creativity, rather than logic and rationality, to dominate. Art depicts and represents how people encounter conflict, respond to it, and in some cases, use it to transform their own feelings. It can be used to help a larger group make sense of something destructive or painful, or to bring people together after a divisive event. In many ways, these expressions are more familiar and immediate forms of conflict analysis than more formal frameworks and theories. These allow observers exposure to conflict, and provide ways, sometimes vicariously, to build empathy, humanity, and relationship while they make sense of the conflicts before them.

There are many instances around the globe in which people are using art as direct engagement tools to transform conflict. Improvisational Theatre (Improv), American folk music and protest songs, theatre, and photography are emerging in the PACS literature as alternative examples of the way some people recognize, interpret, and then express their understanding of conflict. In this way, people transform or make sense of their own struggle with conflict, at the individual and often also at the group level.

## ARTISTIC EXPRESSION AND IDENTIFYING CONFLICT

Art has told the story of individual and group interpretations of conflicts across the ages. For example, petroglyphs are world-wide rock carvings that demonstrate pictorially how prehistoric peoples expressed and addressed conflict. The etchings portray battles, mythology, and relationships engaged in conflict and also at peace. In this way, indirect expressions of violence, aggression, injustice, and agency are communicated. In the Middle East, the sacred carvings and elaborate symbols of the hieroglyphs portray the conflicts and resolutions of conflicts among the many relationships within the history and culture of early peoples.

Older art and art forms also reflect conflict transformation. Usually these are the expressions of individuals making sense of experiences that have affected a group. Classical music is an example of how composers have made sense of conflict in their personal relationships, with the state, or with society. The titles of Mozart's compositions, for example, reflect some of these. Other classical music composers responded to difficult life circumstances, or about larger conflicts like war, with music. Tchaikovsky's *1812 Overture*, which includes actual cannons in the score, was written to commemorate Russia's defense against Napoleon's invasion to unseat and conquer Czar Alexander I. The overture is an example of how Tchaikovsky's music united the Russian people at a difficult time in their history, while finding an outlet to express the victorious outcome of the conflict for his countrymen, in a way that was meaningful to him.

Another way that people have used art to unite people as they strive to make sense of conflict is through painting. One of the more well-known paintings about conflict is Pablo Picasso's *Guernica,* the famous depiction of a rural Basque town after the 1937 German and Italian armies tested their blitzkrieg tactics against the sleepy mountain village. In many ways, the painting is the end of something destructive and an expression of building toward the future.

There are numerous well-known examples of music, painting, sculpture, architecture, and other artistic expressions that provide alternative ways to expand understandings of conflict and transformation. Until recently, such areas have not been recognized as ways to consider what other people have "seen" as conflict, or as ways to make sense of it.

## IMPROV THEATRE

As an instrument of conflict transformation, Improvisional Theatre (Improv) contains structures to encourage laughter, healing, and conflict transformation at the individual and group levels. Some of the unique contributions of improv to the practice of conflict transformation are its adaptability, simplicity, energy, and its outcomes of laughter and healing for practitioners and for audiences. Several years after the horrors of the Rwandan genocide, the head of the Rwanda Cinema Center sought a creative form to help people learn to laugh again. Ed Greenberg of the University of California Los Angeles went to Rwanda to provide improvisational theatre game skills. The program in Rwanda was transformational and expanded upon the power of improvisational theater as a tool for social change in a global setting.[1]

Improv has been growing through implementation in educational institutions, non-profits, and public settings around the globe. It has been said that the heart of collaboration is trust, and it is the collaborative nature of Improv that places it as an emerging instrument of conflict transformation.

### The Art of Improv

Improvising in its broadest sense is a metaphor, a path, and a system; it is a *modus operandi* that anyone can learn. Improv is one of many paths that can lead toward the opening of the creative self. The art of improvisation (in contrast, say, to that of writing, singing, or painting) is particular because it teaches people how to be in harmony with one another and how to have fun doing so. Improvisation is practiced as a creative expression not only to express ourselves but to connect with others in a more immediate way. As an art form, Improv is dependent on groups to function, and is most successful when a collective mindset is in place.

Improvisational actors, called improvisers, make up scenes, songs, stories, characters, or entire plays on the spot, with no script or planned scenarios. They work collaboratively in front of an audience who expect to be entertained and amazed, with only their skills, philosophies, and colleagues to guide them. Improv builds collaboration and trust, and in this way, participants are willing to risk failure of performance, while delighting themselves and audiences with their successes. The secret that improvisers know though, is that the failures can be as satisfying and useful as the successes. The Improv stage is the platform and laboratory where the psychology of purposeful living can be understood, expressed, practiced, and taught indirectly.

A foundational tenet of Improv is spontaneity. Improv, unlike other forms of theatre, encourages players to live in the moment, whether playing a basic Improv game, or performing in a long-form scene. This allows improvisers to shed their self-conscious, critical nature and keep their attention on the moment, acting spontaneously based on intuition and inspiration. Initiated by the so-called mother of Improv, Viola Spolin, in the early 1940s, the concept of spontaneity was the spark to create the art form of Improv. Because improvising is based on spontaneous inspiration, almost anyone can easily participate in improv, making it one of the most accessible and inclusive forms of theatre, and particularly important as a mode of conflict transformation.

While not the initial purpose of Improv, nor the main goal of improvisers, humour is an important part of the contemporary Improv experience. Improv does not necessarily depend on specific cultural references, or adult humour, but often draws comedy from relatable experiences of characters and relationships. Humour and the ability to laugh are an important part of conflict transformation, and the types of cross-cultural, highly understandable type of comedy that Improv employs make it a useful tool for diverse groups of people. Improv skills, when applied to conflicts in life, enrich, stabilize, and provide wisdom toward transforming those conflicts while increasing our capacities to consider them, explore them, analyze, and then respond to them.

Increasingly, the world is conducive to the global implementation of improvisational theatre for understanding and making sense of conflict. In a world where concerns for safety and the double-edged sword of technology have reduced and in some cases eliminated face-to-face collaboration and interaction, improv encourages connections and relationships. For example, in recent years, businesses have begun to realize the value of consciously fostering creativity and teamwork within organizations through engaging the techniques, philosophies, and exercises found in improvisational theatre. These are, more specifically, creativity and communication skills like teamwork, coaching, leadership, calculated risk taking, and idea generation. In other words, improv builds on a platform of approaches and agreements designed to create a culture of innovation and collaboration in groups.

Dramatic improvisation has been an indispensable part of the North American school system since the early 1960s. The literature widely documents that improv provides a vital opportunity for people to harmonize and understand the world around them. In this way, it is relevant for a new perspective in PACS. In the processes of improv, people take on different roles to explore unknown situations. This expands their intellectual capacity for creative and critical thought, insight, rumination, playing, being, viewing, empathizing, and encountering an abundance of improvised roles and situations. These are all critical components of meaningful responses to conflict and effective peacebuilding. Furthermore, improvisation opens an effective and powerful medium for people to create an independent and personal narrative. Improvisation is an interactive, communal, creative process that encourages people to live in the moment, to take risks, make choices, and to exercise their creative sensibilities of both self and other.

## Introduction to Improv as Conflict Transformation

The history of improvisation as a form of artistic expression and communication has its roots in the practices we now associate with conflict transformation. Similarly, improvisation is as old as conflict itself and is recorded as early ritualistic displays of primitive cultures contained in thousands of years of religious tradition and writing. Improv is extremely pervasive throughout the history of theatre and literature. Scholars believe that even the early Greek narrative epics like *The Odyssey* and *The Iliad* had their genesis as improvised storytelling. Commedia dell'Arte from the Renaissance was fundamentally improvised comedy, which was structured to follow simple plot lines and scenarios (lazzis), consisting of a handful of stock characters (zannis) who expressed their character traits through the use of masks, absurd physicalizations, and obscene gestures. Even Shakespeare's plays are believed to have been influenced by the extemporaneous additions of his actors, whose impromptu lines would have been adapted into his written scripts. Suffice to say whether as an adjunct to the actual creation or through the performance itself, improvisation has had an impact on the creators and purveyors of theatrical art from centuries past to present day. Most of the art is expressing conflict and working it through.

Improvisation became an ubiquitous staple of modern learning in schools due in part to the progressive education movement initiated by John Dewey, whose views focused on the premise that people learn through the spontaneity of playing and doing. Half a century later, Dewey's theories were advanced by development and free-expression, as well as social and psychological growth. Game-based teaching has been used by American teachers to help young immigrant children master language acquisition. Other games unlock the individual's capacity for creative self-expression. Gavin Bolton viewed dramatic improvisation as an opportunity to gain insight into human situations by imagining oneself in another's situation. Dorothy Heathcoat, the legendary drama educator, took this one step further by espousing a dramatic curriculum that not only personally engaged students within a world of improvisational make-believe, but also sought a type of hyper-awareness from the students, where they could feel, learn, and reflect upon the drama as it happened. Richard Courtney considered improvised drama as being concerned with a student's inner thought and the spontaneous dramatic action which occurs as they engage in their own personal living and human drama. The relevance of this art form to conflict transformation is evident.

The structure of many improv games offers basic technical strategies that can be mastered and implemented with ease in other situations, and so it is emerging as a way to acknowledge social or interpersonal conflicts, and work them through. One of the fundamentals is to move the scene forward by doing away with all sexism, racism, swearing, and homophobic content. People are penalized (by deducting points or by losing their stage time) if they indulge in any of these areas, as every effort is made to create a fun, trusting, and cohesive community of learners. The positive interactive nature of improvisation and its excellent life-applicable techniques and philosophies develop a community in which trust of others, as well as being someone who can be trusted, inspires people to be bold and fearless in their explorations of the conflict and its resolution.

In Improv, the dual emphasis of the understanding self and working within a group is ideal as a conflict transformation tool. Lederach says that "peacemaking embraces the challenge of personal transformation, of pursuing awareness, growth and commitment to change at a personal level."[2] Improv assists improvisers in understanding their own mind, appreciating their personal significance, and building self-confidence. In a conflict transformation setting, this is essential for personal development, and understanding and recognizing one's own identity.

In Winnipeg, Canada, the Peaceful Village[3] is an afterschool tutoring and support program for newcomer youth in various schools. The program employs various arts-based activities as well, including a weekly improv workshop. Participants in this workshop, over a one year period saw dramatic growth in their personal development, as well as understandings of self, essential to the peacebuilding process. Students were happy to improvise using references and comedy related to their cultural identity. Their confidence was built with the improv skills learned, and they were often more comfortable sharing their personal story and understanding its significance, especially for those who came to Canada as refugees or as survivors of war and conflict.

As discussed, the collective nature of improv as a group pursuit adds to its use as a conflict transformation tool. Conflict transformation depends on allowing groups to share perspectives from often tumultuous outside conditions, in a safe and comfortable environment, which also creates community.[4] Improv encourages a great deal of storytelling, through words, sound, movement, and facial expressions in a creative and supportive space. Often, the storytelling can cross language and cultural lines, therefore positioning itself as a strong tool in overcoming conflicts, especially those cultural or ethnic in nature.

Many of the parents of the Peaceful Village Program, as well as other newcomer parents, participated in another program in Winnipeg entitled the Red Threads of Peace.[5] This model involved playback theatre, which had the newcomer adults, who were mostly women, tell their story, and other participants play it back using Improv skills. While many did not speak a similar language, people connected over the shared experiences of being a newcomer in Canada, coming from nations of conflict, and the significant pressure on women. The group nature of Improv created a space for women to transform conflicts into understanding, peace, and harmony.

Improvisation encourages and nurtures individual and group fulfillment and collaboration all at once. Improvisation is human-centric, innocent, and playful—and by its nature, creative. It is fun. It ignites and sustains passion. It encourages individual choices and exploration, even mistakes and, certainly risk taking. It is therefore a unique approach to conflict transformation. Audiences participate in the art by the suggestions they make, but otherwise are able to watch and observe as others express conflict and proceed through the journey of transforming conflicts peacefully—usually with much laughter.

## AMERICAN FOLK MUSIC AND PROTEST SONGS

Musical expression is a way for people to unite when confronted by conflict. It is a way to express objection to conflict, and it has the potential to effect change. The history of music includes important chapters in which conflicts and the struggles for transformation have been captured in the music of the day, in this way acknowledging conflict and exploring ways to respond to it appropriately. Some of these responses have been structural and national policies have been enacted or revoked as a result of American folk music and protest songs. Ballads, jazz, country music, and modern techno music all reflect different struggles, conflicts, and resolutions that make up the fabric of the country. The medium of music can give voice, unity, agency and hope to a group of people seeking to identify, explore, and transform the conflicts they can no longer bear. Music has played a role in social change in the United States. Although the focus here will be American folk music and protest songs, there is much research still to be done regarding the influence of the many other forms of music in conflict transformation.

## Introduction to Music as Social Change

Music has a powerful impact on social movements in terms of education, recruitment, and inspiration. During the French Revolution, for example, the song that became the national anthem of the country united the rebels to take on the cause of a monarch-free France. A portion of the lyrics include: "To arms, citizens / form your army squad / march, march! / Let impure blood water our furrows!" These words united the French people against the national conflict, and at the same time, kept the revolution alive. Other types of music genres like blues, folk, and hip-hop have been leveraged to unify people toward a common goal. During the Great Depression in America in the 1930s, people in the United States again endured a time of strife and hopelessness, and just as the spirituals sustained African American slaves in earlier times, music gave voice and shape to the experiences of conflict. Folk and blues music increased in popularity during the Depression and became the launch for a new era that recognized music as non-violent social protest. In this way and throughout history, music has often been the expression of individual and group conflict experience, and the architecture for transformation.

## Music and Political Change

The politicizing of folk music in the 1930s was largely a response to the aftermath of the Great Depression and the general political climate in the United States. The post-Depression era was also a time when the country experienced mass influxes of European immigrants, which began a major shift and redefinition of American culture. Many people embraced folk music as part of their effort to understand and belong in their new country. As a result, the environment of populism changed and folk music became interpreted as the music of ordinary people. Music of this period portrayed countercultural characteristics, and became a credible venue for artists to freely express their thoughts and perceptions of life, struggles, and politics of the time.

Huddie Leadbetter, also known as Lead Belly, was one of the first folk musicians that popularized protest songs as a way to bring attention to perceived flaws in the government and society. Racism in 1930s in the United States was Lead Belly's music focus, and his music provided a platform for other artists to leverage music as a means to social revolution for conflict transformation, especially to transform the on-going presence of racism.

Another well-known folk artist during this time period was Woody Guthrie. Guthrie also used his music to influence social change. He sang about hardships like living in the dust bowl and the struggles of the working class, which was a commonly shared experience. Along with lyrics about the hardships of the working class life, the songs of Guthrie and Company advocated for world peace and to discourage military involvement of the United States in the World War in Europe. However, the influences of folk music as a tool for conflict transformation were interrupted during the McCarthy Era (1947–1957). In Hollywood, the "Red Scare," was an anti-communist campaign that resulted in accusations toward thirty thousand writers, musicians, actors, and others as using their music medium to promote communist values. About three hundred people were placed on an official list of Communists and were barred from working. Allegedly, iconic and popular folk artists and activists such as Pete Seeger, were blacklisted during the McCarthy Era. Seeger is noted for his songs promoting international disarmament and civil rights. Some of his more popular and representative songs included "Turn, Turn, Turn," "If I Had A Hammer," and "Where Have all the Flowers Gone?"

This was subsequently recognized as the First Folk Revival and was marked by political messages and commentary. The Second Folk Revival of the 1960s was different from the first, and many of the artists sang about conflict transformation in the form of respect for other cultures and races. They sang toward a more harmonious relationship among people so that differences could unite, rather than divide people. During the 1960s, Greenwich Village in New York became a common gathering and collaboration site for musicians with political motivations. Country, Blues, Rhythm and Blues, and Rock and Roll artists came together in masses to learn from each other, play together, and live together. The outcome of this mass collaboration was the emergence of folk-rock, which combined the passion and political influence of folk music with an electric sound. Many artists like Bob Dylan used this seemingly contradictory sound to express their thoughts about conflict. Bob Dylan emerged to stardom with his 1963 record album, *The Freewheelin' Bob Dylan*. Dylan's music focused attention on the injustices endured by African-Americans across the country, and coincides with the height of the civil rights movement in the United States. His music highlighted social injustice, inviting members of his audiences to question their own attitudes about unjust matters like racism. Dylan carefully inserted social justice and the context of the civil rights movement into each song by simplifying the album to four-minute songs, and wrote his classic and powerful protest song "The Times They Are A-Changin'," as an invitation for people to embrace fundamental social change in peaceful ways.

Protest songs are an important part of the music conflict transformation story, as the songs encouraged many people to recognize that attitudes and realities needed to change. Many white urban college students were motivated by the music to join the movement against racial discrimination in the United States. The tumultuous 1960s produced music that encouraged and commented on Cultural Revolution, and which still influences the way people think and act today.

*Practicing Change: The Beatles*

The Beatles emerged on the music scene in 1964 and within one decade became one of the most popular and recognized bands in the world. After the initial Beatlemania craze in the United States, the Beatles became interested in serious politics and shifted their focus to write songs about peace and love by the end of the 1960s. During the height of the civil rights movement, the messages within the protest songs written and performed by the Beatles gained tremendous momentum due to the world-wide popularity of the group.

The Beatles seemed to take the strength of their voice seriously, and instead of pointing out obvious problems in society, the Beatles began writing about self-awareness and love in order to create a stronger community around the world, and in this way, transform conflict. The songs of the era included "All you Need is Love" (1967), written for the BBC's first live global television broadcast, and "Come Together" (1969). The Beatles wrote music about peace, love, and harmony; and they publicly donated money to charities, played benefit concerts, and engaged in a number of similar efforts to transform the conflicts inherent in American society in peaceful ways. The effects of the Beatles' songs on political and social change cannot be underestimated. Although the Beatles were widely regarded as controversial figures, their music inspired audiences around the world to rally against injustice.

*Influencing Change: Vietnam and Woodstock*

The Woodstock Music and Art Festival took place over three days in August 1969, on a dairy farm in the Catskills of New York. Woodstock, as it has become known, protested American participation in the controversial Vietnam War. Joan Baez, the Grateful Dead, The Who, and Jimi Hendrix wrote protest songs specifically against the Vietnam War. The music and lyrics were intended to showcase how violence could never lead to peace. At the same time, John Lennon's song "Give Peace a Chance" (1969) quickly became the anthem to the Vietnam War protest movement. The song was wildly compelling and was sung by half a million protesters in Washington, DC. Paul McCartney has consistently credited Lennon's song for the withdrawal of troops from the Vietnam War.

The role of music in conflict transformation is significant, especially in the United States and Canada. The social and cultural revolution inspired by countless musicians during the 1960s and early 1970s provided major impetus for the greatest social change in civil rights and liberties in the United States since the Civil War of the 1800s.

## Hip-Hop, Conflict, and Encouraging Change

Hip-Hop became popular in the 1970s as a new genre of protest against social injustice. However, while many of the lyrics were abrasive, offensive, and for some people, just plain scary, the songs were written to tell people what was happening in black neighborhoods across the country and express the rage many of them felt in a way that news organizations were not communicating.

Tupac Shakur was one of the most popular and controversial artists of the 1990s. He focused on social and political issues faced around the black communities in the United States and the complexity of problems many African-Americans faced. Tupac, as he is known, used his music and poetic style to promote positive social change. As Tupac became well known in the hip-hop scene he began developing a system of peace between various gangs in California and set standards for the way gangs should act within their communities. He also proposed gender equality and neutral ground for gangs at parties and concerts. Unfortunately, Tupac's manifesto was quickly misinterpreted by the media and gangs despite his explanation of what it meant to be a thug and how it related to people beyond gangs. Tupac continued to write about the black experience in the United States until he was shot and killed in 1996. Despite the misinterpretation of Tupac's guidelines, he came the closest to achieving peace between rival gangs, an achievement that has not been repeated since.

There have been many artists and many forms of music that have helped transform important conflicts. Two current examples are hip-hop artist Chuck D, who, through his music, encouraged people to vote in order to fight systems of intolerance, and Bono, U2's lead singer, has become a major figure in the fight to rid Africa of AIDS. These artists and many more have used their music to help shape public opinion about social issues, tell untold stories of violence, and protest against social injustice.

American folk and protest music has influenced transformative change. Music brings hidden truths to a mass audience that either actively ignored or was ignorant of the problem. Although the choices of which conflict to address or highlight are at the discretion of the artist, typically the emphasized conflicts are those that impose struggle at the group level, so that musical expression becomes the center of a community seeking change. American folk music, like many other forms of music, has influenced conflict transformation by invoking empathy and action in people that do not suffer, and has given a voice and hope for change to the ones that do.

## THEATRE

Theatre as an art represents another way of seeing the world and another way of seeing transformative change. Theatre reminds society that transformation is an integral part of the human experience; playwrights like William Shakespeare and Molière highlight both the tragic and the comic during the sixteenth and seventeenth century, displaying social norms as desirable, laughable, and sentimental. As a social commentary, theatre can be critical and illuminating, providing a powerful lens and diverse perspectives. As an experience, both individually and communally, theatre can send a message of hope that audiences are not alone in how they see or experience their lives. This sense of humanity and relationship is an important element for conflict transformation.

Though the origins of western theatre are unknown, most historians attribute the art form to community-based storytelling and spiritual rituals of early societies.[6] These origins provide a telling foundation for theatre as an expressive medium. It is through historical theatre that events have been commemorated; through medieval plays, that morality could be propagandized; through realism, that humanity has contemplated its reflection; and through theatre of the oppressed, that the common man has challenged political and social structures. As a medium, theatre can be found woven throughout the history of civilizations and existing in many forms. However, at its core purpose, theatre serves to convey a message. In this simple truth lies the power of theatre across the globe: one can say what needs to be said in a medium that encourages others to hear.

### An Introduction to Theatre

Theatre in the present still lives close to its storytelling roots. Historical re-enactments throughout the western world, like the Easter Passion plays, draw upon ideas of what happened long ago. Exploration into the lives of historical figures provides insight into historical and contemporaneous sensibilities surrounding historical conflict, conflicted histories, and the human condition. The participants who perform such depictions and re-enactments, as well as those who receive them, shape the re-telling of these stories. For many communities, these are endeavors of love undertaken entirely by a volunteer workforce with the aim of sharing a story that is important to the community.

This idea of telling the story is the reason why during medieval times theatre was utilized by the Catholic Church as a beacon of morality, outlining the necessary vicissitudes that shape of the soul of man.[7] Illiterate audiences could be shown the folly of Everyman[8] and be inspired to seek the church, religiosity, and righteousness. In this way, moral values were taken on tour with theatrical pageant wagons, and the message of the importance of regular and consistent participation in church life was emphasized. By including moral messages in plays, theatrical performances exhibit the same qualities of other mass media: co-optation for a particular purpose. The result can be the privileging of specific narratives and potentially reinforcing conflict asymmetry.

## Theatre as Art and Conflict Transformation

As a conflict transformation medium, theatre has also provided a critical role in helping audiences make sense of their own life experiences. This has never been truer than at the inception of onstage realism, marked in western theatre by Henrik Ibsen's *A Doll's House,* first performed in Copenhagen in December, 1879.[9] Theatrical realism was a general movement in nineteenth-century theatre from the time period of 1870–1960, intended to bring real life resonance to texts and to performances. Through onstage or theatrical realism, theatre builds upon human experience to provide a space for reflection and contemplation. Examining the harsh realities of conflict-driven narratives, audiences are given a lens through which moral decisions are contemplated, made, and evaluated. This holds particularly true in modern western performance, during which participating artists typically use a cause and effect narrative model to guide the process of building a play or building a community experience. The mode of realism distills stories down to their most universal elements, and builds the lives of characters based upon reactions to events and their environs, just as real life conflict is set in the context of events and environs.[10]

The relationships of these on stage conflict participants reach into audiences to weave narrative strands into the fabric of conflicted societies. This places not only the story, but the how and the why of its telling into the hands of its subjects.[11] These politically and socially charged movements are of community. They are grassroots efforts driven by both theory and practice, within the intersection of theatre as an aesthetic art, and the engagement of peace and conflict. In many ways, they echo the work in problem definition and narrative incorporation advocated in post-conflict societies through the work of peace builders like Dan Bar-

On,[12] and that of *The Junction*, a Northern Ireland-based community-relations organization whose project, *Towards Understanding and Healing*, utilizes storytelling and positive encounter dialogue to enable people to make sense of the violent conflicts they have endured.

*Theatre Peacebuilding Projects*

Perhaps the most exciting innovations within this interdisciplinary study include such projects as the Fringe Benefits' Theatre for Social Justice Institutes (TSJ).[13] Not the first, nor the only of its kind, Fringe Benefits' TSJ focuses on creating or devising work within communities, dovetailing acts of community building with local social justice movements. Reminiscent of Baol's methodology[14] of reaching into the shared consciousness of communities of oppression, Bowles and Nadon research and refine a process that is responsive to the present and the presence of every participant.[15]

Along with supported training opportunities, theatre companies like Puente Theatre[16] in Victoria, British Columbia, Canada, and The Justice Theater Project,[17] within the nongovernmental sector have emerged as arts organizations focused on creating opportunities for communities to explore, reflect, and organize around peacebuilding concepts. Such organizations allow for peacebuilding elements like Rothman's[18] resonance and invention to deal directly with extant protracted identity-based conflicts within their communities.

These empowering and recognition-based projects are the culmination of an art form as old as the campfire. The continued exploration of storytelling as an expression of the human condition is likely to garner more connections to possible applications within conflict transformation and peacebuilding, which need not stop with the use of role-playing in training situations. Peacebuilding efforts within the discipline of theatre can run deeper than joint history textbooks and tolerance.[19] While these efforts can be worthwhile, they miss a vital transformational element because they work on an external level. Current trends in the arts, and especially in theatre, indicate that process-based approaches can provide unique opportunities for intervention and transformation within pre- and post-conflict societies and communities.

# PHOTOGRAPHY

Photography defines how humanity sees itself, which makes it exceptionally relevant to peacemaking and conflict transformation. Photography is important because it functions as a permanent visual record in social and cultural interaction of who, what, where, and how something has been perceived. It has the ability to carry into the future a visual moment that, each time it is viewed, evokes an emotional and intellectual response akin to experiencing it again in real life. For those involved in conflict transformation, the potential for peacebuilding grows with each revisiting and re-experiencing of the event.

Photography is a means to capture and re-experience what is seen in the moment, and seeing is the strongest of the five senses. In fact, seeing makes up 83 percent of sensory input![20] Photography is un-clocked, so that the slice of time it captures lives beyond the moment of perception, and allows people to share what they see with others perpetually into the future. It is free from spatial restrictions because it exists apart from its subject matter and can be transmitted and shared anywhere. Photography also condenses within itself more details of perception than can be consciously observed in the moment itself. For all these reasons photography has great potential as a means for peace and the transformation of human conflict.

There is an increasing use of photography as a means to explore and understand conflict. For example, Howard Zehr, who is known for his work with restorative justice, has used photography, and in particular photographs of people who have been part of crime, in order to help people better understand each other. His two books, *Doing Life: Reflections of Men and Women Serving Life Sentences*[21] and *Transcending: Reflections of Crime Victims*,[22] contain photographs that capture the humanity of the subjects. There are many ways to explore and facilitate conflict transformation, and photography, although it is not new, is an expanding horizon in the study of peace and conflict as it captures people in a moment in time and offers new ways to consider what is seen.

*How Photography Facilitates Peace and Transforms Conflict*

1. Photography utilizes the dominant sense: seeing.

Humankind has historically depended on sight to sense danger, choose a mate, and gather food. Imagery enters the brain and is chiefly processed by the right hemisphere because its function is to receive new information. The new information is then compared to stored images, a function of the left hemisphere, looking for similarity and familiarity, and to name, count, measure, and categorize the input. The right hemisphere is like a wide-angle lens that sees the big picture; the left hemisphere is like a telephoto lens that focuses in on details of that big picture. The hemispheres work in concert to analyze what is seen and offer an integrated picture. One must be aware of the delicate balance between big picture and details to avoid distorted or reductionist conclusions.[23]

2. Photography is non-verbal and is humanity's dominant means of communication.

Breakdowns in communication (mostly verbal) are a major source of human conflict. Between 66 percent and 93 percent of all human communication is non-verbal and since photography speaks that language it has greater potential to address conflict.[24]

Photography's non-verbal nature has an advantage over verbal solutions in the practice of conflict transformation. Verbal means of dialogue and problem solving alone are prone to mistrust, denial, deception, secrecy, minimization, intellectualization, displacement, and rationalization.[25] Photography serves as an effective tool to authentically share experiences and feelings. It has the ability to create a visual bridge across these verbal pitfalls and facilitate genuine transformation. The field of Phototherapy has long recognized that photography has the ability to transport a person from a state of anxiety to a state of relaxation and to access often hard-to-reach feelings. It is also noted to be especially effective in raising multicultural awareness, supporting diversity, and conflict resolution training.[26]

3. Photography is a time machine.

Photography captures a fleeting slice of time and place and exports it to permanence. Photography is outside of time and space, allowing people to re-experience its contents repeatedly, anytime, anywhere. Photography is a re-presentation of a visual reality, not the reality itself. It has been called the "weightless, invisible envelope"[27] because it contains and delivers an important message. "Selective" or "unattended blindness"[28] allows it to be invisible while its message is transferred, just as one becomes unaware of the television set or the movie screen over time.

4. A photograph is a container packed with information.

A photograph captures and fixes enormous amounts of visual information for later analysis, mostly unseen at the moment of its capture and helping to answer the question "why?" Photography is particularly important to peacebuilding because it functions as a permanent contextual record of who, what, where, and how something has been perceived. For these reasons it is a valuable tool in visual anthropology.[29] Over time and with each viewing, a photograph maintains a representation of a physical reality and can evoke responses on emotional and intellectual levels which are similar to an experience in reality.

Photography has the capacity to continue to provide significant contributions to the patterns of peace and conflict. Photography facilitates positive change by capturing and reflecting attitudes, values, and perceptions. At the same time, photography increases general understanding about culture, which then has the potential to nurture compassion and empathy for others. This is conflict transformation.

## SUMMARY

Through the perspectives of peace and conflict students, several prominent approaches to conflict transformation from the world of art and music provided testament to the diversity and relevance of the PACS field. Theatre and Improv have casts and audiences, which are both indirect ways for addressing conflict through expression. Both sides are forced to come together and to engage in scenes as a way to improve the relationships highlighted on the stage. This builds community, communication, and trust, which are important elements for transformation. Music, as seen through the history of American folk music and protest songs, can be a tool to raise awareness of issues and to engage people toward change. Photography bears witness to conflict in many forms, and provides alternative ways to tell stories and experiences of conflict and peace. In this way, individual internal conflict can be transformed along with group conflict transformation.

There are other forms of expression not explored here that also ignite the hearts of PACS practitioners and students, and contribute to conflict transformation. These include poetry, film, documentaries, sports, and dance. Around the globe, there are many artistic forms of expression for the conflict experience.

## QUESTIONS

1. In what ways do the arts outlined in this chapter present conflict differently than the earlier chapters of the book?
2. Listen to your favourite music for references to interpersonal conflict. What is the essence of these conflicts, and how do the artists propose to transform the conflicts?
3. Go through the photographs on your phone or in a personal or family album. Note the impact they have on you personally. How do they make you think and feel? How do they define you as a human being? What impact do they have on your individual identity and purpose in life? If someone who didn't know you saw these personal images how do you think they would sum you up as a human being?
4. Examine the performance schedule for your local theatre company. This year, what is the message that particular company will be sending regarding conflict transformation?
5. Attend a local arts performance from one of the categories in this chapter. What is the conflict being explored? How does the medium you observed extend your understandings of conflict transformation?
6. On your next drive or walk to school or work watch for images you see along the way. What are the messages they convey? Select one or two and evaluate them with these questions:
    a. Does the image contribute to human conflict, structural or passive violence, or inequality?

b. Does it foster peace, human potential for reconciliation, and wellbeing, equality?

c. What is the effect of daily exposure to these images
and how do they unconsciously affect your social
identity?

7. Visit your local art gallery. Look for pieces on display that represent and tell the stories of peace and conflict. How does this particular medium affect understandings of conflict for both artist and
viewer?

8. Consider a national historical issue that has garnered significant
public attention. How did the expressive arts portray the conflict?
How have the expressive arts assisted you in making sense of this
conflict?

9. Write a short play or a song about this conflict. Be certain to explore principles of conflict transformation in your work.

10. Attend an Improv show and participate as an audience member.
How did your experience align with the expanded notion of Improv as relationship building?

## NOTES

1. Laughter For A Change. (2014). At http://www.laughterforachange.org/about-us/improv-history/.

2. "Peacemaking embraces the challenge of personal transformation, of pursuing awareness, growth and commitment to change at a personal level." See John Paul Lederach, *Preparing for Peace*: 19, 20.

3. For more information on more ways that the Peaceful Village is transforming interpersonal conflict for youth, see http://www.msip.ca/the-peaceful-village/.

4. "Empowerment of self was intimately wrapped up with empowerment of oth-ers through creating community." (*Preparing for Peace*, 21).

5. http://playbackwinnipeg.blogspot.ca/.

6. Brockett, O. G. and Hildy, F. J., (1998), *History of the Theatre* (8th ed.). San Fran-cisco, CA: Pearson.

7. Ibid.

8. Gassner, J. (2000). *Medieval and Tudor Drama: Twenty-four Plays*. New York: Ap-plause Theatre & Cinema Books.

9. Brockett & Hildy (1998).

10. See Boleslavsky, R. (1949). *Acting: The First Six Lessons*. New York: Theatre Arts Books; Hagen, U. and Haskel, F. (1973). *Respect for Acting*. New York: Macmillan; Meisner, S. and Longwell, D. (1987). *Sanford Meisner on Acting*. New York: Vintage Books; and Stanislavsky, K. (1980). *An Actor Prepares* (E.R. Hapgood, Trans.). London: Eyre Methuen.

11. See the literature of theatre practiners Boal, A. (1993). *Theatre of the Oppressed* (C. A. McBride, Trans.). New York: Theatre Communications Group; Cohen, C., Var-ea, R. G., and Walker, P. (Eds.). (2011). *Acting Together: Performance and the Creative Transformation of Conflict* (Vols 1–2). Oakland, CA: New Village Press.

12. Bar-On, D. & Kassem, F. (2002). "Storytelling as a way to work-through intract-able conflicts. The TRT German-Jewish experience and its relevance to the Palestin-ian—Israeli context." *Journal of Social Issues*, 60(2), 289–306. DOI: 10.1111/j.0022-4537.2004.00112.x; and Auerbach, Y. (2009). "The Reconciliation Pyramid—a Narra-

tive-Based Framework for Analyzing Identity Conflicts." *Political Psychology*, 30(2), 291–318. DOI: 10.1111/j.1467-9221.2008.00692.x

13. Bowles, N. & Nadon, D. (2013). *Setting the stage for social justice: Collaborating to create activist theatre*. Carbondale, IL: Southern Illinois University Press. Retrieved May 20, 2014, from Project MUSE database.

14. Baol's (1993).

15. See Bowles & Nadon (2011).

16. Puente Theatre Society. (2013). *About Puente Theatre*. Retrieved May 20, 2014, from http://www.puentetheatre.ca/about.html.

17. *The Justice Theater Project*. (2012). Retrieved May 20, 2014, from http://www.thejusticetheaterproject.org/.

18. Rothman, J. (1997). *Resolving identity-based Conflict in Nations, Organizations, and Communities*. San Francisco: Jossey-Bass.

19. Zheng, Wang. (2009). "Old Wounds, New Narratives: Joint History Textbook Writing and Peacebuilding in East Asia." *History & Memory*, 21(1), 101–126.

20. Stolovich, H., Keeps, E. (2011) *Telling Ain't Training*. American Society for Training and Development, Alexandria, VA. pp. 19–22

21. Zehr, H. (1996). *Changing Lenses: A New Focus for Crime and Justice*. Scottsdale, PA: 1996

22. Zehr, 2001

23. McGilchrist, I. (2009). *The Master and his Emissary, the Divided Brain and the Making of the Western World*. New Haven, CT.: Yale University Press.

24. Mehrabian (1972).

25. Stevens and Spears (2009) have observed, Stevens, R. & Spears, E. (2009). "Incorporating photography as a therapeutic tool in counseling." *Journal of Creativity in Mental Health*, 4:3–16.

26. Weiser, J. (2007) "Using photo therapy techniques in art therapy and other counselling practices." *Canadian Art Therapy Association Newsletter* 6: 4, p. 7

27. Barthes, R. (1981). *Camera Lucida, Reflections on Photography*. New York: Hill & Wang, p.5.

28. Mack, A. and Rock, I. (1998). *Inattentional Blindness*. Boston: MIT Press.

29. Collier, J. & Collier, M. (1986). *Visual Anthropology, Photography as a Research Tool*. Albuquerque, University of New Mexico Press.

# Conclusion

## *Transformative Change*

Peace and Conflict Studies is about understanding and transforming conflict and building sustainable peace through theory, research, and practice. Strong relationships are at the center of PACS work, so that while the context of analysis extends to the global level, the base expertise is local. Conflict work begins among community members and strengthens the peace processes through the development and transformation of individuals and groups.

The interdisciplinary nature of PACS leads to a creative reconfiguration of knowledge and engagement practices. The primary practices of the field focus on creative and nonviolent social change through conflict transformation. For there to be positive transformative change, it is critical that we continue to explore ways to transform conflicts before they manifest, and simultaneously provide meaningful healing for those in conflict and post-conflict situations. Knowledge development is deep and circular in its nature. Theory informs research and the development of practice models. Research strongly influences and is influenced by peacebuilding practices. Through the layering of the abstract with practice paradigms, models and processes unique to PACS have been developed. Improving relationships through the recognition of conflict for transformative change undergirds further expansion of models for knowing and responding.

The earliest theorists explored the relationship between war and peace and recognized its complexity. Scholars like Adam Curle and Johan Galtung realigned the focus for study from conflict to peacebuilding. John Paul Lederach entrenched the notion of conflict transformation and developed the Inquiry model as a graphic illustration of how conflict is transformed through change processes. Models and frameworks developed by international scholars and practitioners like Jay Rothman, Sean Byrne, and Maire Dugan are similarly based on research with people in situations of entrenched conflict in order to better understand conflict and to provide appropriate and meaningful peacebuilding interventions. Frameworks have been extended to include Indigenous principles and community engagement, which also reflect the circular nature of conflict and peace. These models and frameworks animate many emerging academic theses and dissertations.

The field of PACS is expanding to further engage multiple ways of learning and knowing. Inquiry is no longer restricted by the historical analysis and rigid traditions of the academy, as knowledge is expanding in important directions, led by impassioned and curious scholars around the globe. As we design our way forward, we need to highlight the voices of the silenced by asking what voices are missing. If they are not heard, lasting peace cannot occur. The depth of our knowledge and our practice has increased as we have brought forward the voices of Indigenous communities. Our understanding of the intersection across the personal and the public has increased with the inclusion of women and girls.

Practitioners seek to transform conflict and empower individuals and groups at all levels of relationship. Work within the field is leading to the continuous cultivation of new knowledge that challenges the existing war cultures and peace paradigms. The theories and frameworks that characterize the field encompass that which is the best from other fields. PACS workers seek to apply all of this knowledge with wisdom, sensitivity, appropriateness, and scholarship, so that the practices of conflict transformation effect change in unprecedented ways.

Community engagement, listening to local voice, Appreciative Inquiry, and restorative practices represent the themes of inclusion and participation that weave through PACS, echoing some of the main themes of theory and research methods. Storytelling remains a primary medium through which new voices are heard. The stories make sense of our past and transform our painful conflict experiences into the bonds that strengthen communities to shape the future.

Practices highlight the sincere effort by peace practitioners to develop asset-based, engaged communities. PACS as a field of practice is broad and supports engagement in the change process. Recognizing different types of conflict, learning one's own conflict style, and learning that there is a broad and proven repertoire for meaningful intervention equip practitioners for the transformation of conflict. The practices of ADR, mediation, negotiation, and facilitation can be used in multiple forms and contexts toward the creation of effective, transformative, and sustainable change. Expanding the frameworks for analysis supports exploration of the complex factors that influence transformative change. The skills and techniques as outlined distinguish peace and conflict practitioners from others, and these are the skills and techniques that are transforming conflict around the world.

Through art, theatre, and music, people are finding that healing from conflict and engaging in transformative change can be found in ways that are uniquely meaningful for them, for their families, for their communities, and for their nations. These are expressions of alternative ways that people think through their experiences of conflict. This kind of constructive and creative peacebuilding is a testimony to the power of research and practice stemming from PACS.

The PACS field prepares individuals to think critically, and to recognize the underlying causes of conflict and the complexity of developing and promoting peaceful and transformative alternatives to violence. Underlying each is the need to always practice as our genuine selves and to emote respect to all present. The bottom line is that we cannot learn if we do not listen to the verbal and the nonverbal. We cannot heal if we are not heard. True listening is a very difficult skill to develop. Peace cultures are defined by the presence of justice, equality, respect for life, and care for the physical environment. These take time. As the field continues to flow out from its core into the many dimensions of life and interaction, there may possibly be no greater work than to apply our knowledge, passions, and strengths for transformative change.

# Bibliography

*About the Junction*. (n.d.). Retrieved May 21, 2014, from http://thejunction-ni.org/index. php/about.

Argyle, Michael, and Monika Henderson. *The Anatomy of Relationships: And the Rules and Skills Needed to Manage Them Successfully*. Harmondsworth: Penguin Books, 1985.

Asset-based Community Development Institute website: http:// www.abcdinstitute.org/.

Atalay, Sonya. *Community-Based Archaeology: Research with, by, and for Indigenous and Local Communities*. Oakland, CA: University of California Press, 2012.

Auerbach, Yehudith. "The Reconciliation Pyramid—A Narrative-based Framework for Analyzing Identity Conflicts." *Political Psychology*, 30, No. 2, 2009: 291-318. DOI: 10.1111/j.1467-9221.2008.00692.x.

Augustine, Stephen, J. "Oral Histories and Oral Traditions," in *Aboriginal Oral Traditions: Theory, Practice, Ethics*. In Renée Hulan and Renate Eigenbrod, Editors. Halifax: Fernwood Publishing, 2008.

*Australia*, Directed by Baz Luhrmann. United States: Twentieth Century Fox Film, 2008. DVD, 165 min.

Avruch, Kevin, and Peter W. Black. "The Culture Question and Conflict Resolution." *Peace & Change, 16*, 1991.

Bandy, Susan J., and Anne S. Darden. *Crossing Boundaries: An International Anthology of Women's Experiences in Sport*. Champaign, IL: Human Kinetics, 1999.

Barash, David P. *Approaches to Peace* (Third Edition). New York: Oxford University Press, 2014.

Barash, David, and Charles Webel. *Peace and Conflict Studies*. Thousand Oaks: Sage, 2002.

Barash Bush, Robert, and Joseph Folger. *The Transformative Approach to Conflict*. San Francisco: Jossey-Bass, 2005.

Bar-On, Dan. *Tell your Life Story: Creating Dialogue among Jews and Germans, Israelis and Palestinians*. Budapest: Central European University Press, 2006.

Bar-On, Dan, and Fatima Kassem. "Storytelling as a Way to Work-Through Intractable Conflicts: The TRT German-Jewish experience and its relevance to the Palestinian—Israeli context." *Journal of Social Issues*, 60(2), 2002: 289-306. DOI: 10.1111/j.0022-4537.2004.00112.x.

Barthes, Roland. *Camera Lucida, Reflections on Photography*. New York: Hill & Wang, 1981.

Baxter, Leslie. "Dialectical Contradictions in Relationship Development." *Journal of Social and Personal Relationships, 7*, 1990: 69–88.

Baxter, Leslie. "Dialogues of Relating." In Rob Anderson, Leslie A. Baxter, and Kenneth N. Cissna (Editors), *Dialogues: Theorizing Difference in Communication Studies*. Thousand Oaks, CA: Sage, 2004: 107: 124.

Becker, Lily. "An Overview of Groups and Groupwork." In Lily Becker (Editor), *Working with Groups*. Cape Town, South Africa: Oxford University Press, 2005: 7–30.

Becker, Lily. "Groups and Organizational Life." In Lily Becker (Editor), *Working with Groups* Cape Town, South Africa: Oxford University Press, 2005: 66–81.

Becker, Lily (Editor). *Working with Groups*. Cape Town, South Africa: Oxford University Press, 2005.

Becker, Lily, and Madeleine Duncan. "Thinking about Groups." In Lily Becker (Editor), *Working with groups*. Cape Town, South Africa: Oxford University Press, 2005: 31–51.

Becker, Lily, Willem de Jager, Madeleine Duncan, and Monica Spiro. "Conclusion: Groupwork--A unifying language." In Lily Becker (Editor), *Working with Groups*. Cape Town, South Africa: Oxford University Press, 2005: 216–219.

Bens, Ingrid. *Facilitating with Ease! Core Skills for Facilitators, Team Leaders and Members, Managers, Consultants, and Trainers.* San Francisco, CA: Jossey-Bass, 2005.

Bercovitch, Jacob, and Jackson, Richard. "Negotiation or Mediation? An Exploration of Factors Affecting the Choice of Conflict Management in International Conflict" 17, No. 1. *Negotiation Journal,* January, 2001: 59–77. Article first published online: 2 JUL 2007. DOI: 10.1111/j.1571-9979.2001.tb00227.x.

Boal, Augusto. *Theatre of the Oppressed* (C. A. McBride, Trans.). New York: Theatre Communications Group, 1993.

Boleslavsky, Richard. *Acting: The First Six Lessons.* New York: Theatre Arts Books, 1949.

Borden, Robert. "Social Instigation and Control of Aggression." *Global Peace/War Issues,* 1980.

Bowles, Norma, and Daniel-Radon Nadon. *Setting the stage for social justice: Collaborating to create activist theatre.* Carbondale, IL: Southern Illinois University Press, 2013. Retrieved May 20, 2014, from Project MUSE database.

Brown, Barbara, Carol Werner, and Irwin Altman. "Choice points for dialecticians: A dialectical-transactional perspective on close relationships." In B. Montgomery and Leslie Baxter (Eds.), *Dialectical Approaches to Studying Personal Relationships.* Mahweh, NJ: Erlbaum.1998: 137–154.

Brown, Juanita, and David Isaacs. *The World Café: Shaping Our Futures through Conversations that Matter.* San Francisco, CA: Berrett-Koehler Publishers, Inc., 2005.

Brockett, Oscar G., and Franklin J. Hildy. *History of the Theatre* (8th Edition). San Francisco, CA: Pearson, 1998.

Bruhn, John. *The Sociology of Community Connections.* New York: Springer, 2005.

Burgess, Heidi. "Negotiation Strategies" *Beyond Intractability,* January, 2004. http://www.beyondintractability.org.

Burgess, Guy and Heidi Burgess. "Limits to Agreement: Better Alternatives," 1998. Available at Conflict \research Consortium http://www.colorado.edu/conflict/peace/problem/batna.htm.

Burton, John. *Deviance, Terrorism, and War: The Process of Solving Unsolved Social and Political Problems.* Oxford: Martin Robertson, 1979.

Burton, John. *World Society.* Lanham MD: University Press of America, 1987.

Burton, John. *Conflict: Resolution and Provention.* London: Macmillan, 1990a.

Burton, John (Editor). *Conflict: Human Needs Theory.* New York: St. Martin's Press, 1990b.

Burton, John. "Controlled Communication to Analytic Problem Solving." In F. J. Ronald (Editor), *Intactive Conflict Resolution.* Syracuse: Syracuse University Press, 1997:19–37.

Burton, John. "Conflict Resolution as a Political Philosophy." In Dennis Sandole and Hugo van der Merwe (Editors). *Conflict Resolution Theory and Practice: Integration and Application.* New York: Manchester University Press, 1993.

Burton, John and Dennis Sandole. "Generic Theory: The Basis of Conflict Resolution." *Negotiation Journal, 2,* No. 4, 1986: 333–344.

Bush, Kenneth. "What We Have Learned about Storytelling: On Story, Culture, and Evaluation." In Irish Peace Centres, *The Evaluation of Storytelling as a Peace-building Methodology.* Belfast, NI: International Conflict Research Institute, 2011: 65–74.

Bush, Robert A. Baruch, and Joseph Folger. *The Promise of Mediation: The Transformative Approach to Conflict.* San Francisco, CA: Jossey-Bass, 2005.

Bushe, Gervase R. "Appreciative Inquiry: Theory and Critique." In D. Boje, B. Burnes, and J. Hassard (Editors). *The Routledge Companion to Organizational Change*. Oxford, UK: Routledge, 2011.

Byrne, Sean. "International Mediation: Observation and Reflections." In Alexia Georgakopoulos (Editor), *The Handbook of Mediation: Theory, Research and Practice*. Routledge, NY: forthcoming 2016.

Byrne, Sean. "The Politics of Peace and War in Northern Ireland." In Judy Carter, George Irani, and Vamik Volkan (Editors), *Regional and Ethnic Conflicts*. Upper Saddle River, New Jersey: Pearson Prentice Hall, 2008b.

Byrne, Sean and Jessica Senehi. *Violence: Analysis, Intervention and Prevention*. Athens OH: Ohio University Press, 2012

Byrne, Sean, and Lora Keashly. "Working with Ethno-political Conflict: A Multi-modal Approach." In Tom Woodhouse and Oliver Ramsbotham (Editors), *Peacekeeping and Conflict Resolution*. Taylor and Francis: London, 2002

Byrne, Sean, and Neal Carter. "Introduction to Social Cubism," *ILSA Journal of International & Comparative Law*, Summer, 8, 2002.

Chaitin, Julia. "Narratives and Storytelling." In *Beyond Intractability*, eds. Guy Burgess and Heidi Burgess. Conflict Information Consortium, University of Colorado, Boulder. Posted: July 2003. Available at http://www.beyondintractability.org/essay/narratives.

Cheldelin, Sandra, Daniel Druckman, Larissa Fast, and Kevin Clements. *Conflict*. New York: Continuum, 2008.

Chernick, Richard and Barbara Reeves Neal. "Design Your Resolution Process," *California Bar Journal*, August 2013. Accessed July 8, 2015. http://calbarjournal.com/August2013/Opinion/RichardChernickandBarbaraReevesNeal.aspx.

Clausewitz, Carl Von. *On War*. (Edited and translated by Michael Howard and Peter Paret). The Center of International Studies: Princeton University, 1989.

Clayton, Patti, Robert Bringle, Bryanne Senor, Jenny Huq, and Mary Morrison. "Differentiating and Assessing Relationships in Service-learning and Civic Engagement: Exploitative, Transactional, or Transformational." *Michigan Journal for Community Service Learning, 16* no. 2, 2010: 5–22.

Cloke, Kenneth, and Joan Goldsmith. *Resolving Conflicts at Work: Ten Strategies for Everyone on the Job*, (3rd edition) San Fransisco, CA: Jossey Bass, 2011.

Cobb, Sheila. "A Narrative Perspective on Mediation: Toward the Materialization of the Storytelling Metaphor." In *New Directions in Mediation: Communication Research and Perspectives*. J. P. Folger and T.S. Jones, Editors. Thousand Oaks: Sage, 1994.

Cohen, Cynthia, Roberto G.Varea, and Polly Walker (Editors), *Acting Together: Performance and the Creative Transformation of Conflict* (Vols 1–2). Oakland, CA: New Village Press, 2011.

Cohen, Ira. J. *Theory: Antony Giddens and the Constitution of Social Life*. London: Macmillan, 1989.

Collier, John Jr., and Malcolm Collier. *Visual Anthropology, Photography as a Research Tool*. Albuquerque: University of New Mexico Press, 1986.

Combs, Cindy C. *Terrorism in the Twenty-First Century* (Fourth Edition). Upper Saddle River: Pearson Prentice Hall, 2006.

*Community Boards: Building Community through Conflict Resolution*, available at communityboards.org, n. d.

Conway, M. "Terrorist Web Sites: Their Contents, Functioning, and Effectiveness." In *Media and Conflict in the Twenty-First Century*. Edited by Philip Seib. Palgrave Macmillan, 2005.

Cooperrider, David L., and Suresh Srivastva. "Appreciative Inquiry in Organizational Life." In Richard Woodman and William A. Pasmore, W.A. (Editors), *Research in Organizational Change and Development*. Stamford, CT: JAI Press, Vol. 1, 1987: 129–169.

Cronin, Audrey Kurth. *How Terrorism Ends: Understanding the Decline and Demise of Terrorist Campaigns*. Princeton: Princeton University Press, 2009.

Darnell, Simon. C. *Sport for Development and Peace: A Critical Sociology*. London: Bloomsbury Academic, 2012.

Davies, J. C. "Aggression, Violence, Revolution, and War." In J. N. Knutson (Editor), *Handbook of Political Psychology*. San Francisco: Jossey-Bass, 1973.

Decontie, Jeffrey Walter. "Indigenous Identities and Nation-Building within Canadian Urban Centres: Relevance for Algonquin Nationhood," Unpublished Master's Thesis, University of Winnipeg, 2013.

Denning, Stephen. *The Springboard: How Storytelling Ignites Action in Knowledge-era Organizations*. New York, NY: Routledge, 2011.

de V Smit, Andre. "Groups and organizational life." In Lily Becker (Editor), *Working with Groups*. Cape Town, South Africa: Oxford University Press, 2005: 66–81.

Dostilio, Lina, Sarah Brackmann, Kathleen Edwards, Barbara Harrison, Brandon Kliewer, and Patti Clayton. "Reciprocity: Saying What We Mean and Meaning What We Say," *Michigan Journal of Community Service Learning*. 19 no. 1, 2012: 17–32.

Dougherty, James E., and Robert L. Pfaltzgraff Jr. *Contending Theories of International Relations: A Comprehensive Survey* (5th Edition). New York: Pearson, 2001.

Dubois, Joel. "Myths, Stories & Reality." California State University, Sacramento, CA, 2008 Available at: http://www.csus.edu/indiv/d/duboisj/WM/WM_MSR.html.

Dumlao, Rebecca, and Emily Janke. "Relational Dialectics: Understanding and Managing Challenging Dynamics in Campus-Community Partnerships." *Journal of Higher Education Outreach and Engagement, 16*. no. 2 (2012): 151–175.

Duncan, Susan. "Restorative Justice and Bullying: A Missing Solution in the Anti-Bullying Laws." *New England Journal on Criminal & Civil Confinement*, Vol. 37, (June 6, 2011):701. 2011. University of Louisville School of Law Legal Studies Research Paper Series No. 2011–2009.

Egerton, Charles. "Photography and Intergroup Conflict Transformation." *Global Journal of Peace Research and Praxis*. Greensboro, NC: University of North Carolina Greensboro. 1, No. 1, 2015.

Engelberg, Isa N., and Dianna R. Wynn. *Working in Groups*. (Sixth Edition). Upper Saddle River: Pearson, 2011.

Enos, Sandra, and Keith Morton. "Developing a Theory and Practice of Campus Community Partnerships." In *Building Partnerships for Service-Learning*, edited by Jacoby & Associates (San Francisco: Jossey-Bass, 2003). 20-41.

Esman, Milton. *Ethnic Politics*. Ithaca: Cornell University Press, 1994.

Ewald, Wendy. *The Best Part of Me: Children Talk about their Bodies in Pictures and Words*. NY: Little Brown, 2002.

Ewald, Wendy, and Alexandra Lightfoot. *I Wanna Take me a Picture: Teaching Photography and Writing to Children*. Boston. MA: Lynhurst Books, 2001.

Fisher, Ronald. J. "Needs Theory, Social Identity and an Eclectic Model of Conflict." In John Burton (Editor), *Conflict: Human Needs Theory*. New York: St. Martin's Press, 1990: 89–114.

Fisher, Roger, and William Ury. *Getting to Yes: Negotiating Agreement Without Giving In*. London, UK: Penguin Group, 1981.

Fisher, Roger, William Ury, and Bruce Patton. *Getting to Yes: Negotiating Agreement without Giving In*. 3rd Edition. New York, NY: Penguin Books, 2011.

Fitzgerald, Ross. "Human Needs and Politics: The Ideas of Christian Bay and Herbert Marcuse." *Political Philosophy, 6*, No. 1, 1985.

Flaherty, Maureen. *Peacebuilding with Women in Ukraine: Using Personal Stories to Envision a Common Future*. Lanham: Lexington, 2012.

Friere, Paulo. *Pedagogy of the Oppressed*. New York: Continuum, 1970.

Furco, Andy. 2005. "A Comparison of Traditional Scholarship and the Scholarship of Engagement." In J. Anderson, J., and John Aubrey Douglass (with A. Agogino and K. L. Komar). *Promoting Civic Engagement at the University of California: Recommendations from the Strategy Group on Civic and Academic Engagement*. Berkeley, CA: Center for Studies in Higher Education, 2005.

Funken, Katja. "The Pros and Cons of Getting to Yes-Shortcomings and Limitations of Principled Bargaining in Negotiation and Mediation." *Zeitschrift fur Konfliktmanagement*, 2002. Accessed at http://aryme.com/docs/adr/2-4-294/The%20Pros%20and%20 Cons%20of%20Getting%20to%20Yes.pdf.

"The Future of Court ADR: Mediation and Beyond." Last modified June 24, 2011. http://law.marquette.edu/courtadr/.

Galtung, Johan. "A Structural Theory of Aggression." *Journal of Peace Research, 1*, No. 2. 1964: 95–119.

Galtung, Johan. "International Development in Human Perspective." In John Burton (Editor), *Conflict: Human Needs Theory* (pp. 301–335). New York: St. Martin's Press, 1990b: 301–335.

Galtung, Johan. *Peace by Peaceful Means: Peace and Conflict, Development and Civilization.* London: Sage, 1996.

Galtung, Johan. "Violence, Peace and Peace Research." *Journal of Peace Research, 6*, No. 3, 1969: 167-191.

Gassner, John. *Medieval and Tudor Drama: Twenty-four Plays.* New York: Applause Theatre & Cinema Books, 2000.

Giddens, Anthony. *The Constitution of Society.* Cambridge: Polity Press, 1984.

Giddens, Anthony. *Politics, Sociology and Social Theory: Encounters with Classical and Contemporary Social Thought.* Cambridge: Polity Press, 1985.

Gilpin, Robert. *War and Change in World Politics.* Cambridge: Cambridge University Press, 1981.

Goldstein, Joshua S., Sandra Whitworth, and Jon C. Pevehouse. *International Relations.* New York: Pearson Longman, 2007.

Gurr, Ted Robert. "Minorities, Nationalists, and Islamists: Managing Communal Conflicts in the Twenty-first Century." In Chester. A. Crocker, Fen. O. Hampson and Pamela Aall (Editors), *Leashing The Dogs of War. Conflict Management in a Divided World.* Washington, DC: United States Institute of Peace Press, 2007: 131–160.

Guthrie-Shimizu, Sayuri. *Transpacific Field of Dreams: How Baseball Linked the United States and Japan in Peace and War.* Chapel Hill: University of North Carolina Press, 2012.

Hagen, Uta, and Frankel Haskel. *Respect for Acting.* New York: Macmillan, 1973.

Hamerlinck, P., and J. Plaut. *Asset-based Community Engagement in Higher Education.* Minneapolis: Minnesota Campus Compact, 2014.

Holt, Nicholas. L. "Positive youth development through sport." London: Routledge. *The Justice Theater Project*, 2008. Retrieved May 20, 2014, from http://www.thejust icetheaterproject.org/.

Horgan, John. *Leaving Terrorism Behind.* London, Routledge, 2008.

Horgan, John. *Walking Away from Terrorism: Accounts of Disengagement from Radical and Extremist Movements.* London: Routledge, 2009.

Horkheimer, Max. *Critical Theory.* New York: Seabury Press, 1982.

Hook, Steven W. *Democratic Peace in Theory and Practice.* Kent, Ohio: Kent State University Press, 2010.

International Committee of the Red Cross (ICRC). *Addressing the Needs of Women Affected by Armed Conflict.* ICRC: Geneva, 2004.

Irish Peace Centres. *The Evaluation of Storytelling as a Peace-building Methodology.* Belfast, Northern Ireland, 2011.

Israel, Barbara, Amy Schulz, Edith Parker, and Adam Becker. "Review of Community-based Research: Assessing Partnership Approaches to Improve Public Health." *Annual Review of Public Health* 19, (1998): 173–202.

Jabri, V. *Discourses of Violence: Conflict Analysis Reconsidered.* New York: Manchester University Press, 1996.

Janke, Emily. M. "Community Participation is not a Proxy for Reciprocity." *eJournal of Public Affairs, 2*, No. 2: 2013.

Janke, Emily M., and Patti Clayton. *Excellence in Community Engagement and Community-engaged Scholarship: Advancing the Discourse at UNCG.* Greensboro, NC: University of North Carolina at Greensboro, Vol. 1, 2011.

Jeong, Ho-Won. *Understanding Conflict and Conflict Analysis.* Los Angeles: Sage, 2008.

Johannsen, Agneta. "Post-conflict situations: The example of the war-torn societies project." *Berghof Handbook for Conflict Transformation.* Berlin, Germany: Berghof Research Center for Constructive Conflict Management, 2001.

Johnstone, Gerry, and Daniel W. Van Ness (Editors), *Handbook of Restorative Justice.* Cullumpton, UK: Willan Publishing, 2011.

Johnstone, Keith. *Improv for Storytellers.* London: Faber and Faber, 1999.

Jordan, Cathy, Sarena Seifer, Lorliee Sandmann, and Sherill Gelmon. "CES4Health.info: Development of a Mechanism for the Peer Review and Dissemination of Innovative Products of Community-engaged Scholarship. International." *Journal of Prevention Practice and Research,* 1 no. 1 (2009): 21–28.

Jussim, Lee, Richard Ashmore, and David Wilder. "Social Identity, Intergroup Conflict and Conflict Reduction." In Richard. D. Ashmore (Editor), *Introduction: Social Identity and Intergroup Conflict.* New York: Oxford University Press, 2001: 3–14.

Justice, Thomas, and David W. Jamieson. *The Facilitator's Fieldbook.* New York, NY: American Management Association, 2012.

Katz, Neil H., John Lawyer and Marsha Sweedler. *Communication and Conflict Resolution Skills.* Dubuque: Kendall/Hunt Publishers, 2011.

Kleiboer, Marieke. *The Multiple Realities of International Mediation.* Boulder, CO: Lynne Rienner, 1998.

Kolb, David. *Experiential Learning: Experience as the Source of Learning and Development.* Englewood Cliffs: Prentice Hall, 1984.

Koppett, Kat. *Training to Imagine: Practical Improvisational Theatre Techniques to Enhance Creativity, Teamwork, Leadership and Learning.* Sterling, Virginia: Stylus Publishing, 2001.

Kretzmann, Jody, and John McKnight. *Building Communities from the Inside Out: A Path Toward Finding and Mobilizing a Community's Assets.* Chicago: ACTA, 1993.

Kriesberg, Louis. "The Growth of the Conflict Resolution Field." In Chester Crocker, Fen Osler Hampson, and Pamela Aall (Editors), *Turbulent Peace: The Challenges of Managing International Conflict.* Washington: United States Institute of Peace Press, 2001: 407–426.

Kriesberg, Louis. *Constructive Conflicts* (Second Edition). Lanham: Rowman & Littlefield Publishers, Inc., 2003.

Lambert, Joe. *Digital Storytelling: Capturing Lives, Creating Community* (4th Edition). Centre for Digital Storytelling, New York, NY: Routledge, 2013.

Lax, David, and James Sebenius. "The Power of Alternatives or the Limits to Negotiation." In *Negotiation Theory and Practice,* J. William Breslin and Jeffery Z. Rubin (Editors), Cambridge, MA: The Program on Negotiation at Harvard Law School, 1991: 97–114.

Lax, David, and James Sebenius. "The Manager as Negotiator: The Negotiator's Dilemma: Creating and Claiming Value." In *Dispute Resolution,* 2nd ed. Stephen Goldberg, Frank Sander and Nancy Rogers (Editors), Boston: Little Brown and Co., 1992: 49–62.

Lederach, John Paul. *Preparing for Peace: Conflict Transformation Across Cultures.* Syracuse, NY: Syracuse University Press, 1995.

Lederach, John Paul. *Building Peace: Sustainable Reconciliation in Divided Societies.* Washington, DC: United States Institute of Peace Press, 1997.

Lederach, John Paul. *The Journey Toward Reconciliation.* Scottsdale, PN: Herald Press, 1999.

Lederach, John Paul. *Little Book of Conflict Transformation: Clear Articulations of the Guiding Principles by a Pioneer in the Field.* Intercourse, PA: Good Books, 2003.

Levy, Jack S., and William R. Thompson. *Causes of War.* Chichester, West Sussex, U.K.: Wiley-Blackwell, 2010.

Lewicki, Roy, David Saunders, and John Minton. *Essentials of Negotiation*. Boston, MA: McGraw-Hill, 1999.

Lewicki, Roy, David Saunders, and Bruce Barry. *Negotiation*. Boston, MA: McGraw-Hill, 2014.

Lordan, Nuala, and Mary Wilson. "Groupwork in Europe: Tools to combat social exclusion in a multicultural environment." In Sue Henry, Jean East, and Cathryne Schmitz (Editors), *Social Work with Groups: Mining the Gold*. New York: The Haworth Press, 2002: 9–21.

Mack, Arien, and Irvin Rock. *Inattentional Blindness*. Boston: MIT Press, 1998.

Maguire, Patricia. *Doing Participatory Research: A Feminist Approach*. Amherst, MA: The Center for International Education, School of Education, University of Massachusetts, (1987): 38.

Marini, Margaret M. "Sex and Gender: What Do We Know?" *Sociological Forum*, 5, No. 1. 1990: 95–120.

Matyok, Tom, Hannah Mendoza, and Cathryne L. Schmitz. "Deep Analysis: Designing Complexity Into Our Understanding of Conflict." *InterAgency Journal*. 5 No.2. Summer, 2014: 14–24.

Mazurana, Dyan, and Keith Proctor. "Gender, Conflict and Peace." Occasional paper. Somerville: World Peace Foundation at the Fletcher School, 2013. Available at http://fletcher.tufts.edu/~/media/Fletcher/Microsites/World%20Peace%20Foundation/Gender%20Conflict%20and%20Peace.pdf.

McCarthy, William. "The Role of Power and Principle in Getting to Yes." In *Negotiation Theory and Practice*. J. William Breslin and Jeffery Z. Rubin (Editors), Cambridge: The Program on Negotiation at Harvard Law School, 1991: 115–122.

McGilchrist, Iain. *The Master and his Emissary, the Divided Brain and the Making of the Western World*. New Haven: Yale University Press, 2009.

McIntyre, Alice. "Meaning, Violence, School and Community.: Participatory Action Youth Research with Urban Youth." *The Urban Review* 32 no. 2 (2002): 149.

McIntyre, Alice. *Participatory Action Research*. San Francisco: Sage, 2008.

McNiff, Jean, and Jack Whitehead. *Action research principles and practice*, 2nd ed. London: Routledge/Falmer, (2002): 4.

McTaggart, Robin. "Issues for participatory action researchers." In *New Directions in Action Research*, edited by Ortrun Zuber-Skerritt. London: Falmer Press, 1996.

McTaggart, Robin. "Principles for Participatory Action Research." In *Adult Education Quarterly*, 41 (1991): 20, as cited in Alice McIntyre (2008). *Participatory action research*. San Francisco: Sage.

Mehrabian, Albert. *Nonverbal Communication*. Chicago, IL: Aldine-Atherton, 1972.

Meisner, Sanford and Dennis Longwell. *Sanford Meisner on Acting*. New York: Vintage Books, 1987.

Melé, Domènec, and Josep M. Rosanas Power. "Freedom and Authority in Management: Mary Parker Follett's "Power-With" *Philosophy of Management*.

Meyer, J. "Action research." In K. Gerrish and A. Lacey (Eds.), *The Research Process in Nursing*. Oxford: Blackwell, 2006.

Mills, Geoffrey. *Action Research: A guide for the teacher researcher*. 5th ed. London: Pearson, 2013.

Mitchell, Stephen. A., and Margaret Black. *Freud and Beyond: A History of Modern Psychoanalytic Thought*. New York: Basic Books, 1995.

Morrison, Brenda. "Bullying and Victimization in Schools: A Restorative Justice Approach." *Trends and Issues in Criminal Justice*. No. 219 (February, 2002). Available at http://aic.gov.au/documents/0/B/7/%7B0B70E4C9-D631-40D2-B1FA-622D4E25BA57%7Dti219.pdf.

Nachmanovitch, Stephen. *Free Play: Improvisation in Life and Art*. New York: Penguin-Tarcher, 1990. ISBN 0-87477-631-7.

Nacos, Brigitte Lebens. *Mass-mediated Terrorism: The Central Role of the Media in Terrorism and Counterterrorism*. Lanham, MD: Rowman & Littlefield, 2002.

Neufeld, Gordon, and Gabor Mate. *Hold On To Your Kids: Why Parents Need to Matter More than Peers.* Toronto: Alfred A. Knopf Canada, 2004.

Nester, William R. *Globalization, War, and Peace in the Twenty-first Century.* New York: Palgrave Macmillan, 2010.

Nicotera, Ann M., and Laura K. Dorsey. "Individual and Interactive Processes in Organizational Conflict." In John Oetzel and Stella Ting-Toomey (Editors), *The Sage Handbook of Conflict Communication.* Thousand Oaks: Sage, 2006.

Nolan-Haley, J.M. *Alternative Dispute Resolution in a Nutshell.* St. Paul, MN: West Publishing Company, 2013.

Northrup, Terrell A. "The Dynamic of Identity in Personal and Social Conflict." In *Intractable Conflicts and Their Transformation.* Louis Kriesberg, Terrell A. Northrup, and Stuart J. Thorson, (Editors). Syracuse, New York: Syracuse University Press, 1989.

Nudler, Oscar. "On Conflicts and Metaphors: Toward an Extended Rationality." In John Burton (Editor), *Conflict: Human Needs Theory.* New York: St. Martin's Press, 1990: 177–204.

O'Brien, Connie. "Community Groups and 'Peacebuilding from Below.'" In Lily Becker (Editor), *Working with Groups.* Cape Town, South Africa: Oxford University Press, 2005: 52–65.

O'Hagan, Liam. *Stories in Conflict: Towards Understanding and Healing.* Yes! Publications: Londonderry, NI, 2008.

O'Kane, Rosemary H. T. *Terrorism.* Harlow: Pearson Longman, 2007.

Onashowewin Justice Circle. Available at http://www.onashowewin.com/.

Participatory action research: A feminist perspective and practice reader. (2013). Womin: African Women Unite Against Destructive Resource Extraction. Retrieved from http://webfactoryinternational.co.za/preview/womin/participatory-action-research.html.

Peer Mediation Programs: Facts and Statistics. Retrieved from: https://sites.google.com/site/peerMediationprograms/home/facts-and-statistics.

Pranis, Kay. *The Little Book of Circle Processes: A New/Old Approach to Peacemaking.* Intercourse, PA: Good Books, 2005.

Pranis, Kay, Barry Stuart, and Mark Wedge. *Peacemaking Circles: From Crime to Community.* St. Paul: Living Justice Press, 2003.

Puente Theatre Society. *About Puente Theatre.* Retrieved May 20, 2014, from http://www.puentetheatre.ca/about.html.

Putnam, Robert. *Bowling Alone: The Collapse and Revival of American Community.* New York: Simon and Schuster, 2000.

Reimer, Laura E. PhD Dissertation. *Dropping out of School: Exploring the Narratives of Aboriginal People in One Manitoba Community through Lederach's Conflict Transformation Framework.* University of Manitoba, August 21, 2013. Available at http://mspace.lib.umanitoba.ca/handle/1993/22052.

Reimer, Laura, "Conflict Transformation: Canadian Democracy and Aboriginal Relations," *Global Journal of Peace Research and Praxis,* 1 (2014, 2015): 41. Available at http://www.partnershipsjournal.org/index.php/prp/issue/view/74.

Remen, Rachel. N. "Helping, Fixing or Serving?" *Shambhala Sun.* September, 1999.

Restorative Justice Online. Available at http://www.restorativejustice.org/programme-place.

Rice, Brian. "Relationships with Humans and Non-Humans Species and How They Apply toward Peace-Building and Leadership in Indigenous Societies." In Thomas Maytok, Jessica Senehi and Sean Byrne (Editors), *Critical Issues in Peace and Conflict Studies: Theory, Practice, and Pedagogy.* Lanham: Lexington, 2011: 199–277.

Ridgeway, Celia L., and Shirley Correll. "Unpacking the Gender System: A Theoretical Perspective on Gender Beliefs and Social Relations." *Gender and Society, 18,* No. 4, 2004: 510–531.

Risman, Barbara. J. "Gender as a Social Structure: Theory Wrestling with Activism." *Gender and Society, 18,* No. 4, 2004: 429–450.

Rosenblum, Naomi. *A World History of Photography*. NY: Abbeville Press, 2007.

Ross, Mark Howard. *Cultural Contestation in Ethnic Conflict*. New York: Cambridge University Press, 2007.

Ross, Rupert. *Returning to the Teachings: Exploring Aboriginal Justice*. Toronto: Penguin Books, 1996.

Rothman, Jay. *Resolving Identity-based Conflict in Nations, Organizations, and Communities*. San Francisco: Jossey-Bass, 1997.

Rothman, Jay. *From Confrontation to Cooperation: Resolving Ethnic and Regional Conflict*. Aria Group Publications, http://www.ariagroup.com, 2012.

Rubenstein, Richard. "Sources." In S. Cheldelin, Sandra, Daniel Druckman, and Larissa Fast (Editors), *Conflict: From Analysis to Intervention* (Second edition). New York: Continuum, 2008: 55–67.

Ryan, Pat. *Storytelling in Ireland: A Re-awakening*. Londonderry, NI: The Verbal Arts Center, 1995.

Sabourin, Teresa. *The Contemporary American Family: A Dialectical Perspective on Communication and Relationships*. Thousand Oaks: Sage, 2003.

Salem, Walid, and Edy Kaufman. "From diagnosis to treatment. Towards new shared principles for Israeli-Palestinian peacebuilding." In Dennis Sandole, Sean Byrne, Ingrid Staroste-Sandole, and Jessica Senehi (Editors), *Handbook of Conflict Analysis and Resolution*. New York: Routledge, 2008: 301–312.

Salinsky, Tom. *Improv Handbook: The Ultimate Guide to Improvising in Theatre, Comedy, and Beyond*. New York: Continuum, 2008. Print. ISBN 978-0-8264-2858-5 http://www.laughterforachange.org/about-us/improv-history/.

Saltmarsh, John, Matt Hartley, and Patti Clayton. *Democratic Civic Engagement White Paper*. Boston: New England Resource Center for Higher Education, 2009.

Sandole, Dennis. J. D. "The Biological Basis of Needs in World Society: The Ultimate Macro-Macro Nexus." In J. Burton (Editor), *Conflict: Human Needs Theory*. New York: St. Martin's Press, 1990: 60–88.

Sandole, Dennis. J. D. *Capturing The Complexity of Conflict. Dealing With Violent Ethnic Conflicts of the Post-Cold War Era*. New York: Pinter, 1999.

Saltmarsh, John, Matt Hartley, and Patti Clayton. *Democratic Civic Engagement White Paper*. Boston: New England Resource Center for Higher Education, 2009.

*Saving Mr. Banks,* Directed by John Lee Hancock. United States: Walt Disney Pictures, 2013. DVD, 125 min.

Schellenberg, James A. *Conflict Resolution: Theory, Research, and Practice*. New York: State University of New York Press, 1996.

Schirch, Lisa. *Ritual and Symbol in Peacebuilding*. Bloomfield, CT: Kumarian Press, 2005.

Schön, Donald. *The Reflective Practitioner: How Professionals Think in Action*. New York: Basic Books, 1983.

Schwarz, Roger. *The Skilled Facilitator : A Comprehensive Resource for Consultants, Facilitators, Managers, Trainers, and Coaches*. San Francisco, CA: Jossey-Bass, 2002.

Sebenius, James K., "Six Habits of Merely Effective Negotiators." In *Harvard Business Review*. April, 2001: 87–95

Seib, Philip M., and Dana M. Janbek. *Global Terrorism and New Media: The Post-Al Qaeda Generation*, London: Routledge, 2011.

Senehi, Jessica. "Building Peace: Storytelling to Transform Conflicts Constructively." In Dennis Sandole, Sean Byrne, Ingrid Sandole-Staroste, and Jessica Senehi, (Editors), *Handbook of Conflict Analysis and Resolution*. New York, NY: Routledge, 2008: 199–212.

Senehi, Jessica. "Constructive Storytelling: A Peace Process." *Peace and Conflict Studies*, 9, No. 2, 2002: 41–63.

Senehi, Jessica, "Constructive Storytelling in Inter-communal Conflicts: Building Community, building peace." In Sean Byrne, Cynthia Irvin, Paul Dixon, Brian Polkinghorn, and Jessica Senehi (Editors), *Reconcilable Differences: Turning Points in Ethnopolitical Conflict*. West Hartford: Kumarian Press, 2000: 96–114.

Senehi, Jessica. "Language, Culture and Conflict: Storytelling as a Matter of Life and Death," *Mind and Human Interaction* 7, No. 3 (1998): 150–164.

Senehi, Jessica, Maureen Flaherty, Cindy Kirupakaran, Llyod Kornelsen, Mavis Matenge, and Olga Skarlato. "Dreams of Our Grandmothers: Discovering the Call for Social Justice Through Storytelling." *Storytelling, Self, Society.* 5, No. 2, 2009: 90–106.

Sinclair, Honourable Justice Murray. "What Do We Do About the Legacy of Indian Residential Schools?" *Sol Kannee Lecture*, University of Manitoba, September 29, 2014. You Tube, https://www.youtube.com/watch?v=qTiB13H0tic.

Sisneros, Jose, Catherine Stakeman, Mildred Joyner, and Cathryne L. Schmitz. *Critical Multicultural Social Work.* Chicago, IL: Lyceum Books, Inc., 2008.

Sites, Paul. "Needs as Analogues of Emotions." In John Burton (Editor), *Conflict: Human Needs Theory.* New York: St. Martin's Press, 1990b: 7–33.

Smith, Linda Tuhiwai. *Decolonizing Methodologies: Research and Indigenous Peoples.* New York: Zed Books, 1999.

Snyder, Anna. "Gender Relations and Conflict Transformation Among Refugee Women." In Dennis J. D. Sandole, Sean Byrne, Ingrid Sandole-Staroste, and Jessica Senehi (Editors), *Handbook of Conflict Analysis and Resolution.* New York: Routledge, 2009: 43–52.

South Africa. *Truth & Reconciliation Commission,* 2009. Available at http://www.doj.gov.za/trc.

Stanislavsky, Konsantin. *An Actor Prepares* (E.R. Hapgood, Trans.). London: Eyre Methuen, 1980.

Staub, Ervin. "The Psychology of Perpetrators and Bystanders." *Political Psychology, 6,* No. 1, 1984: 61–85.

Stern, Paul C., and Daniel Druckman. "Evaluating Interventions in History: The Case of International Conflict Resolution." In *International Conflict Resolution After the Cold War*, Paul C. Stern and Daniel. Druckman, (Editors). Washington, DC: National Academy Press, National Research Council, 2000.

Stevens, R., and Evans Spears. "Incorporating Photography as a Therapeutic Tool in Counseling." *Journal of Creativity in Mental Health*, 4, 2009:3–16.

Stolovich, Harold, and Erica Keeps. *Telling Ain't Training.* American Society for Training and Development, Alexandria, VA, 2011.

Stone, Douglas, Bruce Patton, and Sheila Heen. *Difficult Conversations: How to Discuss What Matters Most.* New York: Penguin, 2000.

Strand, Kerry, Nicholas Cutforth, Randy Stoecker, and Sam Marullo. *Community-based Research and Higher Education: Principles and Practices.* San Francisco, CA: Jossey-Bass, 2003.

Stutzman Amstuz, L., and J.H. Mullet. *The Little Book of Restorative Discipline for Schools: Teaching Responsibility: Creating Caring Climates.* Intercourse, PA: Good Books, 2005.

Taylor, Laura, and John Paul Lederach, "Participatory action research and strategic peacebuilding." *Unpublished manuscript.* 2009.

Tir, Jaroslav, and Michael Jasinski. "Domestic-level Diversionary Theory of War: Targeting Ethnic Minorities." *Journal of Conflict Resolution* 52 No. 5, 2008: 641–664.

Trainin-Blank, Barbara. "Different Strokes: Art and Photo Therapy Promote Healing." *New Social Worker*, 6, No. 2, 2009.

Truth and Reconciliation Commission of Canada. www.trc.ca.

UNICEF, "Alternative Discipline," (n.d.) Accessed January 5, 2015 at http://www.unicef.org.

University of Manitoba. Arthur V. Mauro Centre. *Winnipeg International Storytelling Festival,* 2014. Accessed at http://umanitoba.ca/colleges/st_pauls/mauro_centre/outreach/storytelling/about.html.

Ury, William. *Getting Past No: Negotiating in Difficult Situations.* New York: Bantam Books, 1991.

Van de Ven, Andrew. *Engaged Scholarship: A guide for organizational and social research.* Oxford: Oxford University Press, 2007.

Vayrynen, Tarja. *Culture and International Conflict Resolution. A Critical Analysis of the Work of John Burton*. Manchester and New York: Manchester University Press, 2001.

Volkan, Vamik. "Psychoanalytic Aspects of Ethnic Conflict." In Joseph V. Montville (Editor), *Conflict and Peacemaking in Multiethnic Societies*. Lanham, MD: Lexington Books, 1990.

Volkan, Vamik. *Bloodlines, From Ethnic Pride to Ethnic Terrorism*. Boulder: Westview Press, 1997.

Volkan, Vamik. "The Tree Model: Psychopolitical Dialogues and the Promotion of Coexistence." In Eugene Weiner (Editor), *The Handbook of Interethnic Coexistence*. New York: Continuum, 1998: 342–358.

Volkan, Vamik. "Transgenerational Transmissions and Chosen Traumas: An Aspect of Large-Group Identity." *Group Analysis, 34,* No. 1, 2001: 79–97.

Waltz, Kenneth. *Man, the State, and War*. New York: Columbia University Press, 1959.

Wang, Carolyn, and Mary Ann Burris. "Empowerment through Photo Novella: Portraits of Participation." *Health Education & Behavior*, 21, No. 2, 1994: 171–186.

Warters, William. *Mediation in the Campus Community: Designing and Managing Effective Programs*. San Francisco, CA: Jossey-Bass, 2000.

Watkins, Jane N., and Bernard J. Mohr. *Appreciative Inquiry: Change at the Speed of Imagination*. San Francisco: Jossey, 2001.

Weisbord, Marvin, and Sandra Janoff. *Future Search: Getting the Whole System in the Room for Vision, Commitment, and Action* (3rd Edition). San Francisco: Berrett-Koehler Publishers, 2010.

Weiser, Judy. "PhotoTherapy Techniques in Counseling and Therapy—Using Ordinary Snapshots and Photo-interactions to Help Clients Heal their Lives." Parksville, BC: *Canadian Art Therapy Association Journal* 17, No. 2, 2004: 23–53.

Weiser, Judy. "Using photo therapy techniques in art therapy and other counseling practices." *Canadian Art Therapy Association Newsletter* 6, No. 4, 2007: 4–7.

Whitfield, Geoffrey. *Amity in the Middle East: How the World Sports Peace Project and the passion for football brought together Arab and Jewish youngsters*. Brighton: Alpha Press, 2006.

Whitfield, Geoffrey. V. *Dynamics of a journey to conflict prevention and peace in Israel and Palestine through an Olympic sport*. Lexington, KY: Emeth Pres, 2012.

Wilkinson, Paul. *Terrorism*. Singapore: Marshall Cavendish Editions, 2012.

Wilmot, William, and Joyce Hocker. *Interpersonal Conflict*. New York: McGraw-Hill Companies, 2014.

Wilson, Shawn. *Research is Ceremony: Indigenous Research Methods*. Halifax, Canada: Fernwood Publishing, 2008.

Winslade, John, and Gerald Monk. *Narrative Mediation: A New Approach to Conflict Resolution*. San Francisco, CA: Jossey-Bass, 2000.

Wolff, Stephen. *Ethnic conflict: A global perspective*. Oxford, UK: Oxford University Press, 2006.

Wood, Julia. *Interpersonal Communication: Everyday Encounters*. Belmont, CA: Thompson Wadsworth, 2007.

Zartman, William. "Explaining Disengagement" In *Dynamics of Third Party Intervention: Kissinger in the Middle East*, edited by J. Rubin. New York: Praeger, 1981.

Zartman, William, and Saadia Touval. "International Mediation." In Chester Crocker, Fen Osler Hampson and Pamela Aall (Editors), *Leashing the Dogs of War: Conflict Management in a Divided World*. Washington: United States Institute of Peace Press, 2007: 437–45

Zehr, Howard. *Changing Lenses: A New Focus for Crime and Justice*. Scottsdale: Herald Press, 2005.

Zehr, Howard. "Doing Justice, Healing Trauma: The Role of Restorative Justice in Peacebuilding." *Peace Prints South Asian Journal of Peacebuilding* 1, No. 1 (Spring, 2008): 3.

Zehr, Howard. *The Little Book of Restorative Justice*. Intercourse, PA: Good Books, 2002.

Zheng, Wang. "Old Wounds, New Narratives: Joint History Textbook Writing and Peacebuilding in East Asia." *History & Memory*, 21, No. 1, 2009: 101–126.

# Index

# About the Authors

**Laura E. Reimer**, MPA, PhD, is an assistant professor at the University of Winnipeg in central Canada, where she teaches in political science. Her research merges education and public sector governance with peace and conflict studies. She has a particular interest in Indigenous issues and in how people, including Indigenous or Aboriginal people, experience public policy in social service areas, especially education. A former school board member, Laura authored Leadership and School Boards I and II (published by Rowman Littlefield) to increase student and public knowledge about the role of school boards. She has written several book chapters, book reviews, and published in peer-reviewed journals. Laura's innovative dissertation developed and tested a new methodology to ask Canadian Aboriginal people to share their stories of why they dropped out of school. She served her post-doctoral fellowship at the University of North Carolina Greensboro, where she met the co-authors, and remains a research fellow with the Center for Newcomers to North Carolina at UNCG and with the Arthur V. Mauro Centre for Peace and Justice in Canada, exploring the relationships between public policy and PACS.

**Cathryne L. Schmitz**, PhD, MSW, professor and chair, Department of Peace and Conflict Studies, and professor, Department of Social Work, at the University of North Carolina Greensboro, is an affiliate faculty in women and gender studies and a research fellow with the Center for Newcomers to North Carolina. Her scholarship focuses on analysis of the privilege/oppression nexus, critical multiculturalism, environmental sustainability, leadership, interdisciplinary education, global engagement, organizational development and community building, and peacebuilding. She is engaged in intercultural global education and knowledge building. She has numerous publications and is currently focusing in the areas of peace assessment, environmental justice, and organizational/community transformation.

**Emily M. Janke**, PhD, is an associate professor in the Peace and Conflict Studies Department and the founding director of the Institute for Community and Economic Engagement at the University of North Carolina Greensboro. Her scholarship explores different levels of community-university partnerships, including reciprocal engagement principles and practices, leadership and organizational change in higher education, the nexus between community engagement and economic development, and the next generation of engagement scholars. Emily is a recipient of the

Early Career Researcher Award given by the International Association for Research on Service-Learning and Community Engagement, the John Saltmarsh Award for Emerging Leaders in Civic Engagement given by the American Democracy Project of the American Association of State Colleges and Universities, and the Civic Engagement Professional of the Year Award given by North Carolina Campus Compact. She is a visiting scholar at the New England Resource Center for Higher Education and on faculty at the Engagement Academy for University Leaders.

**Ali Askerov**, PhD, is an assistant professor of peace and conflict studies at the University of North Carolina Greensboro, and author of numerous articles and papers. Dr. Askerov has lived and travelled around the world. Educated in Canada and the United States, his research interests include ethnic conflicts, peace education, peace journalism, political violence, human rights, theories of international politics, media and terrorism, history of political thought, Middle Eastern studies, and Russian studies.

**barbara Strahl**, PhD, earned her doctorate in conflict analysis and resolution from Nova Southeastern University. Her research focused on restorative justice and reintegration of offenders into community. She is an experienced practitioner, mediator, facilitator, and professor, nationally recognized for her dedication to the fields of peacemaking, conflict transformation, and restorative and social justice. barbara teaches at the University of North Carolina Greensboro in the postgraduate Peace and Conflict Studies Department and at Nova Southeastern University in the Health Science doctoral program. She was part of the Kroc Institute team who designed the UNCG undergraduate Peace and Conflict Studies Program. Besides numerous articles, barbara is a contributing author to *Crimes against Humanity in the Land of the Free: Can a Truth and Reconciliation Process Heal Racial Conflict in America*? Involvement in the field of conflict resolution has led her to serve on numerous boards, including the National Association for Community Mediation (NAFCM), where she served two terms as board chair. She is a founding director for the Nevada Mediation Group. barbara lives in the southwest United States with her husband and rescued animals where she is also a glass artist, reiki master, and outdoor enthusiast.

**Thomas Matyók**, PhD, is an associate professor and Director of Graduate Studies in the Department of Peace and Conflict Studies at the University of North Carolina Greensboro. His research focuses on the education and training of conflict workers and peacebuilders, institutions of peace, the role of religion in peacebuilding and conflict management, and the design and deep analysis of conflict. Tom possesses substantial knowledge of international, cross-cultural, and organizational conflict resolution processes. Tom's research and practice in the area of conflict worker education focuses on merging the academic study and practice of the strategic and tactical levels of conflict intervention and peacebuilding.

Tom was the lead editor of: *Critical Issues in Peace and Conflict Studies: Theory, Practice, and Pedagogy* and *Peace on Earth: The Role of Religion in Peace and Conflict Studies.*